AGILE PRODUCT DEVELOPMENT FOR MASS CUSTOMIZATION

How to Develop and Deliver Products for Mass Customization, Niche Markets, JIT, Build-to-Order and Flexible Manufacturing

DAVID M. ANDERSON
with an Introduction by B. Joseph Pine II

McGraw-Hill

New York   Chicago   San Francisco   Washington, D.C.   Auckland   Bogotá
Caracas   Lisbon   London   Madrid   Mexico City   Milan
Montreal   New Delhi   San Juan   Singapore
Sydney   Tokyo   Toronto

Library of Congress Cataloging-in-Publication Data

Anderson, David M., P.E.
    Agile product development for mass customization:
    how to develop and deliver products for mass
    customization, niche markets, JIT, build-to-order
    and flexible manufacturing.
/ David M. Anderson
    p. cm.
    Includes index.
    ISBN 0-7863-1175-4
    1. New products. 2. Product management. I. Title.
HF5415.153.A53   1997
658.5'75—DC20   96–38548
                               CIP

McGraw-Hill

*A Division of The **McGraw·Hill** Companies*

3 4 5 6 7 8 9 0 DOC/DOC 3 2 1 0 9
Printed and bound by R. R. Donnelley & Sons Company.

McGraw-Hill books are available at special quantity discounts to use as
premiums and sales promotions, or for use in corporate training programs. For more information, please write to the Director of Special
Sales, McGraw-Hill, 11 West 19th Street, New York, NY 10011. Or con-
tact your local bookstore.

This book is printed on recycled, acid-free paper containing a
minimum of 50% recycled de-inked fiber.

To my loving and supportive wife, Lin,
my companion in life and a real source of inspiration

CONTENTS

Chapter 4

Chapter 5

Chapter 7

Building Products Quickly with Agile Manufacturing   175

Chapter 10

Designing Mass Customized Products   247

PREFACE

MASS CUSTOMIZING PRODUCTS

This book will show companies how to develop products that can be easily customized for niche markets or individual customers. The ultimate application of this approach will allow companies to mass customize products to produce custom products at mass production speed and efficiency.

Many readers, if not most, may use this book primarily to help them better handle variety. Few products today can be manufactured like mass-produced Model T's, without any need for product variation or customization. Most manufacturers are forced to customize products, to some degree, for increasingly selective customers or to compete in niche markets. If products and processes are not designed for this, then coping with this variety will be a slow and costly ordeal.

The book is written with the broadest definition of Mass Customization, which includes the entire spectrum from addressing niche markets efficiently to actually providing a unique, custom product for every customer. It will show how to concurrently develop agile products for flexible manufacturing processes that can quickly and easily build custom or niche market products. Mass Customization, per se, is the ultimate application of the principles taught in this book. Companies can apply these principles effectively anywhere along the spectrum: to pursue niche markets or build-to-order strategies; to help with their efforts in flexible manufacturing, just-in-time, and setup/inventory reduction; to help rationalize and consolidate product lines; and to help reduce the cost of variety.

OUTLINE OF THE BOOK

The book is organized into five parts: Executive Overview; Existing Products; The Challenges of Mass Customizing Products:

Cost and Speed; Developing Mass Customized Products; and a concluding Epilogue.

Part I, Executive Overview, presents the paradigm shift to Mass Customization. Chapter 1, by Joe Pine, presents Mass Customization as a formidable competitive strategy with many examples. Joe then makes the case that Mass Customization is the new imperative in product development.

Chapter 2, The Mass Customization Vision, presents an example that has all the mass customization elements that will be discussed in this book. The example is structured to be very "doable" in that it does not depend on high levels of automation or high volume. The two illustrations (Figure 2-1 and 2-2) show the degree of product customization, the factory layout, the information flow, and an elegantly simple concept for manual assembly of mass customized products. Following the illustrations are descriptions of how mass customization is achieved for all the elements of the production system. These are summarized in the table shown in Figure 2-3.

Part II, Existing Products, focuses on the existing product line. Chapter 3 begins with a discussion of current customization attempts. If products and manufacturing processes are not designed for Mass Customization and if companies are operating in the Mass Production paradigm, then costs will rise exponentially with the amount of variety offered. These costs are what we call the *cost of variety,* which is the cost of *attempting* to offer customers variety with inflexible products that are produced in inflexible factories and sold through inflexible channels. After a discussion of the drivers of variety costs, a cost of variety model is presented followed by explanations of the various elements.

Chapter 4 presents methodologies to *rationalize* (consolidate) existing product lines. Market forces may have encouraged, or forced, companies to offer wide varieties of products or customization, even if they cannot do it quickly and inexpensively. If the company is operating in the Mass Production paradigm with large lots and lengthy setups, it simply will not be able to offer much variety in a timely and cost-effective manner. Under these conditions, which are present in most companies, product lines must be rationalized. The methodologies presented show how to analyze the product lines by 12 criteria and how to segregate products into four categories ranging from the "cash cows" that can remain in the mass production mode to the "dogs" with such high variety costs that they should be dropped.

Chapter 5, Standardization, is a bridge between existing products and new products that are to be designed for Mass Customization. Standardization is the prerequisite to any of the agile paradigms: Mass Customization, Agile Manufacturing, Just-in-Time, Flexible Manufacturing, Build-to-Order, and efficiently manufacturing niche market products. To build products "to order" or to mass customize, factories must be flexible enough to build in "lots of one" without setup delays to retrieve parts, find instructions, change fixtures, and reprogram equipment. Thus, it is imperative that agile companies standardize on parts, processes, tools, features, raw materials, and procedures. This chapter contains many practical methodologies for standardization.

Part III addresses the challenges on Mass Customization: cost and speed. This part answers the critical question: "How can anyone really build custom products at the speed and cost of Mass Production?"

Chapter 6, Putting the "Mass" in Mass Customization, shows how to address the cost challenge of Mass Customization, which may seem hard to comprehend for some people. The solution to this apparent paradox can be found by analyzing cost on the basis of total cost. As will be pointed out in Chapter 5, versatile parts and modular architectures may contain parts and modules that may be somewhat more expensive than their mass production counterparts. However, the total cost will be less because of the savings in "overhead" from eliminating nonvalue activities such as setup, inventory, kitting, repairing recurring defects, excessive tooling, wasted machine tool utilization, inefficient use of floor space, materials administration expenses, and excessive service cost from too many parts and procedures.

Chapter 7 addresses the other challenge of Mass Customization: speed. In the Craft Production paradigm, custom goods took longer to make than mass production goods. People who think in the craft production mentality have a hard time comprehending how a mass customization operation can quickly produce custom products. Mass Customization uses flexible or agile manufacturing to build a wide variety of products in any batch (lot) size without stopping production to change the setup. Thus, given the same equipment capacity, a mass customization plant may run at the same output rate as a mass production plant while the equipment is running. However, the mass production plant must stop production to change over to other products, unless it is dedicated to one product, which is very rare today. Thus, the equivalent mass customization plant will actually run faster because the plant is running and producing products all the time.

Chapter 7 presents a 15-step process for implementing agile manufacturing capabilities.

Part IV shows how to develop products for mass customization, niche markets, build-to-order, and flexible manufacturing environments.

Chapter 8 discusses product line planning: How to decide which product families would be suitable for mass customization. Chapter 8 then presents the mass customization order fulfillment process as contrasted with current reactive processes. The information flow is presented from configurators to parametric CAD through CAD/CAM to the flexible factory described in Chapter 7.

Since concurrently designing families of products and compatible flexible manufacturing processes is the most demanding product development challenge, Chapter 9 presents an overview of the author's *whole company synergy* approach, based on his product development seminars.

Chapter 10 shows how to design mass customized products, starting with product definition for families of products. Then, the product line architecture is determined, which will determine various ways of customizing products: modules, adjustments, and dimensional (permanent cutting or mixing to fit) customization. A 16-step process is presented to develop mass customized product lines.

The Epilogue concludes with an essay by Joe Pine on the future of mass customized products.

CUSTOMIZED READING SCENARIOS

Readers may customize their own reading scenarios. Company executives and senior managers can get an overview by reading Chapter 1 on the strategic implications of Mass Customization and Chapter 2, which shows how a mass customization operation works, assuming that all the steps in the rest of the book have been followed.

Any company that produces more than a single "Model T" product would benefit from reading Chapter 3 on understanding the current variety/customization situation and corresponding cost of variety. Implementers who will be rationalizing the product line and standardizing parts, materials, and processes should read Chapters 4 and 5, which are the how-to chapters that can be used as a guide for rationalizing products and implementing standardization.

Companies that need a better understanding about cost and how to lower total cost, especially the cost of variety, should read Chapter 6, Putting the "Mass" in Mass Customization. Companies that have activity-based cost management systems and that base all decisions on total cost criteria may skim through this chapter and focus on issues related to the cost of variety.

Companies that need to improve the flexibility of their factories, reduce lot size to one, reduce inventories, and improve machine tool utilization should read Chapter 7. Companies that have strong flexible or agile manufacturable capabilities may skim through and focus on gaps between their "islands of agility."

Companies that need to design products for Mass Customization will need to thoroughly implement the lessons of the design Chapters: 8, 9, and 10. Remember, success in any product development endeavor is proportional to *how well these principles are followed.*

Strategic planners and those interested in "futurist" thinking should read the Epilogue on the future of Mass Customization.

Dr. David M. Anderson, P.E.   B. Joseph Pine II
Management Consultant   Founder
Anderson Seminars & Consulting   Strategic Horizons LLP
P.O. Box 1082   5239 Lynd Avenue
Lafayette, CA 94549-1082   Cleveland, OH 44124-1030
(510) 253-0900   (216) 449-9180
fax: (510) 283-1330   fax: (216) 449-9182
andersondm@aol.com   shllp@aol.com

PART ONE

EXECUTIVE OVERVIEW

CHAPTER

INTRODUCTION

Mass Customization

The New Imperative in Business

B. Joseph Pine II
Founder, Strategic Horizons LLP

Of the many profound changes to which businesses must respond to succeed in today's turbulent climate, none is more difficult, more perilous, nor more vital than being customer-focused. But the initiatives of most companies—measuring customer satisfaction, implementing quality function deployment, putting together cross-functional teams that span marketing, manufacturing, and development; and so forth—are in fact *market*-focused, not customer-focused. In product development, even when individual customers *are* sought, it is done to create better averages rather than customized goods. The imperative today is to understand and fulfill each *individual* customer's increasingly diverse wants and needs—while meeting the co-equal imperative for achieving low costs. The critical role for executives, managers, and engineers within the product development community is harnessing new technologies, manufacturing capabilities, and management techniques to efficiently serve each customer uniquely.

Like it or not, customers (whether consumers or businesses) are becoming more demanding about getting exactly what they need, while increasing competitive intensity—arising in particular from the globalization and convergence of industries—dictates that costs keep decreasing as well. Where companies used to pursue either a low-cost or a high-differentiation strategy, today companies are increasingly finding that they must adopt strategies embracing *both* efficiency *and* customization. Instead of mass producing standardized goods (and services) or incurring high costs to produce great variety, companies are discovering they can combine the best of both strategies to mass customize their products.

Mass Customization, in short, is the *mass* production of individually *customized* goods and services.* As a technological capability, the ability to mass customize products was anticipated in 1970 by Alvin Toffler in *Future Shock,* delineated (as well as named) in 1987 by Stan Davis in *Future Perfect,* and in 1993 fully fleshed out in my first book, *Mass Customization.*[1] What has emerged in the present is much more than Toffler foresaw 25 years ago, more than Davis envisioned less than 10 years ago, and even more than I could describe just 3 short years ago. Mass Customization is the new imperative in business, one that puts the identification and fulfillment of the wants and needs of individual customers paramount within the company without sacrificing efficiency.

A FEW EXEMPLARS

Many companies are already effectively meeting this challenge. Levi Strauss & Co., for example, has created Personal Pair™ jeans, which (for only about a $10 premium) are tailored to individual consumers along four dimensions: waist, hips, rise, and inseam. The enabling PC-based technology (developed by Custom Clothing Technology Corp. of Newton, Massachusetts, since purchased by Levi Strauss) selects a piece of stock inventory to ensure the consumer likes the fit and then transmits the custom order to Levi's factory in Mountain City, Tennessee, for production. In-store or at-home delivery generally takes less than two weeks.

---

* The term *mass customization* is capitalized when it refers to a system of management, business model, or paradigm for governing corporations and their decision-making processes (as is Mass Production and other such paradigms) and is not capitalized when it refers to operational activities.

In creating Personal Pair, Levi Strauss increased its number of manufacturable sizes by two orders of magnitude: from about 40 to more than 4,000, with five additional options on color/finish and two more on leg cut. But that level of customization is nothing compared to what other companies are doing. Consider window manufacturer Andersen Corp., of Bayport, Minnesota, which has millions and very possibly billions of possible window configurations and saw the number of unique end items shipped explode from 10,000 in 1980 to more than 188,000 in 1995! To handle this rapidly increasing level of customization, Andersen developed a multimedia system called the Window of Knowledge™. The system features an icon structure of more than 50,000 possible window components to let distributors collaborate with end customers in *designing their own* windows and to interactively see exactly how potential designs would look—with such added touches as videos of beautiful, cloud-swept vistas viewed through the on-line windows. This sophisticated design tool automatically generates error-free quotations and manufacturing specifications and transmits completed orders directly to Andersen's factory. The process infrastructure the company put in place also allows it to put new products into its distributors' hands overnight.

While the goods created by both Andersen and Levi Strauss are sold to consumers, Mass Customization has also made inroads in heavy industrial applications. For example, ChemStation, of Dayton, Ohio, mass customizes industrial soap—something most competitors consider to be a commodity—for factory floors, car washes, restaurants, and other commercial outlets. It independently analyzes each customer's needs and then uses its patented "H7" technology and exclusive process to customize the concentration strength, pH-level, enzyme concentration, foaminess, color, odor, and so forth, for that customer. These unique formulations are delivered in bulk in ChemStation's own plastic storage tanks—with the ChemStation logo emblazoned on the front for all to see—that are provided to customer sites to eliminate the need for drums. The company further enhances its overall service simply by ensuring that customers never run out of their particular formulation. By constantly monitoring its tanks at customer sites and thereby learning each customer's usage pattern, the company presciently replenishes inventory before a customer ever has to ask—eliminating any need for the customer to create or even review orders.

As just one more example of the many manufacturers that have embraced Mass Customization, consider the case of Ross Controls, a 70-year-old Troy, Michigan-based manufacturer of pneumatic valves and other air control systems used in heavy industrial processes in the automobile, aluminum, steel, and forestry industries. Through its "ROSS/FLEX" process, Ross learns about its customers' business needs, collaborates with them on precisely tailored designs that will help them meet those needs, and then quickly and efficiently produces their customized products, often replicating that customer's own design across various production lines. By integrating its efficient customization capabilities with the ability to learn about each customer's needs over time, Ross develops a connection to customers that grows with every successive interaction.

To make this happen, the company instituted an integrator position that productively combines marketing, engineering, and manufacturing functions into one person. The integrator's primary task is to "mine the knowledge" of his assigned customers and let them see their knowledge of what is required in their manufacturing process embedded into physical solutions. Interestingly, because the integrator's responsibilities are so antithetical to the normal engineer's way of working—one person must talk with customers, engineer the valve designs, and then determine the manufacturing specifications (including the tool paths for the CNC machines)—Ross found it had to hire new engineers from college *who had not yet learned that engineers were supposed to only do engineering,* and not all that marketing and manufacturing "stuff" as well!

CHANGES IN THE LANDSCAPE OF THE NEW FRONTIER

I subtitled my first book *The New Frontier in Business Competition* because, when I completed it in 1992 Mass Customization was indeed the new frontier: While many companies were moving in that direction and many industry markets were clearly demanding it, only a few companies had truly figured out how to efficiently customize down to the level of individual customers. None of the exemplars above, for example, were mentioned in that book because they had not yet made significant progress (and in the case of Levi Strauss, it was not yet even a gleam in the eye of Sung Park, founder of Custom Clothing Technology Corp.).

Much has changed since then. Not only are more companies mass customizing their products, but as the examples above show, they are doing so to a breadth and depth that is often astonishing compared to what could be done just five short years ago. Much has also changed in my view of what Mass Customization truly is. I described it in my first book as a new system of management (or paradigm) whose controlling focus was "variety and customization through flexibility and quick responsiveness."[2] My intent was to contrast it with the system of Mass Production, to show that this decades-old paradigm—while the reason behind the economic dominance of the United States during much of this century—was no longer appropriate in industries undergoing the high degree of market turbulence characteristic of most markets today. I used the explosion of product proliferation during the 1980s to show that the old system of Mass Production wasn't working anymore, and we needed to move to a new system that began with greater and greater variety and, through a reinforcing feedback loop with customers, blended in more and more customization until every customer was able to purchase a unique good or service.

While that is what often occurs, most companies use product proliferation to forestall true customization, trying desperately to maintain the heritage of Mass Production in the face of rapidly fragmenting markets. Today we can now be very clear: *Variety is not the same as customization.* Variety is producing a product and putting it in finished goods inventory in the hope that some customer will come along and desire it. In contrast, it is customization only if it is produced in *response* to a *particular* customer's desires. (The term *individual customization* is in fact redundant!) Variety is about giving more customers more choices in the hope that they can find something close to what they need. But often we overwhelm customers with so much proliferation that they throw up their hands at having to go through a lengthy decision-making process with little or no support and simply walk away. Fundamentally *customers do not want choice; they just want exactly what they want.* Your task is to figure out (often through collaboration) exactly what they need and then produce it, generally using

design tools (like Andersen's Window of Knowledge) that eliminate the problem of information overload.

And the task of *mass* customization is to do so efficiently, at a
price customers are willing to pay and at a cost that allows for profitable margins. Most companies today handle variety by layering
new work activities on top of existing processes and handle customization through exceptions and expediters—all of which will
add tremendous costs, wasted time, and extra resources. But Mass
Customization is not being everything to everybody; rather, as my
partner at Strategic Horizons LLP, Jim Gilmore, likes to say, it is
doing *only and exactly* what each customer wants, when they want
it. Most mass customizers find that—although there may be a significant up-front investment in developing the products, processes,
and technologies required—mass customized products can cost
nearly the same as mass produced ones, and sometimes less, when
markets become fragmented enough that mass production techniques can no longer effectively predict what customers desire.

Further, most customers are willing to pay a premium (often
10 to 50 percent) simply because customized products *have greater
value* than standardized ones—they more closely match each individual's needs. Margins, therefore, often increase greatly, especially once a company realizes the gains from eliminating the carrying
costs of finished goods inventory, having customers not walk
away when they can't get what they want, and not having to put
some product on sale because no one wanted it. Think of the financial gains in your company that could be realized through the
elimination of finished goods inventory alone!

THE NEW IMPERATIVE

Because of these tremendous advantages, Mass Customization is
moving from being at the frontier to fast becoming an imperative
in industry after industry. It is the next logical progression in business competition.

This can be seen clearly through a framework originally
developed by two University of North Carolina professors (currently visiting at the International Institute for Management
Development in Switzerland)—Bart Victor and Andy Boynton—
and extended in collaboration with me. This framework, given in

Figure 1–1, defines four distinct *business models*—four different ways of succeeding in business.[3] The *Invention* model includes craft producers, entrepreneurs, units of large companies, and others that compete on high differentiation. These organizations constantly create new products as well as the processes by which they are produced: Both product and process change are very dynamic.

For centuries all businesses were craft producers that basically followed the Invention model—if any customer wanted something the company didn't know how to make, an artisan would figure out how to make it and tailor it to the customer's individual tastes. With the Industrial Revolution and in particular Henry Ford's development of the assembly line came the capability for *Mass Production*. Here, everything is stable: These organizations find the one best way to produce a given product and then move down the learning curve as fast as possible to do it. Both product and process change come only very slowly to ensure fixed costs are recouped. Every once in a while (typically four to five years or longer), mass producers would have to depend upon some other Invention organization (usually their own R&D labs) for a new product to be mass produced.

FIGURE 1–1

The New Competitive Reality

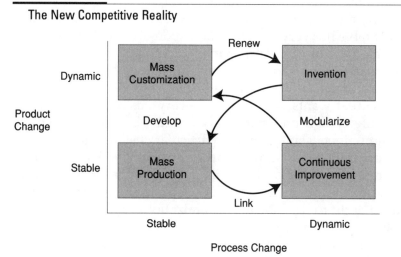

Source: Bart Victor, Andrew C. Boynton, and B. Joseph Pine II.

Mass producers were thus very dependent on Invention organizations to create new products, and Invention organizations were often dependent on mass producers to provide a ready market for their highly differentiated creations.[4] This synergy between Mass Production and Invention organizations worked very well for a very long time; it was at the heart of America's economic success during this century. But Japanese companies (in particular but not exclusively) figured out that if they continually improved their processes, they could achieve *both* lower costs *and* higher quality than the typical mass producer. By embracing dynamic process change, they could gain a significant advantage over their competitors. This was so different from the old ways of doing things that it took American producers a long time to figure out exactly what it was. Now most companies subscribe to the *Continuous Improvement* business model (at least in principle, if not fully in practice), incorporating such innovations as statistical process control, cross-functional teams, total quality management, and customer satisfaction measurements, to name just a few. At its ideal, organizations following this model have a process life cycle of one execution: Every execution is different—and better—than the last.

While companies everywhere seem to be making great strides in quality by focusing on Continuous Improvement, many firms are already moving beyond this to the *Mass Customization* business model.[5] Stable but very flexible and responsive processes provide a dynamic flow of products, enabling companies to achieve *both* low costs *and* high individual customization. In this business model, the organization's primary thrust is to identify and fulfill the individual wants and needs of every customer. Ideally, the product life cycle is one unit: Every product is different from the last—and uniquely suited to that particular customer's needs.

Organizations can move between business models, but based on the research of Victor, Boynton, and myself, as well as direct client experience, there is a definite order to the transformations that must occur to reach Mass Customization. The first such transformation, from Invention to Mass Production, is called *development* and is a well-known activity. It requires articulating and stabilizing the product and process, making them definable and repeatable for high-volume, low-cost production.

The resulting Mass Production organization has historically been very hierarchical and bureaucratic, with very little information flow between functions. To enable the organization to switch to Continuous Improvement, these vertically separated functions must be *linked* through cross-functional teams, information sharing, and a horizontal process focus. The result is a set of tightly coupled, high-quality processes capable of constant improvement.[6]

To move to Mass Customization requires that products be *modularized* to provide unique combinations for any customer. This enables companies to efficiently deliver individual modules of customer value—whether it be a particular length of pant, a specific pitch of a window, a certain pH factor in industrial soap, or an exacting pneumatic valve connection—within the structure of a total product architecture.

Further, the tightly coupled processes created through Continuous Improvement should also be broken apart and modularized, so that, at its ideal, specific process modules can dynamically link to other process modules as required to create the unique end-to-end value chain that will best satisfy each individual customer. This results in a dynamic network where linkages between people and processes are loosely coupled to enable the mass customization of goods and services.

Mass Customization organizations also have to be able to *renew* themselves, to realize when they cannot satisfy a particular customer or cannot go after a particular market opportunity with their current envelope of customization. This causes them to reinvent a new product module or a new process or to link to an organization inside or outside the firm to provide the new capability required. And at times, firms may have to overthrow their entire product or process architecture—before their competitors do—and reinvent one that will once again provide a distinct competitive advantage.

Although the organization will never want to "live" in Mass Production again, it does have to go through the activities outlined above for each new product, process, or organization module created in Invention. Each one still has to be developed and stabilized, linked to the rest of the organization and be made of high quality, and finally be made to fit the modular architecture for Mass Customization.

This, then, is the new competitive reality. It is an ongoing cycle of business transformations that requires a rapid and fluid movement between each successive business model—not a one-time selection of any particular model. Those firms that can manage this transformation cycle better than their competitors will be uniquely positioned to succeed in today's increasingly turbulent environment. The entire set of business transformations can be seen through one of the true pioneers of Mass Customization discussed in my first book: the Motorola Paging Products Group in Boynton Beach, Florida. During the 1980s, Motorola as a company moved beyond the traditional mass production of electronic products to embrace a Continuous Improvement mind-set. It implemented many quality and cycle time improvement programs, with the company's vaunted Six Sigma program (which strived to reduce defects to 3.4 parts per million) becoming the most well known. But when Japanese competitors significantly stepped up the competitive requirements through their own Continuous Improvement programs, the Paging Group went beyond the competition to Mass Customization at an organizational level.

In just 18 months, Motorola created an (almost) fully automated manufacturing system that could produce any one of 29 million different combinations of pagers in Boynton Beach within an hour and a half of the order being taken via a sales representative's laptop computer anywhere in the country. This drastically changed the nature of competition in the industry, leading to Motorola's position as the sole surviving American producer of pagers and as the holder of more than 40 percent of worldwide market share. But it didn't stop there.

Since that project, code-named Bandit to encourage its members to "steal" from any source inside or outside the company to create the best possible manufacturing system, the Paging Group has gone far beyond its original capabilities. It has created what it calls the "Fusion Factory" because it unifies and integrates engineering, manufacturing, and marketing into one enterprise system that, at an operations level, looks and acts remarkably like the framework in Figure 1–1.[7] Because of the information technology infrastructure that the Paging Group has put in place, engineers can invent new module designs on a computer-aided design system (renewal), simulate the performance of that "virtual" design using various electronic tools (development), ensure that the manufacturing processes exist with sufficient raw materials inventory and capacity to physically create the module in concert with the rest of the pager manufacturing processes (linking), build the complete product specifications and dynamic manufacturing instructions on-line (modularization), and send them to the Fusion Factory for production. As a testament to how far Motorola has come, one of its customers (a vice president of a paging services firm) told me how his designers collaborated with the Paging Group to design a new feature peculiar to their consumers. The Motorola engineers left on Friday afternoon with an agreed-to description of the feature and came back Monday morning with working pagers!

One clear result of the success of Japanese competitors and others that embraced the Continuous Improvement model was the tremendous force for change it became. Company after company in industry after industry *had* to increase their quality and lower their costs to compete in the face of a clearly superior business model to Mass Production. But a second result, perhaps less clear but of equal importance, is that all of this improvement *taught customers to become more demanding.* Once they discovered they could get both low costs and high quality from one company, they stopped putting up with poor service from others and began demanding that companies provide goods and services exactly as promised. Indeed, these two effects were reinforcing, driving each other to greater and greater levels, until today in most industries Continuous Improvement only gets companies into the game.[8] Quality is no longer a differentiator.

We are nowhere near that point yet with customization, but companies in the next decade will be faced with *the same precise predicament.* Once customers begin to see that they can get products made just for them that almost exactly match their needs at a price they are willing to pay, you can believe that they are going to ask for it elsewhere. Mass Customization is indeed moving out of the frontier and becoming an imperative.

THE NEW IMPERATIVE IN PRODUCT DEVELOPMENT

The good news is that Mass Customization need not be a repeat of the short-lived competitive-advantage game, at least not if it is done right. There are so many degrees of freedom for what, how, where, and when a company customizes that it can open a large amount of competitive space. And much of that freedom depends upon what occurs in product development. For any company to realize the full potential of this business model, those responsible for bringing new products to market must fully embrace it as an imperative as well. Without the support, diligence, and effort required to create products that can be mass customized, no company will fare well.

There are a number of issues concerning how best to do this for any particular company, ranging from the nature of the product to how it is represented to customers; from how to create an infrastructure to produce it, to how to determine when to renew it. These crucial issues are discussed below.

Customized versus Customizable versus Customizing

The first such issue is deciding whether to create products that can be customized for individual customers or standard products that can be *adapted* for or by customers to meet their specific needs. Adaptive products come in two flavors, customizable and customizing. With *customizable* products, the customer (or perhaps an intermediary) selects from various options that are present within the product the one that most meets the customer's needs at this time. Perhaps the simplest customizable product to think about is the graphic equalizer, a stereo component that allows customers to select the precise amount of different frequency bands they desire to hear. And perhaps the most common customizable products today are personal computer applications that over the past decade have become highly customizable, with tool bars, preference menus, power modes, and other increasingly sophisticated ways of enabling users to customize the software to their liking.

With *customizing* products, it is the product itself that adapts to the user. This can range from something as simple as the Gillette Sensor razor that, thanks to a system of flexible springs, "automatically adjusts to the contours of your face" (as the advertising attests) to something as complicated as a Matsushita washing machine that has optical sensors, weight sensors, and fuzzy logic to determine which of 600 cycles would best wash each particular load of clothes.

In either case, because one product can be adapted to a large number of users—and can be further customized to each use—this causes no extraordinary changes in manufacturing as do customized products. It is, therefore, the most comfortable path to customization taken by those still ensconced within the heritage of Mass Production. Automakers, for example, have been constantly adding adaptive (both customizable and customizing) features that embed multiple permutations within a standard design—a particularly valid development strategy because cars are often driven by multiple people. Recent announcements include an Autostick feature on Chrysler Eagle Visions that allows drivers to switch between automatic and standard transmission; push-button memories on Lincoln Continentals to adjust seating positions for two different drivers; and, furthering that innovation, a "self-adjusting comfort seat" under development by Johnson Controls that wraps around and adjusts to the proper pressure points of any driver.

While an appropriate first step for mass producers, there is a real danger here. It is imperative for any development organization not to blindly latch onto adaptive products as the solution for all time. This would foreclose many facets of customization that are or will become very important to customers, such as body styling, height adjustments, accessorization, and feature choices with automobiles. Adaptive products do not place a company within the Mass Customization quadrant of Figure 1–1; they are not created in response to a particular customer's needs, but they are produced one time for everyone. Increasingly, as more and more companies embrace Mass Customization, customers will come to expect that products be produced just for them.

The most feasible approach is generally to provide some degree of both customization and adaptability, particularly for sophisticated or complex products with a high degree of functionality. One company that does a superb job of managing both of these facets is lighting-control manufacturer Lutron Electronics Co., Inc., of Coopersburg, Pennsylvania. Many years ago Lutron was the first in its industry to embed microprocessors in its products to give people great control over their own lighting environments. Customers can achieve maximum productivity (in offices) or design appropriate moods (in homes) at different times for different occasions. For example, Lutron's GRAFIK Eye™ product connects different lights in a room and enables the user to choose instantly among combinations for alternative lighting effects he has programmed, such as party, reading, family, and romantic "scenes" in a living room. Lutron not only embeds adaptive features into its lighting controls, but it also collaboratively creates new designs to meet particular customer needs, such as integrating controls into security systems and matching any color sample the customer desires. It is the effective combination of customized and adaptive features within its product lines that makes Lutron the number one company in its industry.

Product Architectures

To efficiently customize products for individual customers requires a *product architecture.* This architecture determines what universe of benefits the product is intended to provide to customers and then within that universe what specific permutations of functionality will be provided at this time. These permutations are in turn defined by a modular schema that specifies what types of components can be used and what linkage system will connect them to create specific products for specific customers.

In speeches and workshops with clients, whenever I talk about modularity I bring up Lego® building blocks and ask, "What can you build with Legos?" The answer, of course, is "anything you want!" because of the large number of different kinds of blocks and a simple, elegant system of tabs and holes that enables them to be instantly snapped together. Every product architecture needs to standardize these two elements: a set of modules and a linkage system for snapping them together. Without standardization here, no company can hope to efficiently customize anywhere. Modularity, once again, is *the key* to mass customizing in product development.[9]

Process Infrastructures

Modularity, as mentioned earlier when discussing the movement from Continuous Improvement to Mass Customization, applies not only to products but also to the processes by which they are manufactured. Product developers must work with manufacturing engineers and operators to create a *process infrastructure* that automates the linkages between modular process capabilities—atomic units of value that the company knows how to efficiently perform. Each of the exemplars discussed earlier employs such an infrastructure that enables it to be as effective as possible in ascertaining what customers need, to be as efficient as possible in linking customer-unique capabilities, and to match the two as effortlessly as possible.

Many R&D functions are implementing groupware to share information and resources. While that can be a very good start at breaking down the walls of communication that have grown up around the "Not Invented Here" syndrome, today's groupware offerings in no way fill the needs required of process infrastructures. Groupware, at least as it has thus far been implemented, is suitable only for Invention, not Mass Customization, because it is fundamentally based on ad hoc activities. Existing tools have no notion of process capability modules that are essentially sitting in inventory, waiting to be called upon to fulfill the next customer's wants and needs. Rather, what a company needs are work flow management, coordination software, enterprise networks, common customer views (such as with image processing or shared databases), computer-integrated manufacturing, and agile manufacturing capabilities—what are generically categorized here as process infrastructures—that can all be used to automate the linkages between processes and the relationships between people, enabling exactly the right resources to be brought together to cost-effectively service a customer's unique wants and needs.

Creating such an infrastructure requires a significant financial investment and implementation effort. This may be difficult—if not impossible—to cost-justify by current financial procedures because it is impossible to forecast exactly what process capabilities customers will want at any particular time. While academia and consultants are making progress on how to do this better (such as strategic options theory), when it comes right down to it, companies thus far have had to make a commitment to Mass Customization based on faith (that's right: faith!) in their own ability to create the future, rather than their own perception of what worked in the past. Top management must be convinced that the future will be a battle over who can best efficiently serve each customer uniquely—or there may not be enough of a future to worry about.

Product Representation

One key element of a process infrastructure is a design tool that matches customer need with company capabilities. Without one, it is too easy to overwhelm customers (or their proxies: distributors and sales reps) with so many permutations and combinations that they can't figure out which one is right for them. Design tools let customers "play with the possibilities." This is not, however, like dumping the Legos on the floor and saying, "OK, let's build your product!" Rather, design tools must manage the complexity that, on the one hand, allows you to tailor your products to individual customers, while on the other threatens to choke your customers' ability to quickly, easily, and without hassle find exactly what they want.

Andersen Corp.'s Window of Knowledge is a very sophisticated design tool provided to distributors to enable their collaboration with homeowners on custom window design. Its success is predicated on highly trained personnel that know windows, know customer needs, and know how to use the design tool to guide customers to the right solution. Without such a person, the process would resemble Lego-dumping and would not be effective.

Less complex products, however, need less complex solutions, such as that provided by MusicWriter of Los Gatos, California, when it began mass customizing sheet music. It digitized the music notations of each song and placed them in disk storage within an electronic touch-screen kiosk. Rather than browse through hundreds of different choices by hand (several thousand in larger stores), customers simply walk up to the kiosk and start typing in the title or composer. The system automatically presents and narrows their choices as they type until exactly the right piece is found. It can then play back and display the available versions, transpose the song to any key desired, and immediately print each customer's exact choice.

MusicWriter is great at listening to customers' expressed wants, but successful design tool efforts must also aim to surface unarticulated customer needs. Few people, for example, can walk into an eyewear store and truthfully state the exact shape of frames they desire; Paris Miki draws this out of each interaction with consumers *without* forcing them to wade through scores of frames in inventory on the shelf. The Tokyo-based eyewear company, one of the largest in the world, spent five years creating the Mikissemes Design System that analyzes a digital picture of each consumer's face, along with a set of interview statements that the consumer selects to indicate the look he is trying to achieve, and then suggests the shape of eyeglasses that is just right for that consumer. Once he makes his final choice—including the option of looking at alternatives or even taking a mouse and changing the frame design himself—Paris Miki can produce the rimless glasses in about an hour.

Learning Relationships

As Paris Miki has found, making known what was previously unknown—even to the customer himself—develops not only a better product offering but also a stronger relationship with that customer. And in today's hotly contested competitive environment, the most worthwhile asset of any corporation may be its long-lasting relationships with its customers.

A rapidly expanding array of interactive technologies—including electronic kiosks, on-line services, e-mail, fax response, World Wide Web sites, and so forth—enables companies to efficiently dialogue with thousands, and potentially millions, of individual customers. By interacting with them on a personal basis, companies can better learn the wants, needs, and preferences of each, and can then fulfill those preferences with better tailored goods and services. This combination of mass customization in operations, with what Don Peppers and Martha Rogers call one-to-one marketing, forms the basis of a *learning relationship* that grows, deepens, and becomes smarter over time.[10] The more the customer teaches the company, the better it can provide exactly what he wants—when, where, and how he wants it—and the more difficult it will be for him to be enticed away. Even if a competitor were to build the exact same capabilities, a customer already involved in a learning relationship with a firm would have to spend an excessive amount of time and energy teaching the competitor what the firm *already knows.*

This is exactly what Ross Controls does. Its integrators work with customers to ascertain their strategic needs and then see that those needs are fulfilled via unique valve configurations. The ROSS/FLEX process has become so effective that one $20 billion division of General Motors—the company that seems to have patented supplier squeezing!—won't buy pneumatic valves from anyone else and won't let its suppliers go elsewhere either.

Learning relationships are a singularly powerful competitive advantage. Their many benefits include:

- *Increased margins.* Because your products are tailored precisely to customer needs, your customers receive greater value and are thus willing to pay a premium price.
- *Increased revenue per customer.* Because you know more about your customers than any competitor, they keep coming back to you every time they are in the market for what you offer.
- *Increased number of customers (at lower acquisition costs).* Because your customers are so pleased with the experience, they will tell their friends and associates, many of whom would try it and join in, and they would tell others, and so on, and so on.
- *Increased customer retention.* The more each customer teaches you about his individual wants, needs, and preferences, the more difficult it will be for him to obtain an equivalent level of service from a competitor.

Renewal

Learning relationships enable companies to essentially *keep their customers forever*—with two provisos. First, once in such a "monopoly" relationship the company must not jack up its prices; and second, the company must continue to learn from its customers and fulfill what it learns with more precisely tailored products. This in turn requires that the company be able to *renew* its product architecture and process infrastructure in response to specific customer requirements that cannot yet be met. As discussed above, this means "leaving" the Mass Customization model and returning to Invention to create something truly new.

This does not mean that every customer whim must be satisfied, nor that every real requirement must be fulfilled. However, a company should determine what to do with every requirement through a decision-making process like the following:

1. Does this fit within the universe of possibility we have defined? If not, do not fulfill it. But do track it along with all other unfulfilled requests to determine when the present product architecture should be abandoned in favor of a more encompassing one.

2. If so, does this make sense to do right now? Consider such factors as the lifetime value of the customer and how much this decision will hurt or help the relationship, the willingness of the customer to help pay for the development, which other customers would desire this functionality, how much time and costs are involved, and the current capacity of the organization for renewal. If not, schedule it for later or for reexamination at some point, again tracking the requirement for further consideration.

3. If so, invent the module for this particular customer. And then determine whether this module should "remain" in Invention or should be developed, linked, and modularized to be added as a standard module to the product architecture or a standard capability to the process infrastructure. Many of the same factors as cited in point 2 above come into play here.

When faced with new customer demands, many product development groups will seek to invent new products only when many requirements are known and understood. The beauty of Mass Customization is that the modular architecture and/or infrastructure enables this to be done incrementally, one module at a time, at very low costs. Instead of massive development efforts—which often end up with a large share of the time spent reinventing what someone else somewhere has already done—new modules can be created and dynamically linked into an existing architecture with a fraction of the effort. This is exactly what Motorola does so well with its Fusion Factory, or what Ross does every time it works with a customer to determine how its pneumatic valves can enable that customer to realize strategic value. They don't completely reinvent a new pager or a new valve; they work from existing designs to reuse 80 to 90 percent (or even 95 or 99 percent!) of what they've used before, and then spend their truly creative work only on what *has* to be innovated to meet that particular customer's needs.

That is the power of embracing Mass Customization within product development. It is becoming an imperative precisely because that power can either be used by you for your customers or it will be used against you by your competitors.

The choice is yours. But you can't hope to take advantage of that power until you master what Dave Anderson has to say in the rest of this book about reducing the cost of variety, rationalizing existing product lines, standardizing parts and processes, making decisions based on total cost, achieving operational flexibility, and concurrently designing families of products and processes around modular architectures. My final word of advice is simply this: Start now!

NOTES

1. See Alvin Toffler, *Future Shock* (New York: Bantam Books, 1970), pp. 261–322; Stanley M. Davis, *Future Perfect* (Reading, MA: Addison-Wesley Publishing Company, Inc., 1987), pp. 138–190; and B. Joseph Pine II, *Mass Customization: The New Frontier in Business Competition* (Boston: Harvard Business School Press, 1993).

2. Pine, ibid., p. 44.

3. It is very interesting to see how this framework has evolved. To trace that evolution, see Andrew C. Boynton and Bart Victor, "Beyond Flexibility: Building and Managing the Dynamically Stable Organization," *California Management Review*, Fall 1991, pp. 53–66; Pine, *Mass Customization*, pp. 215–221; A. C. Boynton, B. Victor, and B. J. Pine II, "New Competitive Strategies: Challenges to Organizations and Information Technology," *IBM Systems Journal*, 32, no. 1, (1993), pp. 40–64; B. Joseph Pine II, Bart Victor, and Andrew C. Boynton, "Making Mass Customization Work," *Harvard Business Review*, 71, no. 5 (September–October 1993), pp. 108–19; B. Joseph Pine II, Bart Victor, and Andrew C. Boynton, "Aligning IT with New Competitive Strategies," in *Competing in the Information Age: Strategic Alignment in Practice*, Jerry N. Luftman, ed, (New York: Oxford University Press, 1996), pp. 73–96; and Bart Victor and Andrew C. Boynton, *The Right Path: The Transformation of Organizational Knowledge for Competitive Advantage* (Boston: Harvard Business School Press, 1997, forthcoming).

4. The idea that Mass Production and Invention organizations were dependent on each other was first articulated by MIT Professor Michael Piore, my advisor at the Sloan School of Management. It was applying this insight to the framework that led us to discover-

ing the figure-8 path that leads from Invention, through Mass
Production and Continuous Improvement to Mass Customization
and back again to Invention. For discussions on the concept of
"industrial dualism" see Michael J. Piore, "Dualism as a Response
to Flux and Uncertainty" and "The Technological Foundations of
Dualism and Discontinuity," in *Dualism and Discontinuity in
Industrial Societies*, Suzanne Berger and Michael J. Piore, ed
(Cambridge, England: Cambridge University Press, 1980), pp.
13–81.

5. For a fuller description of the differences between Continuous
Improvement and Mass Customization and of the difficulty in mak-
ing this transformation, see B. Joseph Pine II, "Challenges to Total
Quality Management in Manufacturing," in *The Quality Yearbook*,
1995 edition, James W. Cortada and John A. Woods, ed. (New York:
McGraw-Hill, Inc., 1995), pp. 69–75.

6. In fact, process improvement is rarely if ever constant, but rather it
is episodic. As explained by Marcie J. Tyre and Wanda J. Orlikowski
in "Exploiting Opportunities for Technological Improvement in
Organizations," *Sloan Management Review,* 35, no. 1 (Fall 1993), pp.
13–26, a burst of activity is followed by a time of gradual stability,
followed by another burst once new challenges surface (or unresolved problems become too great to ignore). In essence, those organizations that have mastered Continuous Improvement really
"bounce" between that model and the more stable Mass Production
model on an episodic basis.

7. For a complete description of Motorola's Fusion Factory, see Russ
Strobel and Andy Johnson, "Pocket Pagers in Lots of One," *IEEE
Spectrum* 30, no. 9 (September 1993), pp. 29–32. Since this article was
written, it appears that Motorola went too far with the automation
of its current architecture of pagers and has had trouble responding
to demand for features outside of that modular architecture. As
good as its Paging Products Group is—and it is among the best of
mass customizers—its current experience is a testament to the need
to renew not just capabilities but architectures as well (what can be
called macro-renewal).

8. Note that this is the same thing that happened in the movement
from Craft to Mass Production. Once customers got used to having
low costs in automobiles and textiles, they began demanding it
across other industries (including service industries, for which back
offices became the equivalent of assembly lines). As a result, thousands upon thousands of craft producers went out of business, and
millions of craftsmen became assembly-line workers, just as many

people have been "reengineered" and "downsized" out of their jobs in the past two decades because of the inability of their companies to provide what their customers wanted at a price they were willing to pay.

9. There are at least six different ways of modularizing and a myriad ways of doing each depending on a company's particular circumstances; see Pine, *Mass Customization*, pp. 196–212. Other good resources on this are Karl T. Ulrich and Steven D. Eppinger, *Product Design and Development* (New York: McGraw-Hill, 1995) and G. D. Galsworth, *Smart, Simple Design: Using Variety Effectiveness to Reduce Total Cost and Maximize Customer Selection* (Essex Junction, VT: Omneo, 1994). The six types of modularity discussed in *Mass Customization* are based on earlier work by Ulrich and one of his students.

10. For more information on learning relationships and on Ross Controls in particular, see B. Joseph Pine II, Don Peppers, and Martha Rogers, "Do You Want to Keep Your Customers Forever?" *Harvard Business Review* 73, no. 2 (March–April 1995), pp. 103–114. Although written for marketers, all product developers should also read Peppers and Rogers fine book, *The One to One Future: Building Relationships One Customer at a Time* (New York: Currency Doubleday, 1993).

CHAPTER

The Mass Customization Vision

Few products today can be manufactured like mass-produced Model T's, without any need for product variation or customization. Most manufacturers are forced to customize products to some degree for increasingly selective customers or to compete in niche markets. However, if products are not designed well for this and if manufacturing is not flexible enough, then customizing products will be a slow and costly ordeal.

The next paradigm, after the century-old Mass Production, is *Mass Customization*, which is the ability to design and manufacture customized products *at mass production efficiency and speed*. This book will show how to develop products that can be quickly and inexpensively customized for niche markets or even for individual customers.

Success will depend on strong product development methodologies that enable multifunctional design teams to concurrently design whole families of products and flexible manufacturing processes. Products must be designed around common parts, versatile modules, standardized interfaces, common fixturing geometries, and standard processes. To assure the required manufacturing flexibility, products and processes must be concurrently designed to eliminate all setup steps, such as kitting, retrieving parts or tools, changing fixtures, manually positioning parts, or finding instructions.

The results will be well worth the investment. Companies that use these techniques will experience *ultra-fast* development of modular products, the agility to quickly respond to changing markets and opportunities, delivery superiority, price premium opportunities, lower overhead costs, and better satisfaction of customer needs.

A MASS CUSTOMIZATION MODEL

This chapter shows how Mass Customization can be implemented by way of an example product that has all the mass customization elements that will be discussed in this book. The example product is an electronic system. This generic category includes all types of computers, instruments, communication devices, audiovisual equipment, electronic games, small appliances, and so forth. Specifically, this example will be based on a small instrument that can be customized with unique software and many different combinations of meters, dials, cases, and various internal parts. However, the mass customization principles described here apply to all products.

This model is structured to be very doable in that it is does not depend on high levels of automation or high volume. The only programmable machine tools used are circuit board assembly equipment and CNC (computer numerically controlled) machining centers, the most common CNC machine tools in industry. The final assembly is manual, which was selected for this example for several reasons. Most companies may not have the volume or the budget for the equipment necessary for automated mass customization. Of course, all the principles demonstrated here can be applied to more automated operations. The whole operation is build-to-order with kanban part resupply (described later), which can be independent of MRP (material requirements planning) systems, which are too dependent on reliable forecasts and accurate bills of materials.

Figure 2–1 shows a close-up view of the manual assembly station. Figure 2–2 shows the overall flow of information and parts for the mass customization operations. The next discussion will describe the manufacture, assembly, and flow of the parts, using

F I G U R E 2–1

Manual Assembly Station for Mass Customization

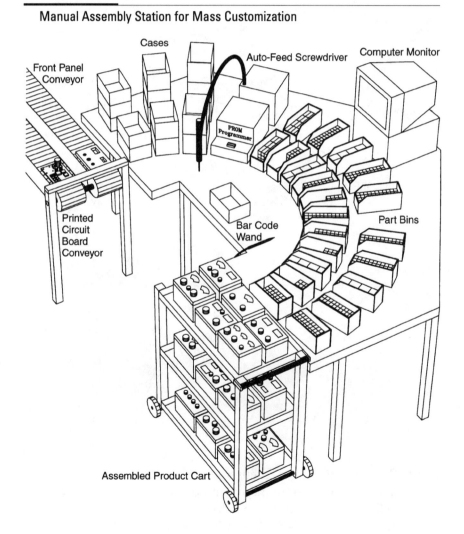

FIGURE 2–2

Overall Flow of Information and Parts for Mass Customization

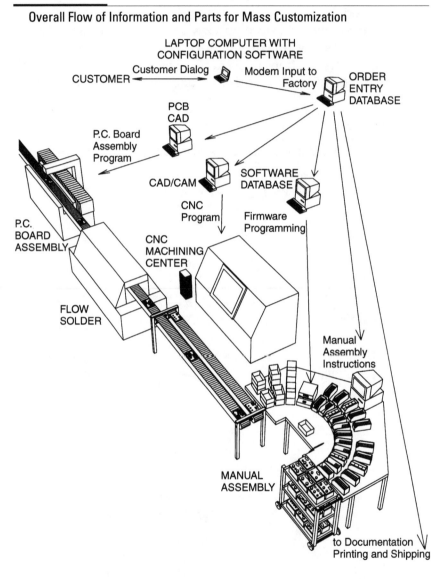

Figure 2–1. The following discussion will describe the information flow that directs the people and machines to manufacture, assemble, and ship the mass customized product, as shown in Figure 2–2. The information flow will be discussed in more detail in Chapter 8.

PARTS MANUFACTURE

The Printed Circuit Board

Versatile Bare Board

Like most electronic systems, the electronic circuitry for this product is manufactured on a printed circuit board (PCB). To optimize flexibility, one cleverly designed "bare board" is used, which can be "loaded" with various sets of components to achieve various levels of functionality and options.

Bare boards consist of layers of fiberglass insulation on which are mounted layers of metal "traces." These traces connect to holes or pads to which the components are soldered after the components are inserted or placed on the board. Because of the inherent setup in its manufacturing process, it is unlikely that bare boards will be able to be built in lots of one. Therefore, the bare boards will be have to be in large enough lots to amortize the significant setup costs of production. This is why mass customizers will want to minimize the number of different bare boards, with these versatile usage scenarios. The bare boards will either be stocked in raw parts inventory or be resupplied by a kanban resupply system, as will be discussed in Chapter 7 and later in this chapter.

A cleverly designed board can accommodate various component placement scenarios: Certain functions can be added or deleted by either placing or omitting certain components. When necessary, zero ohm "resistors" (shunts) can be automatically inserted and soldered to compensate for missing components and to complete the circuitry.

All versions of this instrument are based on the same bare board. All versions have certain minimum functions. Simple versions may require only a few components beyond the minimum. Other versions can have whatever functionality is required by the customer. Multiple versions of one function (e.g., dual channels) are possible by automatically placing appropriate components. The most advanced, complex version will use all the component locations.

Bar Code Identification

Each bare board has a unique bar code that was either laser etched by the bare board vendor or affixed in a preprinted bar code label to the board. The unique bar code numbers are simply sequential at this point, simplifying bar code etching or printing. When the bare board bar code is first read at PCB assembly, its unique number is permanently associated with the current work order. From then on, this bar code number will call up CNC programs for PCB assembly, instructions for manual assembly, packaging information, and shipping directions.

Flexible Manufacturing of the Printed Circuit Board (PCB) Assembly

Most printed circuit boards are assembled by programmable automation equipment that either *inserts* leaded components or *places* surface-mounted components on the bare board. In most manufacturing operations, these versatile machine tools are either dedicated to a single product or used in a batch mode, with expensive downtime used to change parts, fixtures, and programs. However, these computer-controlled circuit board assembly machines can be configured to vary assembly programs and insert components differently for different customer needs. Printed circuit board assembly represents significant opportunities for automatic customization using equipment that may already exist!

For PCB assembly to be flexible, certain rules to eliminate setup must be followed:

1. All bare boards must be the same size (the same form factor) with the same tooling holes to eliminate fixturing setup. Alternately, universal fixtures can be used that can mount multiple board sizes.

2. The component count (for different components) *for the product family* must not exceed machine bin capacity. This depends on component standardization, which will be addressed in Chapter 5.

3. All programs must be able to be downloaded quickly from a file server.

For this instrument, all boards are the same size; all components can be stored permanently in machine bins, and the programs can be quickly downloaded from the order entry database. Component numbers are minimized by combining functions into standard VLSI (very large scale integration) chips and company-specific application-specific integrated circuits (ASICs).

Application Specific Integrated Circuits

One type of component that can be automatically placed on the circuit board is a company-specific or product-specific integrated circuit called an ASIC (application specific integrated circuit). Normally considered only for high-volume products, ASICs can simplify assembly and improve quality and reliability by reducing the number of parts to be assembled. Product quality is determined by the quality level (percent good) *to the exponent of the number of parts.*[1] For example, converting 40 simple integrated circuits to one ASIC changes the exponent from 50 to 1, thus resulting in significant quality improvements. If the quality level of the ICs was 99.9 percent (1,000 defects per million), then the quality degradation would be $(.999)^{50}$ or 95.12 percent, representing a 5 percent quality drop. Replacing these 50 chips with one ASIC would raise product quality almost 5 percent. Doing this several times with ASICs or VLSI devices would result in a significant quality improvement.

The computational needs of *many* company products can be integrated into one (or more) company-specific ASIC. Even if each product uses only one-quarter of the ASIC, all those products will experience assembly and quality benefits. Plus, the ASIC order quantity would be four times that of a single-use ASIC, thus putting the ASIC option within the reach of low-volume producers. Integrating many functions together also saves circuit space and makes it possible to put all circuitry on a single circuit board, thus eliminating card cages and interboard wiring operations.

ASICs that are based on a product family can even be customized with several standard layers and a "custom" layer for a specific product or group of products. One final benefit of ASICs is that they are virtually impossible to reverse engineer, thus making the product harder to copy. The very presence of ASICs in your product may discourage competitors from "cloning" it.

This instrument has one ASIC that covers many routine functions for all instruments. Since several product lines use this chip, order quantities were sufficient for the investment.

Sockets and Connectors

The product can be upgraded, expanded, or customized further by the use of sockets and connectors that are automatically soldered to the circuit board. Firmware can be inserted in a compatible socket (see "On-line Firmware Programming" section below). Similarly, memory can be installed during manufacture or added later by the customer or somewhere along the distribution chain. Connectors can be used to customize a standard "motherboard" with custom "daughter-boards." Upgrade and expansion daughter-boards can be added to these connectors. Versatile daughter-board connectors may be able to extend the product life by adding new functions and technology.

This product uses one PROM socket for firmware and SIMM sockets for memory, which allows various amounts of memory to be built in or added later. Further, the main processor is socketed so that in-circuit emulators can be used for debugging, and so that it can be upgraded later. There is one connector for a current set of daughter-board options and another connector for future options.

Automatic Soldering

If the circuit boards in this operation are the same size and thickness, they can all be automatically soldered, without setup changes, by "wave soldering" equipment for leaded components or "reflow soldering" equipment for surface-mounted components. To avoid setup changes at the soldering stage, circuit boards must be the same thickness and size or "form factor." The only other way to accommodate different size boards without a setup change is to solder them in standard solder fixtures. From a quality standpoint, automatic soldering is one of the most refined of all industrial processes. Many PCB assembly houses routinely achieve defect rates of 3 defects per million. Because of this and the poor quality and reliability performance of hand solder, products should be designed to eliminate hand soldering.

For this example, all circuit boards pass through automatic soldering and cleaning on their way to one of many assembly stations.

Display of Instructions

After automatic soldering, the custom circuit board is placed on a simple conveyor belt, which takes it to the manual assembly station, as shown at the far left of Figures 2–1 and 2–2. When the worker "wands" the board with a bar code wand, assembly instructions are instantly displayed on the computer monitor shown at the far right of Figure 2–1. The last section of this chapter will discuss how these manual assembly instructions are generated.

On-Line Firmware Programming

Custom software can be downloaded into the PROM (programmable read only memory) by the on-line PROM programmer, shown next to the cases in Figure 2–1. The worker picks up the standard PROM "blank" from the parts bin next to the PROM programmer, inserts it into the "zero insertion force" socket of the PROM programmer, and starts downloading software that has been automatically configured for this customer by the software database (shown in Figure 2–2). When PROM programming is completed, the worker inserts the PROM into the awaiting socket in the circuit board before the circuit board is assembled into the case. The circuit board with custom software can be tested by a board level functional tester at this point, if necessary.

An alternative to on-line PROM programming at assembly would be to program the PROM just before it is assembled into the board by the PCB assembly equipment. However, this scenario usually dictates that the PROM be soldered to the circuit board, which may limit upgrade, service, and test options. The PROM could be programmed and automatically inserted into a socket, but the board assembly equipment may not be able to assemble both the sockets and the PROM into the socket without setup changes.

PRODUCT ASSEMBLY

The Case

The worker begins the actual product assembly by choosing one of the three sizes of case (from the three piles shown next to the conveyors in Figure 2–1) based on the instructions on the computer monitor. All versions of the case have the same mounts for the PCB, power supply, and front panel.

The Auto-Feed Screwdriver

Then the worker mounts the circuit board, with its newly programmed PROM chip, in the case with the auto-feed screwdriver shown in Figure 2–1 to the left of the worker. As will be pointed out in Chapter 5, if the entire assembly can be performed with only one size of screw, then all the screws can be oriented and fed though a tube so they are available whenever the power screwdriver is actuated. The screwdriver itself is counterbalanced by a constant force spring overhead (not shown). Fastening torque is preset so that every screw is driven in with the proper torque.

For this instrument, only one screw type is used for all fastening functions. All screws are fastened from above, which matches the screwdriver orientation.

The Power Supply

Next the power supply is mounted in the case with the auto-feed screwdriver. The same power supply is used for all countries since it is a universal power supply that automatically adjusts to various input voltage and can operate at either 50 or 60 hertz (cycles per second). This universal power supply may have cost more than any of the many discrete versions that could have been used. However, reducing several power supplies to a single part offers significant overhead cost savings, as will be pointed out in Chapters 5 and 6. Further, this also helps to make this flexible assembly cell possible, because only one bin slot is required for the power supplies.

Part Assembly

The remaining parts are assembled as required by the instructions displayed on the monitor. All parts are mounted with the same standard screw by the auto-feed screwdriver. All the part bins are arranged in a semicircular pattern to be accessible by the worker.

Kanban Part Resupply

Figure 2–1 shows two rows of part bins, which are set up for resupply by the two-bin kanban system. Initial assembly starts with all bins full of parts. When the part bin nearest the worker is depleted, the full bin behind moves forward, as shown by the middle part bin in Figure 2–1. The empty part bin then is returned to its "source," which could be the machine that made the part, a subassembly workstation that assembled the part, or a supplier. The source fills the bin and returns it to this assembly workstation behind its counterpart, which is now dispensing parts.

The beauty of kanban part resupply is that the system ensures an uninterrupted supply of parts *without forecasts or complicated ordering procedures*, like MRP. The number of parts in a bin is based on the highest expected usage rate and the longest resupply time. The size of the bins is determined by the bin quantity and size of the parts. At the large-part end of the spectrum, some companies use two-truck kanbans, in which parts are drawn from one truck trailer while the other trailer goes back to the supplier for more parts. Alternately, a two-card kanban system can be used where the cards travel back to the source instead of the bins. A quicker version of the two-card system involves reading the bar code on the kanban card. Then an order is transmitted electronically to the source.

For kanban systems to work, there must be enough room to dispense all parts at the point of use. Too many different parts may make kanban infeasible. This, again, emphasizes the importance of part commonality.

It is possible to make more parts available for assembly by stacking the bins like seats in an opera house. However, too many parts may add confusion to the assembly operation and possibly lead to quality problems. One remedy would be to mount signaling devices, such as lights, on each bin. Bin light signals would have to be coordinated with the on-line assembly instructions.

The Front Panel

The other conveyor belt in Figure 2–1 delivers the customized front panel. All versions of the front panel can be milled from a single standard blank by a computer numerically controlled (CNC) machining center, as shown in the center of Figure 2–2. The standard front panel blanks can be made just-in-time or supplied by kanban, either internally or from external vendors.

Based on instructions from the CAD/CAM system (see Chapter 8), the machining center mills out slots for whichever dials, meters, ports, switches, and controls would be required for this order. Note the variety of front panels in the custom products on the output cart at the bottom of Figure 2–1.

To minimize setup changes, all milling can done with the minimum number of cutting tools, for the reasons presented under feature commonality in Chapter 5. Designers need to make sure that the features (holes, slots, etc.) can be machined with the minimum of tools. If holes need to be different sizes, they could still be machined with the same tool. It may take slightly more time to mill a half-inch diameter hole with a quarter-inch diameter end mill, but if this avoids a manual setup change, it might represent a net gain in time, cost, and equipment utilization.

For this instrument, the automatic tool changer changes to a stylus type cutter that spells out the customer company's name, the instrument's function, and its model number into the front panel.

The customized front panel is attached by four standard screws from the auto-feed screwdriver. For labeling that cannot be accomplished by the CNC stylus, adhesive-backed labels are attached based on the instructions on the computer monitor. Custom labels could be printed on-line by a small printer that is directed by the same file server that displays the assembly instruction. More standard labels could be peeled off of one preprinted sheet that contains all possible labels. Unused labels would then be discarded or recycled. This might seem wasteful, but it may cost much more to make dozens of different labels independently available.

The final assembly step is the affixing of a product bar code that is printed out by the workstation file server. This identification label then directs packaging and shipping and identifies the part for field service.

Packaging and Shipping

At packaging, the operator wands the product bar code and follows instructions displayed on the video monitor to insert the appropriate power cord, accessories, and documentation. One set of "standard" documentation for each language is drawn from dual kanban bins. Custom documentation is printed on a laser printer and added to the standard documentation.

After the box is sealed, a computer-directed label printer prints the following information, in the appropriate languages: the customer's name, shipping address, product ID, machine-readable bar code, and any other required markings. Standard protective packaging material is used with clever nesting geometries that accommodate all size cases.

THE INFORMATION FLOW

The whole process starts with the customer. As will be discussed in Chapter 8, the dialog between the customer and the salesperson (top, Figure 2–2) determines the custom product specifications that will satisfy the customer. Configuration software, perhaps running on a laptop computer, ensures that the product specifications are valid, or, in other words, within the capability of the factory to produce the product at the cost and time promised to the customer.

The "configurator" can quickly confirm the configuration and generate price and delivery quotes for customer acceptance. Configurators will be discussed in Chapter 8.

The product specifications are then sent by modem to the factory where they are entered into the order entry database. Often this database is part of the configuration software package. The product specifications are converted into several outputs that direct the following functions (counterclockwise in Figure 2–2).

Printed Circuit Board CAD

Based on the field input, the order entry database determines the functionality requirements of the printed circuit board. Several PCB designs have been prepared to cover every valid combination of product options, all based on the standard bare board and using standard components, which are always in residence in the same bins of the assembly machines.

All PCB versions utilize the same "core" circuitry and components. Products with minimum options may include only the core components. Various option scenarios will determine which additional components are included.

Every anticipated scenario had been created as a unique design with its own assembly program and stored in the PCB CAD database, which can automatically download the appropriate assembly program to the PCB placement or insertion equipment. Unanticipated options can be designed "on the fly" by PCB CAD designers. The configurator, based on the combined knowledge of all PCB CAD designers, has already assured that all accepted orders are within the capabilities of the designers, the design tools, the equipment, and the component set in residence on the assembly machinery.

The actual assembly of the printed circuit board is completely automatic. The single bare board is fed from a stack into the "pass-through" material handling tracks, which route it to all the necessary machines that will load all the specified components, which are permanently loaded, so the machines never have to stop to change them. After automatic soldering, the boards arrive at the manual assembly station described earlier.

CAD/CAM

The CAD/CAM (Computer-aided design/computer-aided manufacturing) station specifies the program that controls the CNC machining center that will machine custom front panels from a single standard blank. The CAD application has a "template" that specifies the standard blank. It also has predrawn "blocks" (sometimes called components or symbols) for every anticipated modification necessary to accommodate various dials, meters, ports, and so forth. With these *parametric* CAD features (see Chapter 8), the order entry database can simply add any specified blocks.

For customizations such as machining the company name or logo in the front panel, the salesperson (or even the customer) can "design" those features, on some advanced configurators, by simply typing in the words, picking the font and size, and then specifying the position. Special fonts or logos can be imported into the configurator or manually into the CAD system. The configurator can then display a graphical representation of the custom front panel and finished product.

CAD/CAM programs, residing on the same computer, can then automatically translate the finished "drawing" into tool path programs and tool changing instructions for the CNC machining center. After the program is downloaded, an operator or robotic mechanism loads the standard blank into a standard fixture. The machining is then automatic. The finished front panel is deburred, if necessary, and sent down the conveyor belt to the manual assembly station.

The Software Database

The software database contains object-oriented modules for all anticipated software requirements. The order entry database specifies which modules are required and directs the software database file server to send this code to the PROM programmer at the manual assembly station.

Unanticipated software requirements can be satisfied by a software engineer who uses a maximum of standard modules and then adds the custom code required. The configurator ensures that any custom code is feasible and within the capabilities of the software engineer, software tools, the PROM programmer, and the PROM memory capacity.

Manual Assembly Instructions

Based on the product specifications coming from the configurator, the order entry database determines which parts need to be assembled. This information is forwarded to the manual assembly instruction file server, which converts it to step-by-step instructions. These instructions are displayed with a combination of graphics and words on the monitor, shown at the far right of Figure 2–1.

For example, one of the first instructions would read: "Take a PROM blank from bin 1, place it in the PROM programmer socket, and start the firmware download by pressing the 'start' button." The next instruction would display a drawing or photograph of the printed circuit board showing where to insert the programmed PROM and the correct orientation of the chip.

SUMMARY

Notice the variety of assembled products on the output cart in Figure 2–1. True Mass Customization was achieved mostly by manual assembly. The only automation production equipment used were the existing PCB assembly machines and a CNC milling machine. See Figure 2–3 for a summary of the various ways this product was mass customized.

FIGURE 2–3

Summary of the Mass Customization Process

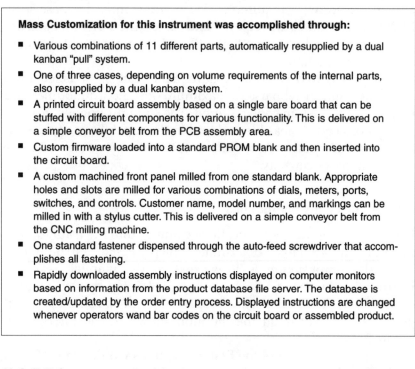

Mass Customization for this instrument was accomplished through:

- Various combinations of 11 different parts, automatically resupplied by a dual kanban "pull" system.
- One of three cases, depending on volume requirements of the internal parts, also resupplied by a dual kanban system.
- A printed circuit board assembly based on a single bare board that can be stuffed with different components for various functionality. This is delivered on a simple conveyor belt from the PCB assembly area.
- Custom firmware loaded into a standard PROM blank and then inserted into the circuit board.
- A custom machined front panel milled from one standard blank. Appropriate holes and slots are milled for various combinations of dials, meters, ports, switches, and controls. Customer name, model number, and markings can be milled in with a stylus cutter. This is delivered on a simple conveyor belt from the CNC milling machine.
- One standard fastener dispensed through the auto-feed screwdriver that accomplishes all fastening.
- Rapidly downloaded assembly instructions displayed on computer monitors based on information from the product database file server. The database is created/updated by the order entry process. Displayed instructions are changed whenever operators wand bar codes on the circuit board or assembled product.

NOTES

1. David M. Anderson, *Design for Manufacturability, Optimizing Cost, Quality, and Time-to-Market* (Lafayette, CA: CIM Press, 1990), pp. 151–155.

PART **TWO**

EXISTING PRODUCTS

CHAPTER

Cost of Variety

UNDERSTANDING CURRENT CUSTOMIZATION ATTEMPTS

Many companies are trying to better satisfy customers by building what customers want, but the companies are not doing it very well. As pointed out in Chapter 1, most companies today are trying to offer *variety* to customers in the mass production heritage by layering new "exception" activities on top of existing processes, but this is not Mass Customization.

In mass production companies, Manufacturing really wants to build a single product in high volume (for economies of scale), but Marketing would like to please customers with many "variations" of "standard" models. This can be expensive and time consuming for Engineering and Manufacturing when the product line is not designed to easily accept those changes. Many companies are customizing by engineering change orders, a very inefficient process.

Some companies offer customers variety by employing "custom engineering" departments, but this high overhead activity can still be inefficient if the product and production processes are not

designed to readily accept the custom engineering. If cost accounting systems do not quantify overhead adequately (as will be discussed in Chapter 6), inherently high overhead activities, like custom engineering, will probably be subsidized by the standard
products, thus distorting decision making on customization.

Some companies are able to do custom products somewhat
quickly, but sacrifice cost and control. These approaches are shown
on the "reactive" side in Figure 3–1. Thus, the challenge is to
achieve *timely* and *efficient* customization of products or mass customization as shown at the "proactive" side in Figure 3–1.

FIGURE 3–1

Customization Contribution for Reactive and Proactive Modes

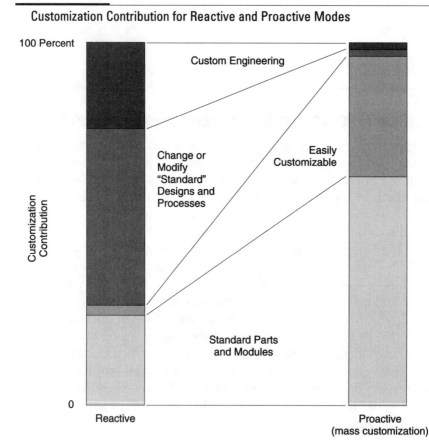

VARIETY

There are two types of variety: *external* variety, which is seen by customers, and *internal* variety, which is experienced inside manufacturing and distribution operations. External variety is often, but not always, good; and internal variety is always bad.

External Variety

There are two categories of external variety. The first category is *useful variety*, which is appreciated by customers. Examples include useful options, stylistic differentiation, and any dimensional variations that satisfy customers better. Useful variety should be maximized within cost and speed capabilities.

The other category of external variety is *useless variety*, which is transparent, unimportant, or even confusing to customers. For instance, a Nissan automobile had 87 steering wheels available, of which 70 types accounted for just 5 percent of the total installed.[1] Useless variety should be eliminated using the rationalization procedures presented in the next chapter.

Internal Variety

This type of variety usually takes the form of excessive and unnecessary variety of parts, features, tools, fixtures, raw materials, and processes. Internal variety can be minimized using the standardization techniques presented in Chapter 5.

After identifying and eliminating variety that is useless or transparent to the customer, mass customizers strive to efficiently produce and distribute the useful variety, while minimizing internal variety.

COSTS OF VARIETY

Many "costs" make up the *cost of variety*, which is generally defined as the sum of all the costs of *attempting* to offer customers variety with inflexible products that are produced in inflexible factories and sold through inflexible channels. This includes the actual costs of customizing or configuring products, the costs of excessive parts, procedures, and processes, and the excessive operations costs caused by trying to offer the customer variety from inflexible factories. Mass Production may be fine for a single product with absolutely no variety, such as the Ford Model T, which was offered in "any color as long as it was black." However, Mass Production is very inefficient at offering the customer variety. This inefficiency is the cost of variety.

The numerous "overhead" costs caused by variety are identified in this chapter. Chapter 6 will present ways to minimize these and other costs. There are also many other nonmonetary costs, such as slow responsiveness to customer needs or changing market conditions. In addition, an ad hoc approach to customization may consume valuable engineering and manufacturing resources that could be better applied to the development of new products that are easier to customize *by design*. Further, documentation integrity may suffer if customization is being achieved by changing or modifying "standard" designs and processes, which is often the largest contributor to the "reactive" approach in Figure 3–1. In the rush to get customization products out the door, the "redline markup" changes may not be documented very well and the modifications may never be entered into the documentation database, thus complicating field service, subsequent customizations, and future product developments.

To be competitive and profitable at offering variety, companies must offer enough external market variety while minimizing internal variety costs (such as costs related to inventory and setup, utilization of equipment and floor space, and materials overhead), and configuration and customization. These internal variety costs will be referred to as *cost of variety.*

Trying to offer market variety in the Mass Production paradigm will cause a high cost of variety, as shown in Figure 3–2. Using the principles of this book, mass customizers can actually offer great market variety with low cost of variety, as shown by the "Mass Customization" line.

Effect of Lot Size on Variety Costs

The key driver of the cost of variety is lot size, sometimes called batch size, which is determined by setup. Setup is any changeover activity that is necessary in batch manufacturing to change parts, fixtures, tooling, equipment programming, or instructions from one product, or product variation, to another.

F I G U R E   3–2

Variety Cost as a Function of Market Variety

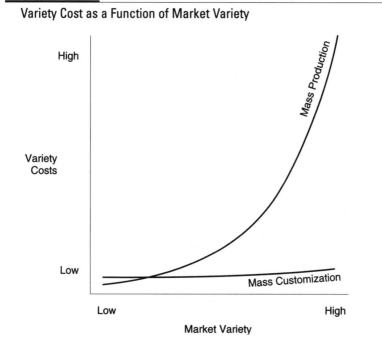

In Mass Production, large setups encourage large lot sizes to amortize the setup charge over the greatest number of products. Large lot sizes drive up many categories of internal variety cost.

Figure 3–3 shows the effect of lot size on work-in-process (WIP) Inventory, floor space, internal transportation, and quality costs due to recurring errors.

WIP Inventory
Work-in-process inventory costs rise as lot size goes up. Usually there is at least one batch of parts before and possibly after every workstation. Thus, if the lot size is 100 and there are 20 workstations, then there would be 2,000 to 4,000 parts in WIP inventory.

Floor Space
Floor space and internal transportation costs (such as forklifts) generally go up with increasing lot size. In Figure 3–3, the step function at lot size of n is caused by the necessity of forklift aisles, which are needed as the lot becomes too heavy or bulky to lift

FIGURE 3–3

Effect of Lot Size on Various Costs

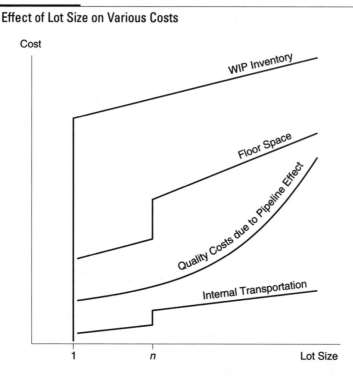

manually. This point n will vary according to the weight and bulk of the parts.

Recurring Quality Costs

Small lot size minimizes the quality costs due to recurring errors that affect the number of parts needing to be scrapped or reworked from recurring defects made upstream. This is known as the "pipeline effect." The longer the pipeline, the greater the vulnerability to unknowingly producing recurring defects. Long pipelines are not only caused by large lots, but are also caused by transportation delays between processing steps such as between a parts plant overseas and a domestic assembly plant.

Consider a factory production line with 10 work stations and a lot size of 100, which results in WIP inventory of 1,000 parts in the line. If a recurring defect occurs in the first step, 1,000 defective parts will be made until the first defective part reaches the last step, say, inspection or final assembly. If transportation delays are added to this scenario, thousands more defective parts might have been made before the first defect part is noticed in the final step. In a just-in-time (JIT) environment, parts would be handed directly between work stations for a total WIP inventory of 10. Recurring defects would probably be spotted even before 10 parts were made because JIT culture encourages everyone to scrutinize parts as they are received from previous operations and immediately remedy problems before they become *recurring* problems. This is why the "quality" curve in Figure 3-3 rises exponentially: The greater the lot size and WIP inventory, the more problems become hidden by inventory, which, in turn, has a compounding effect that causes even more quality problems.

Machinery Utilization

Figure 3–4 shows that machinery utilization cost (the cost of less than 100 percent utilization) improves with lot size, which contributes to the economy of scale enjoyed by mass production. The traditional approach to setup reduction is to minimize the number of setup changes with very large lots. But this practice incurs many other costs that were illustrated in Figure 3–3.

Dedicated machines, with a virtually infinite lot size, can enjoy 100 percent machine tool utilization. However, if setup can be eliminated and if lot size of one is possible, then 100 percent machinery utilization can be achieved, even in low-volume production.

Setup

In high-volume production, setup labor can become quite costly and cause delays in the flow of parts. The traditional approach is to increase the lot size to spread out setup expenses over the maximum number of parts. The *setup labor* curve in Figure 3–4 shows the setup labor decreasing with larger lot sizes. By contrast, in flexible manufacturing environments, setup is eliminated and setup labor costs are zero.

Notice that in both curves in Figure 3–4, the highest cost point of both curves corresponds to a lot size of two, if setup has not been eliminated by flexible manufacturing programs. Unfortunately, this high-cost region of the curve is where many low-volume/high-mix manufacturers operate. Ironically, low-volume producers tend to

FIGURE 3–4

Machinery and Setup Costs as a Function of Lot Size

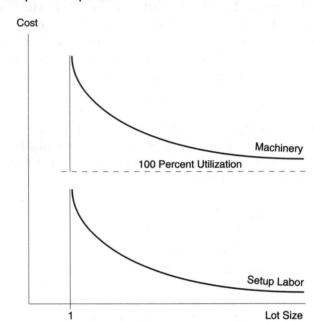

think flexible manufacturing principles benefit only high-volume producers.

Setup expense is not limited to the machinist repositioning different parts on a machine tool. Setup expenses result from any extra effort from anyone in the supply chain who has to do any extra work for a different version of a product: in design, documentation, procurement, part distribution, assembly, or test. Finding drawings or instructions is a setup. This type of set-up may be a greater expense than physical setup for low-volume producers.

COMPUTING THE COST OF VARIETY

Comparison to the No-Variety Scenario

A way to estimate the internal cost of variety is to compare a company's current operation budget to the idealistic case of producing a single product with no variety manufactured with the same volumes as current operations. The difference between current operations costs and the single-product scenario would be equal to the cost of variety.

The "zero variety cost" scenario would assume a single product with no variety, the proverbial "Model T" product. Parts would be made within a just-in-time "pull" system in lots of one. Equipment and personnel would be dedicated to single tasks with 100 percent utilization. There would be no work-in-process inventory. Purchased parts would be supplied from sources "dock-to-stock" (with no incoming inspection). Products would be designed for the minimum part types, part count, and process steps so there would be no setup or kitting. Products would be built to order and shipped directly to customers with no finished goods inventory.

Computation of the Cost of Variety

The other method of computing the cost of variety is to add up all the costs of the individual elements. Figure 3–5 presents a list of some of the key variety costs that may be useful for quantifying the cost of variety.

Most accounting systems do not track overhead costs very well, with the exception of inventory costs. Nevertheless, company managers need to know what the cost of variety is to make decisions to reduce that cost. Investigations may need to be launched to determine, or at least estimate, the cost of variety. The last part of Chapter 6 is devoted to quantifying overhead costs. The following discussion will describe the key elements of the cost of quality as tabulated in Figure 3–5.

Inventory Costs

The value of business inventory for the United States in 1994 was a staggering $1.179 trillion, according to Robert V. Delaney of Cass Information Systems, in St. Louis, Missouri.[2] Manufactured goods had a value of $893 billion in 1994. What it costs to "carry" the inventory is called the *inventory carrying cost*, which is the sum of all the costs for interest, taxes, obsolescence, depreciation, insurance, floor space, handling, damage, tracking, and all the related administration and overhead costs.

FIGURE 3–5

Cost of Variety

Inventory

- Inventory itself
  - Raw materials inventory
  - Work-in-process (WIP) inventory
  - Finished goods inventory: ■ Factory
    - Distribution
    - Dealer/store
- Inventory related
  - Administrative labor, warehouse labor, & data processing expense
  - Floor space costs
  - Write-offs, obsolescence, and deterioration
  - Internal transportation: ■ Equipment (forklifts, carousels, ASRS, etc.)
    - Labor
    - Floor space (forklift aisles)

Setup

- Setup labor cost
- Machinery utilization: the cost of less than 100%, which only exists in Mass Production (for dedicated machinery) and Mass Customization (for flexible machinery working without setup)
- Labor resource utilization
- Kitting: ■ Labor expense
  - Floor space

Cost of Model Changeovers

- Tooling/labor changeover costs
- Plant downtime

Materials

- MRP/BOM administration
- Parts administration/qualification
- Internal parts distribution
- Purchasing: ■ Labor to purchase excessive variety
  - Missed purchasing leverage & economy of scale
  - Expediting cost

Operations

- Tooling, dies and fixtures over the minimum
- Ramp delays caused by too many differences   *continued*

Figure 3–5, concluded

Customization/Configuration

- Plant labor to customize and configure
- Custom engineering
- Documentation expense for each customization and overall documentation roll-up

Marketing

- Product line management, documentation, catalogs, price sheets
- Missed sales from running out of parts or not responding quickly enough with products
- Missed sales from building scarce parts into products that are not selling
- Cost of forecast errors: discounts, rebates

Quality

- Cost of multiple defects, which can occur in batch manufacturing

Service

- Excess service cost due to excessive variety of parts and procedures
- Spare parts logistics of excessive variety

Flexibility

- Cost of flexible manufacturing capabilities and supporting design and information systems

---

Inventory carrying costs are dependent on prevailing interest rates, warehousing cost, and many other factors. Typically, 20 percent of the inventory cost is for interest; 30 percent is for warehousing costs; and 50 percent is for taxes, obsolescence, depreciation, and so forth.[3] Figure 3–6 shows typical inventory carrying costs since 1971. In times of "normal" interest rates, a good rule of thumb would be to assume that inventory carrying cost is the traditional 25 percent. This means the cost of carrying inventory is 25 percent of the value of the inventory per year. For example, $4 million of inventory would cost $1 million per year to carry. Eliminating that inventory could save this amount every year. This is one of the key techniques that mass customizers can use to meet the cost challenge of Mass Customization, as will be discussed in Chapter 6.

Since there may be readily available numbers on inventory costs, this would be a good place to start quantifying the cost of

FIGURE 3–6

Inventory Carrying Cost Since 1971

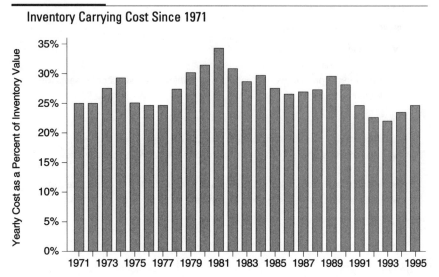

Source: Robert V. Delaney, *Sixth Annual State of Logistics Report* (St. Louis, MO: Cass Information Systems, June 5, 1995), Figure 9, Supporting Data Table I; 1995 figure estimated by Mr. Delaney.

variety. Generally there are three categories of inventory, as tabulated in Figure 3–5: raw materials inventory, work-in-process inventory, and finished goods inventory. It is important to quantify all of these and understand how they cause other problems and raise other costs, as pointed out earlier.

New manufacturing paradigms, such as just-in-time and build-to-order, seek to minimize all forms of inventory through continuous improvement. Just-in-time will replace the old paradigm of "just-in-case" operations where inventory is used throughout the organization to cover up problems, like unreliable sources of supply, poor machine maintenance, and scheduling problems. Inventory not only costs a lot of money to carry, but it also slows down operations, impedes responsiveness and agility, consumes valuable space, and retards the continuous improvement process.

Raw Materials Inventory

Raw materials inventory may have grown to excessive proportions in an attempt to overcome deficiencies regarding consistent sources of supply, anticipated part shortages, incoming inspection, proliferation of materials, sizes, types, grades, finishes, and so forth (see Chapter 5 on standardization), and just plain oversight. Too many categories of inventory are an inventory management burden, which, if not managed properly, may force operations to order more material at expediting prices if the existing material cannot be found quickly. Storing inventory in remote locations can further slow operations and make retrieval more difficult.

Often excessive raw materials inventory is damaged "under its own weight," so to speak. Damage may occur from stacking, handling, moving, "rummaging,"or storing outside, all of which happen more when there are too many raw materials. Deterioration may occur because of humidity, rain, light, dust, vibration, chemical exposure, or simply age. And of course, the longer the raw materials are in inventory, the greater the chance of damage or obsolescence.

WIP Inventory

WIP inventory and its relationship to lot size and setup was discussed earlier. However, WIP inventory does not *automatically* go down with lot size and setup reduction, which *allow* the inventory to go down. Operations people may need to be "weaned" from depending on inventory, "just in case." Although such a practice is not consistent with continuous improvement teamwork, there have been incidents where industrial engineers have simply removed the WIP inventory shelves and tables and moved the workstations closer together to force workers to work without WIP inventory buffers.

Some American automobile manufacturers have made great improvements lately in "lean manufacturing." But when MIT's landmark book on lean manufacturing, *The Machine that Changed the World,* was published in 1990,[4] American automobile manufacturers needed an order-of-magnitude more inventories than their "lean" Japanese competitors!

A Coopers & Lybrand study of five clients that it had helped to implement JIT showed an average WIP reduction of 84.2 percent.[5]

Finished Goods Inventory

All the elements of finished goods inventory must be considered, regardless of where the inventory resides. Factory finished goods inventory is easy to see and quantify because, by definition, it is in the manufacturer's factory or warehouse and is usually the financial responsibility of the manufacturer.

However, the customer must ultimately pay for finished goods inventory, regardless of where it is in the supply chain. Therefore, the cost of finished goods inventory at distributors, dealers, and stores must be considered as part of the cost of variety. Eliminating this inventory with build-to-order and direct distribution could eliminate many carrying costs associated with finished goods inventory and, thus, substantially lower the selling price. Eliminating distribution inventory is one of the main techniques that will enable mass customizers to offer customized products at mass production prices, as will be discussed in Chapter 6.

Inventory Related Expenses

Inventory Administration

In addition to the actual inventory cost itself, several other costs are directly caused by inventory. Inventory requires a certain amount of administrative labor to order, receive, document, catalog, store, retrieve, distribute, and reorder. There may be other costs associated with inventory. For instance, companies that ship automobile batteries from finished goods inventory pay for a crew to keep recharging all the batteries in inventory.

Floor Space

Inventory occupies floor space, the value of which varies according to the need for expansion. Often inventory increases in size and expands when space is plentiful. The inventory corollary to Parkinson's Law would be that "inventory expands to fill the space available." Unfortunately, it always seems to be harder to "reclaim" the space than to fill it in the first place. Nevertheless, inventory reduction programs, especially those starting with product development, can free up much valuable floor space that might delay or eliminate the need to expand or to move as companies grow. Many just-in-time implementations have reduced floor space requirements by 50 percent or more.[6] A summary of seven clients that Coopers & Lybrand had helped to implement JIT showed an average floor space savings of 37.7 percent.[7]

Before making recent improvements, American and European automobile manufacturers needed one-third more floor space for the same vehicle output as their lean Japanese competitors, as shown in Figure 3-7. The American manufacturers needed over three times the floor space for repair, as a percentage of assembly space, and the Europeans needed over three and a half times compared to the Japanese manufacturers.[8]

Empty floor space on the manufacturing floor has a certain value for future flexibility. When Chrysler Corporation converted the old "C/Y" plant to produce the Neon, plenty of open floor space was made available because the Neon has well under 2,000 total parts, compared to over 5,000 on the old C/Y-body cars. This space is now available for future changes and contingencies.[9]

Obsolescence and Deterioration

In just-in-time environments, parts move too quickly to deteriorate or become obsolete. But in "just-in-case" environments, parts and finished products may sit in warehouses so long that they run the risk of deteriorating or becoming obsolete. Historical inventory "write-offs" are a matter of record and can be looked up to help quantify this cost of variety.

Transportation

Finally, many internal transportation costs must be considered as part of the cost of variety. In batch manufacturing, parts are transported in bins, which are often so large that they need to be moved by forklifts. The costs incurred here include the forklifts themselves, the labor to drive and maintain the forklifts, energy and ven-

---

FIGURE 3–7

Floor Space Comparisons, "Lean" versus Mass Producers

	Japanese	American	European
Space (sq. ft./vehicle/year)	5.7	7.8	7.8
Size of repair area (as % of assembly)	4.1	12.9	14.4

Source: IMVP World Assembly Plant Survey, 1989.

tilation costs, and the value of the floor space occupied by the bins themselves and the forklift aisles. Just-in-time "one-piece flow" can eliminate these costs for parts that are small enough to hand off to the next workstation. Similarly, expensive material handling equipment, like carousels, conveyors, and ASRS (automated storage and retrieval systems) may not be necessary in flexible manufacturing environments.

Inventory Statistics

Figure 3–8 tabulates inventory values and inventory turns (ratio of cost of goods sold to average inventory) for selected industries. Leading companies are realizing the value of reducing inventories. American Standard cut inventories more than 50 percent, from $735 million to $326 million, between 1990 and 1994.[10] General Electric cut stocks from $9 billion to $6 billion between 1989 and 1994. CEO Jack Welch estimates that every additional "turn" generates an extra $1 billion in cash, plus more savings in labor and storage.[11]

Inventory management can be expected to improve by implementing inventory reduction programs like just-in-time. Ansari and Modarress studied 31 companies that were implementing just-in-time.[12] Inventory turns for purchased material doubled after implementing JIT; their goals were to almost double again, as shown in Figure 3-9.

Setup

As discussed earlier, setup can be eliminated in flexible operations. Therefore, setup is considered to be part of the cost of variety in inflexible operations.

Setup Labor Cost

Setup labor cost includes all the labor costs to change a production operation from one part or product to another. Typically this involves changing one or more of the following: parts, dies, fixtures, CNC programs, drawings, or instructions. The time it takes to find the parts or instructions are part of the setup time as is the time to position and secure dies and fixtures. Also part of setup labor is the time to build and test the "new" parts to ensure the setup was done properly.

FIGURE 3–8

Inventory and Inventory Turns for Selected Industries with Assets between $50 Million and $100 Million

S.I.C. Code	Industry	Inventory Values	Inventory Turns
3710	Motor Vehicles and Equipment	11,684,000	7.2
3460	Metal Forgings and Stampings	10,740,000	6.9
3570	Office, Computing, and Acct. Machines	10,807,000	5.9
3430	Plumbing and Heating	12,173,000	5.7
3670	Electronic Components and Accessories	11,812,000	5.5
3440	Fabricated Structural Metal Products	15,146,000	5.0
3630	Household Appliances	17,056,000	4.5
3860	Photographic Equipment and Supplies	17,988,000	4.5
3490	Misc. Fabricated Metal Products	14,517,000	4.4
3665	Radio, Television, and Telecom Equip.	14,298,000	4.0
3550	Special Industry Machinery	14,951,000	3.7
3560	General Industry Machinery	13,875,000	3.5
3520	Farm Machinery	20,634,000	3.3
3530	Construction and Related Machinery	20,346,000	3.3
3815	Scientific Instruments	11,835,000	3.2
3845	Optical, Medical, and Ophthalmic Goods	11,403,000	3.2
3725	Aircraft, Guided Missiles, and Parts	18,112,000	3.1
3540	Metalworking Machinery	18,136,000	2.8
	Averages:	14,750,722	4.4

* Inventories include all inventories valued at cost or at the lower of cost or market price.
† Inventory turnover is measured by dividing the cost of goods sold by the average inventory.

Source: *Almanac of Business and Industry Financial Ratios* (Englewood Cliffs, NJ: Prentice Hall, 1996) based on IRS data on 3.7 million U.S. corporations in 179 industries.

Setup time is measured to be all the time between the last part of the previous batch and the *first good part* of the new batch. Thus, setup labor cost is the cost of all the activities that happen in this period. This would even include the cost (value) of idle equipment and people who are forced to be idle because of a setup change.

Kiyoshi Suzaki cited the following dramatic setup reduction examples from his 1987 book, *The New Manufacturing Challenge, Techniques for Continuous Improvement:*"[13]

FIGURE 3–9

Inventory Turnover Improvement as JIT Is Implemented

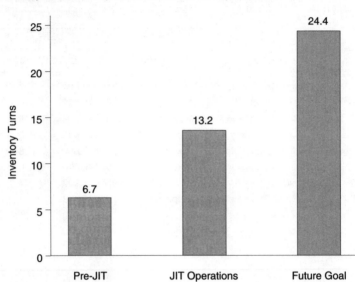

Source: A. Ansari and B. Modarress, *Just-in-Time Purchasing* (New York: Free Press, 1990).

- Toyota reduced the setup on a 1,000-ton press from 4 hours to 3 minutes, an 80-times improvement.
- Yanmar Diesel reduced the setup on a machining line from 9.3 hours to 9 minutes, a 62-times improvement.
- A U.S. chain saw manufacturer reduced the setup on a punch press from more than 2 hours to 3 minutes, a 40-times improvement.
- Mazda reduced the setup on a ring-gear cutter from more than 6 hours to 10 minutes, a 36-times improvement.
- A U.S. electric appliance manufacturer reduced the setup on a 45-ton press from 50 minutes to 2 minutes, a 25-times improvement.

Machinery Utilization

Machinery utilization measurements must be based on *real* utilization: the percent of the plant operation time that the machinery is actually producing good parts or assembling good products. The biggest reason that machinery does not run 100 percent of the time is because of all the time wasted on setup changes. All the setup time discussed above becomes even more costly when an expensive machine is waiting. Another cause of equipment utilization shortcomings is downtime, which, technically, would not be part of the cost of variety. However, equipment dedicated to one part or product typically has much less downtime because of the consistency of the operations and the benefits from a long "learning curve" on a single operation.

The "cost" of poor machinery utilization is calculated by subtracting the utilization rate from 100 percent. This gives the percent of the time the machine is idle. Multiplying this percentage by the yearly equipment cost (lease cost or purchase payments) will result in the cost of poor equipment utilization.

Labor Resource Utilization

Similarly, the utilization of human resources can be higher without setup delays to change fixturing, dies, tools, parts, drawings, or instructions. When products are designed around common parts and standard processing, process tasks are easier to learn and, therefore, people can learn many tasks. Just-in-time environments often utilize people more efficiently by having them tend multiple machines or work at multiple adjacent manual workstations. Flexible environments may have assembly instructions displayed on-line on computer monitors as shown in Figure 2–1.

Kitting

Kitting is the practice of gathering all the parts necessary to build a batch of products. Usually, kitting is done in the raw materials or receiving areas. All the parts for the batch are put in some kind of container and delivered to the production area. Kitting accuracy is important since a shortage of a single part can cause a work shortage. Conversely, excess parts will either be discarded, thus causing waste and complicating parts forecasting, or be returned to raw materials inventory, thus incurring an expense that may exceed the value of the part.

Kitting is unnecessary with JIT "demand-pull" environment since all the parts are distributed at all points of use. Obviously, part standardization is an important prerequisite to be able to do this without excessive logistics cost or floor space demands. Part standardization will be discussed in Chapter 5.

Thus, flexible operations avoid the cost of kitting, which includes the labor to assemble and distribute the kit; the administration cost of the kitting operations; and the cost of the floor space for the kitting activity itself *and for the associated raw materials inventory*. Parts used in just-in-time operations are usually shipped frequently directly to the line in small quantities. When suppliers are certified for this "dock-to-stock" delivery, incoming inspection is unnecessary, thus saving the cost of the inspection and its overhead and floor space.

Cost of Model Changeovers

Even a single product that is built on a dedicated line will incur this variety cost when the line is changed over to the next model. The cost of model changeovers includes the opportunity cost of lost output plus the cost of new equipment, new tooling, and the labor to install it. Every month that an automobile plant is down costs between $65 million and $85 million in pretax profits.[14]

The epitome of Mass Production, the Ford Model T, took eight months to change over to the Model A, with another six months needed to get up to full production. The Model A changeover put 60,000 workers out of work in 1927.[15] One of the largest and most vertically integrated plants in history was not generating any revenue for several months!

Seventy years later, some automobile plants still have very slow changeovers: The 1995 Chevrolet Lumina, built in Oshawa, Ontario, took 87 days to change over from the previous model. In the first month and half, the plant could produce only 288 cars, in limited colors. Full production took another four months. Ford took 60 days to change over to the 1995 Ford Contour and Mercury Mystique in its Kansas City, Missouri, plant.

Concurrently designing products and manufacturing processes, including well-planned changeover scenarios, can drastically shorten changeover times: The 1992 Toyota Camry took 18 days to change over in Georgetown, Kentucky. The 1994 Honda Accord took only three days to change over and reached full production within six weeks.[16]

Materials

The materials elements of the cost of variety include the cost of "excess" variety, that is, the cost associated with parts and raw materials that are beyond the minimum required for a single product factory or a multiproduct factory with products designed around the minimum number of different parts.

MRP/BOM Administration

Planning part deliveries would be easy for the proverbial Model T plant, with a single product, no product variations, and relatively stable demand. As the number of products and variants increased, batch-oriented plants turned to computerization to solve the seemingly bewildering problem of planning the ordering of a wide variety of parts and raw materials. And so was born MRP (material requirements planning) and MRP II (manufacturing resource planning).

However, most companies that have implemented some form of MRP have simply computerized the planning of material requirements or manufacturing resources for existing products and processes, complex as they were. Not only are MRP systems complex, but they also are based on some naive assumptions: reliable sales forecasts, accurate bills of materials (BOMs), correct inventory stock-on-hand counts, and, in some cases, unlimited capacity in all work centers and perfect scheduling flexibility. In reality, sales forecasts are rarely reliable; plus bills of materials and inventory stock-on-hand counts are rarely 100 percent accurate. If sales forecasts are high, then manufacturing builds accordingly and puts the excess in finished goods inventory, incurring more than planned inventory carrying costs and risk, as discussed above. If sales forecasts are low, then operations are faced with a dilemma: build less than the market is demanding or increase the build quantity, on short notice, with expensive and time-consuming expediting. If inaccurate BOMs or stock-on-hand counts omit the procurement of even a few minor parts, this will result in part shortages that can delay production and cause expensive expediting. Some purchasing units try to solve the problem with the wasteful practice of ordering more than needed.

These problems are why MRP systems are difficult to implement successfully. Hayes, Wheelwright, and Clark, in *Dynamic Manufacturing, Creating the Learning Organization*, report that less than a third of MRP systems are ultimately successful.[17]

Industry Week's "Best Plant" annual survey of the 25-top performing candidates reveals which practices are used by leading companies. In the 1994 survey, 100 percent had adopted JIT/continuous-flow production but only 44 percent had a Class A-certified MRP II system.[18]

Parts Administration/Qualification

This is the cost category that captures the cost of part proliferation, which is rampant in many companies. An *Industry Week* article on parts proliferation cited the example of one large U.S.-based manufacturer that forecasted a savings of $300 million during the next 15 years by improving parts management at one division alone![19]

CADIS, Inc., a leading parts-management software/system vendor, conducted a survey of several dozen Fortune 500 manufacturing companies. It found that *not a single company or division had an accurate estimate of the lifetime costs of a part over its life cycle.* Intuitive estimates ranged from $5,000 for a standard part to as high as $60,000 or even $100,000 for a custom part.[20]

Every part, even one costing only pennies, incurs significant overhead costs to enter it into the system, to create new part numbers, to qualify vendors, to release part specifications, and to manage that part for as long as it is actively in the system. Parts used in low volumes, or infrequently, often have much higher than normal costs for purchasing and expediting.

The other element of part administration cost is the qualification function. Every part should be qualified before it is made available to engineers to use in new designs. Part qualification should include the following elements:

- Functional specifications; does the part meet advertised performance specifications?
- Quality/reliability standards.
- Availability for anticipated production and best-case growth scenarios.
- Compatibility with existing parts, processes, and procedures.
- Vendor qualification: manufacturing competence, financial stability, technical expertise, vendor/partner potential; ability to help design teams design parts.

Obviously, the greater the part proliferation, the greater the qualification expense. If a part qualification department is overwhelmed, it may be tempted, or forced, to cut corners. Unfortunately, some companies have no part qualification function, so engineers select a part from trade journal advertisements without any scrutiny of the part or the vendor. Ironically, these situations exist because companies believe they cannot afford the expense. In reality, wise companies realize they cannot afford *not to*, considering the total cost of inferior parts, delayed deliveries, unstable sources of supply, or engineering changes to "design out" unacceptable parts.

Internal Parts Distribution

Common, standard parts can be delivered "dock-to-stock," or directly to the points of use. In dock-to-stock operations, the delivery to the line may be part of the shipment from the source. However, if there are too many part types and the plant is inflexible, then parts must go through a costly sequence of receiving, possibly inspection, warehousing, retrieval, kitting (as mentioned above), distribution, and tracking through the plant. All these steps are usually controlled by expensive information systems. The cost of all these operations is the internal distribution element to the cost of variety.

Purchasing

Many purchasing costs can be avoided with kanban resupply (discussed in Chapter 7) and bread truck deliveries, where suppliers simply keep the bins full and bill the company monthly for parts used. Further, fewer types of common parts used in greater quantities reduce the number of purchasing actions and lead to purchasing leverage and economy of scale. The cost to purchase thousands of different low-volume parts instead of a few high-volume parts is part of the cost of variety, as are expediting costs that are often necessary when inflexible operations try to "plan" procurement in advance for rapidly changing markets.

Expediting costs are usually much less in just-in-time environments. Ansari and Modarress's study of 31 JIT users found that when they achieved their goals, the percentage of time buyers spent on expediting raw materials would be reduced by a factor of

three![21] Figure 3–10 shows the change in the percent of buyers'
time spent on expediting as JIT was implemented.

Operations

Tooling, Dies, and Fixtures
Part of the cost of variety is the cost of tooling, dies, and fixtures
over the minimum, which would be needed for the single product
with no variation. Too often, variety is expanded by simply adding
more tools, dies, and fixtures, which not only cost money to build
but also incur recurring expenses for storage, moving, setting up,
recalibration, and maintenance. Too many dies and molds will discourage improvements aimed at shortening die change times.

Ramp Delays
Too much variety, handled inefficiently, can delay the introduction
of new products by delaying the "ramping up" of production.
Plants that cannot handle variety very well may have to resort to

FIGURE 3–10

Percent of Time Spent on Expediting as JIT Is Implemented

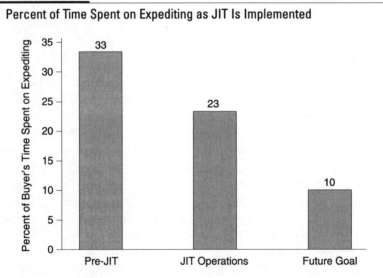

Source: A. Ansari and B. Modarress, *Just-in-Time Purchasing* (New York: Free Press, 1990).

limiting customer variety, just to be able to get products out the door on time. At the beginning of the difficult 1995 Chevrolet Lumina launch, the Oshawa plant only built white cars, "just to keep things simple." Even half a year after the launch, the plant could offer only 7 of the planned 10 colors.[22]

Customization/Configuration Costs

These are the most obvious costs of variety, although few companies really keep track of all the costs of customization and configuration activities on a *total cost* basis.

Plant Labor to Customize and Configure

Usually, the only "customization" cost that is tracked very well is the labor cost to customize products by combining different parts and configuring the resulting products with switches, jumpers, settings, adjustments, and so forth. But part of the cost of configurations is the cost of inaccurate configurations. In the 1980s, Intel Systems Group was using so many jumpers (slide-on connectors that connect adjacent pins) to configure circuit boards that it installed a custom robot to apply all the jumpers *and* to make sure they were installed correctly.

Custom Engineering

Figure 3–1 showed custom engineering as a major expense of the reactive model for offering customization. Usually, custom engineering is done on an ad hoc basis without much prior product line planning. Thus, custom engineering can be inefficient. Poor documentation practices, caused by the usual rush, make custom engineering even less efficient, because subsequent customizations are discouraged from using previous work. Some companies routinely delete electronic CAD file modifications after the customization job is completed.

With a reactive approach to customization, each custom order incurs custom engineering charges. With a Mass Customization approach, all the "custom engineering" is done efficiently up front. Subsequent customization is then done in the factory, often by computer-directed equipment or workers.

Documentation Expense

Treating all customization variations as separate products, with complete bills of materials, instructions, and other documentation for each product, will incur significant documentation expense. One of the author's clients had 1,900 separate BOMs for one product, one for each product variation. The company felt like it was being buried in paperwork. Similarly, documenting all changes and all custom engineering can be expensive, but probably less expensive, in the long run, than not doing so and continually reinventing the wheel. Proper product data management will add more to the documentation cost, but not nearly as much as the cost of not being able to find previous engineering and documentation quickly.

Marketing

Product Line Management and Documentation

If every customization or product variation is treated as a different "product," then there will be many unnecessary marketing costs. Managing a product line of hundreds or thousands of products is much more expensive then managing a single family of products based on several modules and configurations. For the same reasons, documentation expenses, for catalogs and price sheets, would be more expensive for thousands of unique products than for a mass customization family.

Missed Opportunities

A missed opportunity can be considered a cost and this would be part of the cost of variety. Manufacturing operations based on forecasts are notoriously ineffective at producing the right amount of products on time when market demands change rapidly. Forecasting errors often cause product shortages. Bill-of-material errors often cause part shortages, which result in product shortages and expediting expenditures. Complex products with too many different parts have a higher probability of having part shortages, which can lead to product shortages.

Missed opportunities can also be caused by building in scarce parts, such as the newest microprocessor, into products that sit unsold in finished goods inventory. A flexible, build-to-order operation, as proposed by this book, would consume only a scarce part that was going directly to a customer.

Forecasting Errors

The previous section deals with the missed opportunities from not building enough products. Factory output is often greater than demand because of forecasting errors, weak market acceptance, or rigid factory scheduling that will keep building products, whether or not they are needed. Building more products than are needed is sometimes called a marketing defect. The cost of the marketing defects is that excess products have to be unloaded somehow by discounts, rebates, or other deals. When Detroit cannot "move the metal," the phrase that applies is: "Pile them high, and sell them cheap."[23] Inventory carrying costs would also apply to unsold inventory for storage, interest, insurance, taxes, obsolescence, deterioration, and so forth.

By contrast, flexible build-to-order operations build only what has actually been ordered, so there would never be unsold products in inventory.

Quality

Companies that handle variety poorly usually build products in batches, one batch per product or product variation. Manufacturing in batches means having at least one batch of parts between every workstation. As discussed earlier, the pipeline effect can allow recurring errors to occur and infest all the batches in the factory until they are discovered at assembly or inspection.

Eliminating the recurring errors are a big part of the quality improvements generated by just-in-time programs. Huge and Anderson contend that "without even working on quality improvement, reject rates improve proportionally with the reduction in lot sizes."[24] This proportional effect was confirmed by Inman who correlated scrap and rework reduction with lot size reduction, based on a survey of 114 manufacturing firms.[25] He found the ratios (of scrap to lot size reduction) to be 1 to 1.02 for in-house lot size reduction and 1 to 0.98 for vendor lot size reduction. The numerical average of these two numbers is exactly 1:1. Thus, one could conclude that a 50 percent reduction in lot size should lead to a 50 percent reduction in scrap and rework.

Service

The service element of the cost of variety includes the cost of excess service due to an excessive variety of parts and procedures. Ad hoc customization attempts are rarely well documented, thus adding cost to service efforts.

Products designed around too many parts complicate spare parts logistics and, thus, raise this cost. When customers buy capital equipment, they add the cost of spare parts to the purchase price, so, in effect, spare-parts kits should be considered part of the selling price. Excessive part variety forces spare-part kits to be even more incomplete and, thus, incur more risk of downtime, which can be quite a cost for expensive capital equipment.

Flexibility

Up to this point, all these variety costs are those that would be saved if operations were flexible. Achieving this flexibility to handle variety efficiently may incur some cost for information systems and flexible CNC equipment. This is why the curves cross in Figure 3–2; it would not be cost-effective to build Model T's on a flexible line.

Saving all the above variety costs by investing in flexibility is like 20 steps forward and one back: a net gain of 19 steps forward. This "cost" of flexibility should be viewed as an investment rather than a cost. Implementing flexible manufacturing capabilities will be discussed in Chapter 7. Implementing information systems will be discussed in Chapter 8.

NOTES

1. Clay Chandler and Michael Williams, "A Slump in Car Sales Forces Nissan to Start Cutting Swollen Costs," *The Wall Street Journal*, March 3, 1993, p. 1.

2. Robert V. Delaney, *Sixth Annual State of Logistics Report* (St. Louis, MO: Cass Information Systems, June 5, 1995), p. 5.

3. Ibid., Figure 8.

4. James P. Womak, Daniel T. Jones, and Daniel Roos, *The Machine that Changed the World* (New York: Rawson Associates, 1990), p. 92.

5. William A. Wheeler, *III, JIT Client Engagement Results* (Burlington, MA: 1988) Coopers & Lybrand Center for Manufacturing Technology.

6. Daniel J. Jones, "JIT & the EOQ Model: Odd Couples No More!" *Management Accounting* 72, no. 8 (February 1991), pp. 54–57.

7. Wheeler, *JIT Client Engagement Results.*

8. Womack et al., *The Machine that Changed the World.*

9. "Neon Lights Up," *Automotive Industries,* November 1, 1993.

10. Shawn Tully, "American Standard: Profit of Zero Working Capital," *Fortune,* July 13, 1994, pp. 113–14.

11. Shawn Tully, "Raiding a Company's Hidden Cash," *Fortune,* August 22, 1994, p. 86.

12. A. Ansari and B. Modarress, *Just-In-Time Purchasing* (New York: Free Press, 1990), p. 41.

13. Kiyoshi Suzaki, *The New Manufacturing Challenge, Techniques for Continuous Improvement* (New York: Free Press, 1987), p. 43.

14. Scott F. Merlis of Morgan Stanley & Co. quoted in *Business Week,* July 11, 1994, p. 112.

15. Robert Lacey, *Ford, The Men and the Machine* (Boston: Little, Brown and Company, 1986), p. 302.

16. "Motown's Struggle to Shift on the Fly," *Business Week,* July 11, 1994, p. 111.

17. Robert H. Hayes, Steven C. Wheelwright, and Kim B. Clark, *Dynamic Manufacturing, Creating the Learning Organization* (New York: Free Press, 1988), p. 270.

18. Industry Week, *The Complete Guide to America's Best Plants* (Cleveland, OH: Penton Publishing, 1995).

19. Tim Stevens, "Prolific Parts Pilfer Profits," *Industry Week,* July 5, 1995, pp. 59-62.

20. Ibid.

21. Ansari and Modarress, *Just-In-Time Purchasing,* p. 44.

22. "Motown's Struggle to Shift on the Fly."

23. *The Economist,* December 12, 1992, pp. 79–80.

24. E. C. Huge and A. D. Anderson, *The Spirit of Manufacturing Excellence; An Executive's Guide to the New Mind Set* (Homewood, IL: Dow Jones-Irwin, 1988).

25. R. Anthony Inman, "The Impact of Lot-Size Reduction on Quality," *Production & Inventory Management Journal* 35, no. 1 (First Quarter, 1994), pp. 5–7.

CHAPTER

Rationalizing Existing Products

Few readers of this book will be setting up new "greenfield" operations with no existing products, parts, and processes. Most will have to implement these principles into existing organizations. Most product lines evolve haphazardly over time, usually over many careers, agendas, programs, directives, and organizational structures. Product lines tend to grow, not necessarily in the right direction, and part numbers tend to proliferate. Unfortunately, most companies do not have any systematic criteria or procedures to periodically purge product and options.

If there is any question about the adequacy of existing product lines, simply imagine that a well-financed new competitor is now going to simultaneously design an entire coherent product line to compete with your "evolved" product line, using the principles of this book, and choose only the products with the highest potential that would result in the highest company profit and growth. Further, this new savvy competitor will design all the products around common parts and modules and build them in flexible factories that were concurrently designed with the products. Would that be any different from your existing product line and operations? Performing this exercise is actually one of the formal rationalizing techniques presented below.

Almost all product lines could use some *rationalization,* which is the systematic analysis and consolidation of product lines to align them with long-term corporate goals. The purpose of product line rationalization is to identify products that don't fit into a flexible environment, have low sales, have excessive overhead demands, are not really appreciated by customers, have limited future potential, or may be losing money. Rationalization analysis may direct companies to drop these unprofitable products or, if "completeness" is important, farm out their manufacture to others when they are not within company core competencies. This chapter presents such a systematic approach.

This rationalization process should also be applied to product options and variations. Many companies structure bills of materials so that every unique combination of options is a "product." Regardless of how they are defined, options may have escalated and, consequently, could benefit from some scrutiny.

In 1993, Nissan, under serious competitive cost pressures, took a serious look at this issue and realized that, for instance, one model, a midsize sedan, had 87 different steering wheel options, of which 70 types accounted for only 5 percent of the total shipped (demonstrating the Pareto effect). Also, Nissan was forcing its muffler supplier to make over 2,000 kinds of mufflers, the majority of which were used only in a few cars a year.[1]

One solution to option proliferation is to eliminate the low-selling options and to make the popular options standard equipment or combine appropriate sets of options into packages.

Companies must avoid the temptation to base rationalizing decisions on *reported* profitability, if these figures are based on conventional accounting systems. H. Thomas Johnson and Robert S. Kaplan, in their groundbreaking book, *Relevance Lost, The Rise and Fall of Management Accounting,*[2] assert that conventional accounting systems "fail to provide accurate product costs." "The standard product cost systems, which are typical of most organizations, usually lead to enormous cross-subsidies across products." It follows that *enormous cross-subsidies* of product costs will cause enormous distortions in the reporting of individual product profitabilities.

Companies may think that they automatically rationalize products by routinely eliminating products that "drop below the line" of adequate profitability, *as reported by their product costing systems.* However, if product costing generates enormous distortions, then this automatic rationalization may not have occurred or, worse, products that were really profitable may have been erroneously eliminated.

The following section lists several criteria for rationalizing product lines, followed by a detailed description of each technique.

RATIONALIZATION CRITERIA

It is important to rationalize the product line before implementing Mass Customization or any of the agile paradigms: just-in-time, build-to-order, flexible manufacturing, continuous flow manufacturing, or niche market competition. This step would be the parallel to simplifying product designs before automating assembly, and simplifying information structures before computerizing. Failure to perform these basic prerequisites leads to the industrial equivalent of "paving the cow paths."

Rationalizing product lines may improve company profits by eliminating and/or outsourcing products that are currently depressing company profits. It will also lead to a better understanding of company core competencies, help prioritize continuous improvement activities, and facilitate better strategic planning.

When rationalizing products, be sure to rationalize *families of products* rather than single products. Families of products do not necessarily share the same page in the catalog, but do share some *synergy* in design, manufacturing, and distribution. For instance, similar products could be considered together if their processing is almost the same with some minor differences that have little cost or throughput consequences.

The following techniques can be used to rationalize product lines for existing products. The techniques are presented in order of the most objective first and the most subjective last.

1. Sales volume; plot all products in Pareto order.
2. Sales revenue; plot all products in Pareto order.
3. Part commonality; plot products by percentage of common parts.

4. Cost of variety; plot all products in Pareto order.

5. True profitability; plot all products in Pareto order.

6. Polls and surveys; plot responses in Pareto order.

7. Factory processing.

8. Functionality.

9. Customer needs.

10. Core competencies.

11. Clean-sheet-of-paper scenario.

12. Future potential.

Pareto Sorts

It can be useful to sort quantitative information (the first five categories above) and survey results in Pareto order. For consistency, always order Pareto plots with desirable traits to the left and undesirable traits to the right. "Pareto's law" states that usually 80 percent of some result comes from 20 percent of the effort. The general format for Pareto plots is shown in Figure 4–1.

FIGURE 4–1

Pareto Sort Format

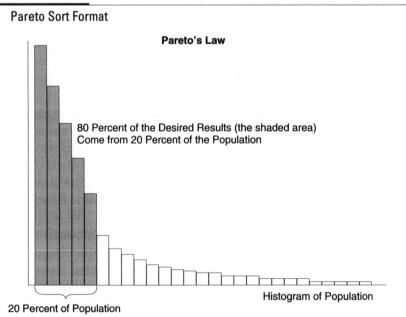

1. Sales Volume

An easy step to start rationalizing the product line is to analyze sales volumes of all the products under consideration using a Pareto sort format that plots out a histogram of all entries in order of highest volume first. The highest-volume products will have higher probabilities of remaining "on the list." The lowest-volume products should be identified for analysis, by all the techniques listed below, to ascertain if they should be eliminated or consolidated with other products. In fact, the lowest-volume products may be found to be unprofitable, if profits are computed using total cost accounting methods (see point 5).

Nissan realized that, by 1993, its model variations had escalated to 2,200 models! The typical Pareto effect was noticed: 50 percent of the models contributed only 5 percent of total sales. *The Wall Street Journal* article that cited these figures quoted a customer who complained, "There are so many different model types, not even the salesmen can remember them."[3]

The same article summarized the model "de-proliferation" goals of some Japanese companies: Nissan planned to reduce model variations by 35 percent; Mitsubishi wanted to cut them by 20 percent; Hitachi's goal was to cut the number of television models in half; and Matsushita planned to reduce the number of Panasonic audio products from 6,000 models to 1,000.

Another useful rationalization metric is sales volume over time. Steady sellers may deserve to be on the list, even if they are not the highest sellers. Plotting sales volume over time may indicate trends that may help make rationalization decisions.

2. Sales Revenue

Similarly, investigate sales revenue and plot, in Pareto order, all products as a function of sales revenue. This information is readily available. The typical "80/20" rule may apply: 80 percent of sales revenue comes from 20 percent of the products. Those 20 percent of the high-revenue products have a higher probability of remaining on the list, possibly unchanged. The other 80 percent of the products merit scrutiny. As an example of this 80/20 rule, Baxter International, the $9 billion health care products and services company, has found that 80 percent of its incremental sales are from large customers with which it already has a relationship.[4]

3. Part Commonality

Part commonality analysis can indicate which products use predominately common parts. Similarly, this analysis can reveal which products use unique, unusual parts.

> *Products that use many common parts inherently have less variety cost than products with unique parts.*

Therefore, part commonality analysis may recommend favorable treatment of products that already use many common parts. Conversely, products that use unique, unusual parts would have higher variety costs and may be considered for elimination or redesign. The latter category can also indicate that certain products don't fit well with existing operations.

One approach can be based on the establishment of commonality or "preferred" parts lists, as will be presented in the next chapter. If a common parts list has been determined, products can be ranked according to the percentage of common parts. Products with a high percentage of common parts could be considered for retention; products with low percentages could be scrutinized further. This technique is even more important if the company is planning to embark on a program to reduce part proliferation.

A less efficient approach, which does not depend on the existence of parts commonality lists, would be to perform a "where used" sort[5] of a key part category and identify parts that are used on very few products. Correlating these seldom-used parts with the products that use them will reveal useful information.

4. Cost of Variety

A cost of variety model was presented in the last chapter. The cost of variety would need to be computed, or at least estimated, for all the products under consideration. Product line rationalization is based on the *relative* cost of variety among all the products. Therefore, for rationalizing activities, the most attention should go to categories that show significant differences among products.

Relative scales could be used, where the "best" product is normalized to equal 1.0 and all the others are assigned numbers to indicate their variety costs as a multiplier of the baseline product, for instance, 1.5 times the baseline product.

5. True Profitability

True profitability can be used as a criterion to rationalize product lines and eliminate marginal or unprofitable products. As pointed out earlier, most cost systems do not automatically give adequate profitability data to be used for rationalizing activity.

Total cost accounting methods, like Activity-Based Cost (ABC) Management (see Chapter 6), can provide realistic indications of profitability. In *Implementing Activity-Based Cost Management*, Robin Cooper et al., refer to "the typical ABC pattern," where several offerings are shown to be highly profitable, most to be at or near break-even profitability, and a few to be highly unprofitable.[6] One Harvard case study (9-186-272) analyzed seven products made by Schrader Bellows. The existing cost system indicated the products had profit margins ranging from 3.76 percent to 10.89 percent. However, when the activity-based analysis was performed, it was shown that one product was just breaking even, three were profitable, and three were actually unprofitable! The product that originally was thought to have the highest profit margin of the group was shown, in reality, to have a negative 59 percent profit margin[7] as shown in the Figure 4–2.

At the minimum, a Pareto listing of *relative* profitability would be helpful in determining which products a company should consider dropping. Again, the product with the highest

FIGURE 4–2

Comparison of Reported Product Cost at Schrader Bellows

Product	Sales Volume	Old Cost System Unit Gross Margin	New Cost System Unit Gross Margin	Percent Change
1	43,562	5.51	6.19	12.3
2	500	3.76	(2.95)	(178.5)
3	53	10.89	(59.45)	(645.9)
4	2,079	4.91	(5.97)	(221.6)
5	5,670	7.95	0.36	(93.4)
6	11,169	5.49	5.57	1.5
7	423	3.74	5.28	41.2

profit could be normalized at the number one with all others compared to that.

6. Polls and Surveys

Often, products that have low true profitabilities may also have a poor compatibility with factory processing. Such incompatibility will probably be noticed by factory managers. Products that have outlived their usefulness, or were never very good to begin with, may be unpopular with factory workers, test technicians, dealers, salespeople, or service representatives.

In the absence of total cost accounting data on true profitability, these people could be queried for their opinions on *what they believe* to be the most profitable and the least profitable products. In fact, such opinions are often the impetus to launch Activity-Based Cost Management programs.[8]

It is advisable, when wording polls and surveys, to avoid the words *profit* or *profitability*, because people may look up profit in a database and be misled by the inaccuracies mentioned above. Since profitability distortions are caused by product costing distortions, ask questions about some indications of the *real* product cost. At the author's suggestions, one division of Emerson Electric asked the people listed above to respond to a survey worded as follows: " List the product types you believe cost considerably more than we say they do (in terms of additional support required, problems experienced, etc.)." The survey results, which fit the Pareto pattern, provided useful information for the rationalization activities.

7. Factory Processing

This category looks at processing compatibility for a range of products. To maximize manufacturing flexibility, it may be necessary to exclude existing products that do not fit a flexible manufacturing environment with respect to common parts, tooling, fixturing geometries, design features, modularity, process steps, product flow, machinery, setup reduction efforts, inventory reduction efforts like just-in-time, and compatibility with CNC equipment.

Be especially skeptical of:

- Older products or products acquired through patent purchases, mergers, and acquisitions.

- Seldom-manufactured products: products "revived from the dead." There is usually a high setup cost to infrequently manufactured products in addition to more learning curve activities trying to remember how to build it. This is an especially sensitive issue if the seldom-manufactured products are also hard to build and are different from the rest of the product line. This is likely since these products are usually older and thus are different from the current product line. Further, older products are usually not designed as well for manufacturability.
- Products with unique processing. Products that require different processing from the rest of the product line might be using older processes or processes that are used too infrequently for the operators and equipment to be at peak efficiency. Seldom-used equipment may be taking up valuable floor space and absorbing capital out of proportion to the value to the plant.
- Products that are harder to build, repair, and service.
- Products that require more labor hours, have higher throughput times, and have higher rework and scrap rates.
- Products that *unexplainably have little competition!* This could be because the products are really so costly to build that the company is selling them at a loss, because it is being misled by its product costing system. Competitors may have rightly concluded they cannot compete at those prices.

8. Functionality

This technique looks for opportunities to consolidate products that have similar functionality. Multiple products performing identical or similar functions could be consolidated by eliminating the "extra" products based on considerations of historical sales, variety costs, profitability, factory processing, design compatibility, or customer needs. Similarly, parts and subassemblies can be analyzed for similar functionality to determine redundancies.

Some related products may be too far apart to evolve into a mass customization family, because of radically different parts, materials, procedures, or processes. For instance, a redesigned product made on different equipment may still be competing with its older counterpart. The old and new products could be consolidated by simply dropping the older product to save all overhead costs associated with carrying each unique product. Similarly, products with slight enhancements or improvements could be consolidated with their basic counterparts by eliminating the basic products. The overhead cost saved from eliminating these older or basic products could pay for the cost of the enhancements or improvements, which could then be offered "free" to customers of the basic model. The enhanced products, at the same price, should be more attractive to customers and thus improve sales and profits.

9. Customer Needs

This technique looks at product line variety from the customer's perspective. Judgment will need to be applied to customer feedback, since most customers will want to maintain their current selections and possibly add more. Complicating this situation is the fact that many marketing departments like to offer "complete" catalogs that satisfy every possible customer need. Since this is the most subjective criteria, it should be considered after knowing data on sales, internal costs, profitability, surveys, factory flexibility, and functionality.

An exception to the above phenomenon is that savvy customers may realize that excessive variety hurts their service operations by complicating training and spare parts logistics.

In some cases, the company will have to offer customers a complete product line. However, the company does not have to design and manufacture all the products. It could still offer to sell (but not build) other companies' commodity products from the catalog. It could arrange to have other companies' products made with its name and logo. It could commission vendors to build its own designs. Vendors could *design and build* products that are needed to "fill the catalog."

10. Company Core Competencies

This rationalization criterion asks the question: "Which products represent core competencies?" with respect to technologies, patents, processing, product development strength, marketing savvy, and so forth. Products representing clear core competencies would be more likely to remain on the list than products representing no core competency.

11. Clean-Sheet-of-Paper Scenario

The other approach is to role-play the scenario mentioned earlier, pretending you, or your brainstorming group, are the well-financed new competitor. Which products would you want to have in your product line? How would you build them flexibly to be able to reach the broadest possible markets? What would you like to do that you cannot do because of existing product line limitations? Start with your discrete product line first and then conduct additional sessions on various degrees of Mass Customization: niche markets, build-to-order, or true Mass Customization.

12. Future Potential

One key principle of mass customization product development is the *leverage* of engineering across many products. Design consistency then becomes a criterion for rationalizing product lines to phase out products that are inconsistent with the dominant trends in product development. In other words, "old paradigm" products may have to go if they are inconsistent with existing or evolving "new paradigm" products.

In the broadest context, assess all existing products and subjectively prioritize them on their future potential with respect to technology, markets, trends, demographics, corporate goals, and mass customization opportunities.

ANALYZING THE RATIONALIZING CRITERIA

Analyze Pareto Plots

Analyze Pareto plots of all products according to the first five objective criteria: sales volume, sales revenue, part commonality, cost of variety, and *true* profitability. Be sure to objectively judge the relevance of available profitability data. Do not blindly import existing finance data to generate profitability Pareto plots for rationalization activities.

The polls and surveys can help shed light on the relevance of existing profitability numbers. If all the polls and surveys on profitability rankings are consistent with existing finance rankings, then the official finance data may be useful. On the other hand, if the polls and surveys are inconsistent with finance rankings, be wary of using existing profitability data for rationalizing. Either delete this category for now, give it a fractional multiplier (to weight it, for example, one half as important as other criteria), or improve the relevance of product costing, as will be discussed in Chapter 6.

Sales Volume and Revenue

Analyze the Pareto plots by concentrating first on the extremes. Very high sales volume and revenue products are probably products that will be retained.

Products with very low sales volume and revenue should be scrutinized using all these criteria. Ask the following questions:

- Why are we building these products that have substantially lower volume and revenue than the others?
- Does their low volume, in itself, make them harder to build because of the time to find the instructions and tooling, set up equipment, and learn how to make it again?
- Are these low-volume products causing more overhead expenditures than is being reported?
- Are these low-volume products a distraction from manufacturing's core competencies?

Persevere until you have satisfactory answers. Do not just accept answers like "we need a complete catalog" or "customers want them." There are other ways to satisfy these concerns, which will be discussed later.

Some products will not always show up in yearly sales data because they are not built every year. These products are definitely candidates for more scrutiny. If necessary, look into past years' productions to make sure these "biennial" products do not get overlooked and slip through the rationalizing process unscathed.

Remember, when total cost accounting is implemented, these "low runners" will probably have much lower *real* profitability than perceived now. The "enormous cross-subsidies" mentioned refer to high-volume products subsidizing low-volume products. As will be shown in Chapter 6, the typical pattern when converting to total cost accounting is that many products that appear to be profitable are really losing money.

Part Commonality Usage

Again, focus attention on the high and low usage products. Products that use mostly common parts may become candidates for mass customization scenarios. Products that use predominately unique parts are probably older or acquired products that may not fit well into flexible operations that mass customize products.

Removing the products with unique parts from the plant, or at least the flexible operations of the plant, may improve the flexibility of ongoing operations or allow ambitious implementations of Just-in-Time, Flexible Manufacturing, Build-to-Order, or Mass Customization.

Cost of Variety

This may be one of the most useful Pareto plots, but it requires sufficient data about the cost of variety, as presented in the last chapter. In the absence of complete cost-of-variety data, focus on the most significant elements, such as inventory costs, setup costs, materials overhead, and customization and configuration costs.

True Profitability

Again, make sure this category is based on total cost numbers. If this is the case, the highest profitability products will probably be retained as cash cows. Scrutinize the marginal or losing products to determine if they should be retained. Remember that a marginal product according to existing cost systems may prove to be a money-loser under more accurate product costing, as shown in an all too common effect in Figure 4–3. When total cost systems are implemented, not only will the shape of the curve change, but also the prioritization order, which is very important for product line rationalization.

When total cost accounting systems are implemented, they discover and correct the cross-subsidies caused by the existing cost systems. The results are a correction in product costing that often resembles the following case study.

After Hewlett-Packard implemented Activity-Based Cost Management in its Boise Surface Mount Center for 57 printed circuit board products, the more accurate costing changed product costing according to the graph shown in Figure 4–4. Fifteen of the products dropped in cost, one stayed the same, and two-thirds of

FIGURE 4-3

Effect of Cost Relevance on Product Line Profitability

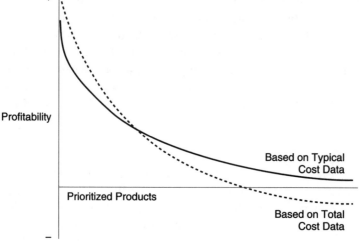

the products went up in cost! One product cost even doubled.[9] The cost drivers used in this implementation will be discussed further in Chapter 6. After making cost corrections, like those shown in Figure 4-4, marginally profitable products would probably turn out to be losing money, as shown by the dotted line in Figure 4-3.

Analyze the Subjective Categories

Attempts should be made to correlate the above Pareto plots and the subjective criteria: polls and surveys, factory processing, functionality, customer needs, core competencies, the clean-sheet-of-paper scenario, and future potential. A good correlation of subjective criteria with the Pareto plots will help verify those plots.

Opposite conclusions indicate a need for more investigation. As pointed out before, if the subjective judgments conflict with profitability data, this might point out a need for more relevant product costing based on total cost methodologies.

Some subjective analyses may suggest action that is not identified by the objective plot data. Potential actions can be investigated by creating a "what if" scenario for each of these decisions

FIGURE 4–4

Cost Corrections after Implementing ABC at Hewlett-Packard

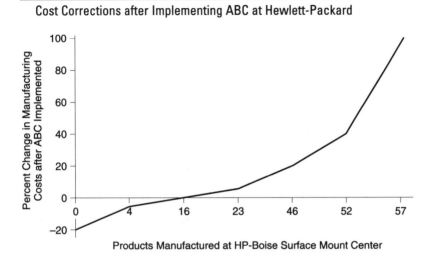

Products Manufactured at HP-Boise Surface Mount Center

under consideration. First, propose the change suggested by the subject criteria. Then, conduct a "what if" analysis to determine what effect the change would have on corporate goals, such as profit or growth. The analysis would need to be based on some common denominator such as money or market growth. It may be necessary to estimate the effect of the change on sales, growth, overhead, responsiveness, and the prioritization of product development, marketing, service, and so forth.

SEGREGATE THE PRODUCT LINE

The next step is to tentatively segregate the product line using the most dominant criteria of the objective Pareto plots. If true profitability data are available and reliable, this may become the most dominant.

For illustrative purposes, variety costs will be used here. Figure 4–5 shows a typical Pareto plot of variety cost as a percentage of total cost. All products are plotted from the lowest at the left to the highest at the right.

Products can be segregated into the following four categories, indicated by the following zones described below and shown graphically in Figure 4–5:

FIGURE 4–5

Segregation of the Product Line Based on Variety Cost

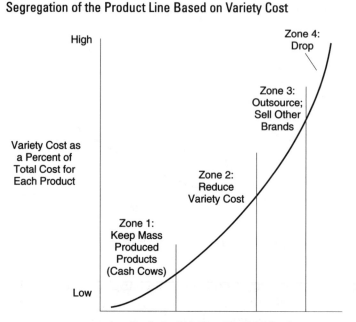

Products, (Prioritized by Total Cost)

Zone 1 Products still suitable for conventional mass production. No change in production *per se* may be required, although other steps resulting from this rationalization may make production equipment more available and may alter optimal batch size and routing.

Zone 2 Potentially compatible families of products with flexible/modular designs, inventory, and tooling that *could* be built on flexible equipment without setup. This is the category that will benefit from consolidation efforts and subsequent redesign of products and manufacturing processes, as will be presented later.

Zone 3 Products that do not fit into either zones 1 or 2 but still need to be in the catalog for completeness, to satisfy loyal customers, or for service obligations. These products may remain in the catalog, *but they do not have to be designed and built-in house.* They could be outsourced and manufactured by a vendor under the company name or label. Or the company catalog could simply carry another source's product to complete the product line, assuring customers about appropriate equivalency.

Zone 4 Products that should be dropped from the product line. If total cost accounting indicates these products are losing money based on current pricing, the price could be raised to ensure that minimum profitability goals are met. Market forces will then decide the fate of these products. However, sales commissions may have to be adjusted if these marginal products are left in the catalog, especially if commissions are based on sales volume rather than profitability.

Alternatively, the decision could be made to simply drop these products from the product line or phase them out. Some companies report that they have to eliminate sales commissions on dropped products to actually halt sales.

The products identified in zone 2 can be designed into a coherent product family using the techniques presented in Part IV of this book. For the products identified in zone 4, run a "what if" scenario for each product or group of related products. Project some trade-off numbers on the revenue lost, the variety costs saved, and the opportunities for better resource allocations. Be sure to use total cost data for these trade-offs. For each zone 3 product, look for alternative sources, propose solutions, and summarize the most likely scenario or scenarios.

For all the above proposed changes, discuss these with all affected parties: marketing, sales, distributors, dealers, customers, service, manufacturing, procurement, and so forth. Overcome resistance to change with a preface about the company's plans to be more agile and how important it is to "clean house" with respect to products that do not fit with new strategies.

The numbers alone may justify such changes, especially if the numbers can be based on total cost data. It may even be possible to lower the price of some of the zone 1 products at the same time because this rationalization is correcting existing cross-subsidies where the zone 1 products were subsidizing zone 3 and 4 products.

If the available numbers do not justify the changes, emphasize subjective issues such as core competencies, future direction, and the need to rationalize the product line to pursue more agile opportunities. It is important to obtain a "buy-in" from all the key players to make the changes with the minimum of adverse effects.

NOTES

1. Clay Chandler and Michael Williams, "A Slump in Car Sales Forces Nissan to Start Cutting Swollen Costs," *The Wall Street Journal*, March 3, 1993, p. 1.
2. H. Thomas Johnson and Robert S. Kaplan, *Relevance Lost, The Rise and Fall of Management Accounting* (Boston: Harvard Business School Press, 1987), p. 2.
3. Chandler and Williams, "A Slump in Car Sales."
4. Rahul Jacob, "Why Some Customers are More Equal than Others," *Fortune*, September 19, 1994, pp. 215–24.
5. Most MRP systems can perform a "where used" sort, which will identify, for a given part, all the products that use that part.
6. Robin Cooper, Robert Kaplan, Lawrence Maisel, Eileen Morrissey, and Ronald Oehm, *Implementing Activity-Based Cost Management* (Montvale, N.J., Institute of Management Accountants, 1992)
7. Robin Cooper and Robert Kaplan, "How Cost Accounting Distorts Product Costs," *World-Class Accounting for World-Class Manufacturing*, ed. by Lamont F. Steedle (Montvale, N.J., Institute of Management Accountants, 1990), p. 122.
8. Ibid, p. 119, under "Accuracy of Product Costs."
9. Mike Merz and Arlene Hardy, "ABC Puts Accountants on Design Team at HP," *Management Accounting*, September 1993, pp. 22–27.

CHAPTER

Early Steps and Prerequisites

Standardization

This chapter presents the prerequisites to developing mass customized products and some early steps companies can implement that will prepare them for subsequent mass customization activities. Since standardization helps all product developments, it should be implemented right away *even if a company has not yet fully committed to Mass Customization.* The methodologies presented in this chapter are not capital intensive and can be easily implemented without many levels of approvals. Further, these steps can be justified on their own merit. The next chapter, "Putting the 'Mass' in Mass Customization," discusses the cost benefits of many of the methodologies presented in this chapter.

Mass Customization means being able to build, in any volume, products that are customized to individuals or market niches *at mass production cost and speed.* The formidable challenge with Mass Customization is to produce an almost infinite *external* product variety without incurring the excessive cost and delays of *internal* variety that would be inevitable if the typical mass production company attempted to customize products.

Thus, the challenge for mass customizers is to reduce the internal variety to the point where products can be built *flexibly* without the cost and time delays of setup changes. This is accomplished by *standardizing* parts, features, materials, and processes *in the design stage.*

This chapter discusses the impact of standardization and setup reduction on flexible manufacturing (Chapter 7), part of the infrastructure that is a prerequisite for Mass Customization. Issues like setup reduction have obvious implications to high-volume producers and are fully discussed.

To operate flexibly in high volume, parts must be *common* enough to be readily available at all the points of use; fixturing geometry must be common enough so that all variations of a part can be positioned the same; design features must be common enough to use the same manufacturing tools; materials must be common enough to avoid stopping production to change materials. If parts cannot be distributed at their points of use, then they will have to be "kitted" together in batches, as discussed in Chapter 3, with enough parts for the number of products to be built. Kitting inhibits flexibility and thus discourages Mass Customization.

All of this incurs significant overhead that is more proportional to variety than to volume, especially for parts that are small and do not have special requirements for inspection, handling, or storage. Consider the difference in material overhead between 100 different resistor types (each with a consumption of 100 a month) and 10 resistor types (each with a consumption of 1,000 per month). Either scenario represents the consumption of 10,000 resistors per month, but the overhead cost to procure and distribute 100 part types would be an order of magnitude greater than for the 10 types.

Standardization of parts is also extremely important to ensure that flexibility will not be compromised by the setup of retrieving parts, changing dies, changing programs, or "double loading" automation machines, which is necessary if there are more parts or tools than bins or receptacles; the machine will then have to be run twice, once to assemble half the parts and again for the remaining half.

The issues that affect low-volume products are more subtle, but equally important. The section below emphasizes that the lessons of this chapter apply to low-volume producers too.

STANDARDIZATION AND THE LOW-VOLUME PRODUCER

For low-volume operations, there is a temptation to ignore standardization and just handle variations ad hoc as they are encountered. But Mass Customization, or even several custom or niche market products, would generate many little variations. The *cumulative* effect of all these "little" variations can cost so much money and time that the company would simply not be able to mass customize products.

Part Distribution
Even if parts are not dispensed from dedicated bins on assembly lines, they would still have to be procured, delivered to the plant, possibly inspected, kitted, routed to the assembly area, and assembled with the right tools.

Procurement of Unusual Parts
If parts are used infrequently, the procurement will be costly and slow. An unusual part may be out of stock, temporarily or even permanently. Delivery for a few unique parts will not be fast, unless expediting charges are paid. Incoming inspection of seldom-used parts, if required, might be time consuming and expensive considering the effort to look up uncommon procedures and find unusual test fixtures.

Assembly Instructions
Assembly might be delayed if instructions or fixtures are hard to find or if workers forgot how to perform the fabrication, assembly, alignment or calibrations.

Shortages
Assembly can grind to a halt for the lack of *any* part; the more types of parts, the more possibilities there are for part shortages. In fact, low-volume production is more likely to cause shortages because of limited sources of supply.

Tools
Low-usage parts do not justify the development of efficient tools to fabricate, assemble, align, calibrate, or test, thus forcing workers to use much slower general-purpose tools. Standardizing proce-

dures for general purpose tools will speed production and minimize confusion and errors.

Testing of Seldom Used Parts
Product testing might be complicated by failures of seldom-used
parts, whose failure modes have not been well understood or documented.

Part/Vendor Qualification
Qualification of parts and vendors will be less thorough if finite
resources are spread thin over a vast variety of parts. Inadequate
qualification of parts can cause major quality problems that affect
every product using a questionable part. Inadequate qualification
of vendors can result in unpleasant surprises; for instance, if it is
discovered that a supplier has gone bankrupt. There may be more
at stake than the loss of a source of supply if investors or authori-
ties close, impound, or seize a vendor's facility, which may contain
its customer's tooling, fixtures, and materials.

Service and Repair
Excessive part variety will complicate service and repair, especially
for the low- volume producer. An unusual part that is no longer used
in current production may cause the factory to "tool up" again, just
for a low-volume part. Purchased parts may have become "orphans"
that are no longer made by any supplier. In this case, the company
must either find new sources or start making the parts in very low
volumes just to ensure availability of replacement parts.

   Depending on service obligations, factories may be required
to stock all parts for the expected lives of all products. This can be
a heavy burden on the low-volume producer who lacks the inherent flow of parts that comes with high volume. Field service may
be more difficult if parts were not common enough to be available
from local suppliers.

Spare-parts Kits
Excessive part variety will force spare-parts kits to be larger, especially for parts that are not included in another machine's spare-
parts kit. A low-volume company that manufactures production or
processing equipment may have only one of its machines in a cus-

tomer's facility. If the machine has many unique parts, the spare-parts kit will have to be large. The cost of a large spare-parts kit must be borne either directly by the customer or indirectly if it is included in the sales price. Unusual parts, not included in the spare-parts kit, represent a vulnerability to the customer.

Thus, lack of standardization, in itself, could be a competitive liability to low-volume producers because it would cause a relative disadvantage with respect to cost, delivery, quality, repair, field service, and, possibly, reputation.

REDUCING INTERNAL COMPLEXITY

An important prerequisite to flexible manufacturing and, thus, to Mass Customization is the reduction of internal complexity, which requires standardization efforts for parts, materials, tools, and processes. Many companies, even some highly respected ones, have allowed their internal variety to become excessive.

Part Proliferation

Recent competitive pressures and currency issues are forcing Japanese automobile manufacturers to reduce cost. One of their thrusts is to investigate and reduce the cost of internal variety. As a result of such an investigation, Nissan realized in 1993 that, in the current model lineup alone, it used 110 different radiators, 300 different ashtrays, 437 dashboard meters, 1,200 floor carpet types, and 6,000 different fasteners![1] This type of variety does not add value to the customer. Of course, customers want their carpets to match interior fabrics and exterior paint, but this could be accomplished with far fewer than 1,200 carpet types.

An electronics company had 1,500 types of resistors, including 120 different kinds, sizes, and tolerances of 1,000 ohm resistors.[2] That company was able to reduce the 1,500 resistor types to less than 200 actively used for manufacturing.

One of the author's clients, who made consumer products, discovered it was using the following numbers of part types: 1,248 wire assemblies, 152 motors, 151 screws, 74 switches, 67 relays, 65 capacitors, 37 valves, 16 transformers, 62 types of tape, and 1,399 different "standard" labels.

Every company has similar horror stories regarding part proliferation. One might ask why, especially considering the following:

- Part proliferation impedes manufacturing flexibility and, thus, discourages mass customization.
- Most part proliferation is unnecessary, as will be shown below.
- Part proliferation generates a great deal of overhead cost.

The Cost of Part Proliferation

Part proliferation is expensive. A Tektronix study determined that half of all overhead costs related in some way to the number of different parts handled.[3] Most companies do not even know how much this cost is in dollars. A survey of several Fortune 500 manufacturing companies[4] revealed that *not a single company or division had an accurate estimate of the cost of a part over its lifetime!* According to Venkat Mohan of CADIS, Inc., who markets parts management software, "intuitive estimates range from $5,000 for a standard part to as high as $60,000 or even $100,000 per part for custom parts."[5] James Shepherd, director of research for Advanced Manufacturing Research (AMR), Boston, says that in electronics, the cost of just entering new purchased components is between $5,000 and $10,000 per component.[6] *The Ernst & Young Guide to Total Cost Management* states, "It is not surprising that manufacturers have estimated the annual administrative cost of each part number to be $10,000 or more."[7]

In addition to these official "materials" costs, excessive part proliferation adds cost to field service and manufacturing in important, but rarely measured, ways related to setup, inventory, floor space, lower machinery utilization, and other flexibility issues.

Part proliferation also lowers assembly productivity. Writing about the automobile industry in a Wharton Business School report, Fisher, Jain and MacDuffie write, "Part variety also appears to have the greatest negative impact on assembly plant productivity."[8]

Why Part Proliferation Happens

Part proliferation happens for the following reasons, which are all easily avoidable:

1. Engineers don't understand. Most product designers do not understand the importance of part commonality and, therefore, do not attempt to design around common parts. An example of this attitude was discovered when the author was soliciting feedback from engineers on a proposed commonality list (which was generated by techniques described below) for resistors. One electrical engineer commented, "Why are we standardizing on resistors? Aren't they cheap and aren't they in the computer?" What this engineer did not realize is that, regardless of a part's cost and the company's ordering/tracking sophistication, every part must be physically delivered to the plant, possibly inspected and warehoused, and then distributed to each point of use. One solution to this problem is training and education that stresses the importance of part commonality to corporate goals.

2. "Not invented here." Sometimes standardization is resisted because of the "not-invented-here" syndrome, but that can be countered by teamwork, training, and encouraging engineers to think "globally instead of locally."

3. Arbitrary decisions. Product designers make *arbitrary decisions* when specifying parts. They may arbitrarily specify a fine pitch 5/16 inch bolt with a button head that is 7/16 inch long when a more common course-pitch 3/8 inch hex bolt that is 1/2 inch long could have done the job just as well. Chapter 9 discusses the general problem of arbitrary decisions in product development.

Electronic engineers at Intel's Systems Group said that for digital circuitry, they did not really need any resistor value between 1,000 ohms and 2,000 ohms. From this feedback, those values were immediately deleted from the list.

4. The minimum weight fallacy. A phenomenon that may be causing arbitrary decisions is the fallacy that all parts have to be sized "just right" to have the minimum weight and be made of the minimum amount of materials. They resist standardization because the standard part is, generally, the next larger size to ensure adequate strength and functionality. The following rules of thumb may help to guide engineers past this obstacle.

If it doesn't fly or move fast, use the next larger size standard part.
If it isn't made of precious metals, use the next larger size
standard part.

5. Qualifying part families. A related cause of part proliferation is the practice of *qualifying* (for entry on approved parts lists) entire *families* of parts, like fasteners, resistors, and capacitors. Intel's Systems Group discovered that out of 20,000 approved parts for printed circuit boards and computer systems, 7,000 had never been used! Over one-third of the approved parts were not used on any product. And yet any engineer could have arbitrarily chosen one of those unused parts and entered a new part into the system without any approval or authorization. In this case, those unused parts were immediately deleted from the approved parts list.

6. Contract manufacturing. Sometimes a shortsighted business strategy undermines standardization efforts. Some companies, in response to downturns, respond to the pressure to "fill the factory" by, in essence, becoming a contract manufacturer. This "use-it-or-lose-it" approach may bring in some additional revenue, but often loses money in the long run. This would be seen if computations included total cost issues such as the overhead expense to support such internal diversity and the substantial learning curve expense needed to gear up to build many new products.

7. Mergers and acquisitions. Another cause of excessive internal variety is the merger of dissimilar products through corporate mergers and the acquisitions of companies, products, patents, and so on. Products that originated in different companies are likely to have very different parts and processes. Thus, manufacturing flexibility should be added to the list of primary factors that determine such decisions.

8. Duplicate parts. When product designers do not know what parts exist, they will often "add" a "new" part to the database, *even when the identical part* already exists. Even if they suspect that the needed part exists, they will probably specify a new purchased part if it takes less time than finding an existing one. They will probably design a new part if it takes less time than finding an existing one. Engineers often find it much harder to search through awkward databases than to design new parts or to select them.

Many companies have hundreds of incidents of duplicates, triplicates, or even several versions of the same part, existing under different company part numbers. There are even more situations where a "close" existing part could have been used instead of introducing a new part.

On the author's suggestion, one aerospace company investigated this and found that it had 900 different types of spacers! Apparently, it was easier to design number 901 than to search through all 900 existing spacers.

When a large machine tool company investigated this phenomenon, it discovered it had 521 very similar gears. The company eventually reclassified all those gears into 30 standard gears.[9] There were 17 times more gear types than necessary! Every gear had an average of 17 functional or exact "duplicates."

Eliminating Multiple Identical Parts

The problem with multiple part numbers for the same part goes beyond the obvious extra material overhead cost of carrying extra parts. Most likely, the similar parts would be ordered separately for each product that needed the parts. This would prevent Purchasing from obtaining quantity discounts and just-in-time deliveries that would have been possible with a consolidated order. Further, the smaller order quantities increase the chances of shortages for a given part. Ironically, the missing part that delays production might be sitting in another bin under a different part number.

The problem becomes more severe in a mass customization environment if different products are using the same part under different part numbers. This may require automation assembly equipment, for instance, for printed circuit board assembly, to load the same part in multiple bins, since bins are assigned by the part number listed on the bill of materials. Even if the machine operator notices that some of the parts seem similar, the operator does not have the time nor the authorization to consolidate parts on the spot. This duplication alone may prevent flexible operations if there are more parts (including duplicates) in the product family than there are bins in the equipment. If this is the case, then parts would have to be reloaded twice for each product, which is the type of setup that must be eliminated for mass customization.

One way to stop the introduction of duplicate parts is to make it easier to *find* existing parts than to release new ones. The two following techniques will do that.

Part Listing

Many parts lend themselves to listing in a logical order as examples show in Figure 5–1. For these parts, simply list all existing parts in order, circulate the lists to the design community, and encourage engineers to use existing parts whenever possible. A procedure will be presented below for determining preferred part designations for these lists.

Part Management Software

Part management software may be needed for parts that do not lend themselves to such ordered listing or in situations where it is hard to find the existing parts because of lack of computerization, awkward database structures, inconsistent descriptions, multiple databases, unstructured data in text fields, and other information system complications.

CADIS-PMX is a part management database and "search engine" that can classify all parts in a hierarchy based on part attributes rather than company part number or supplier catalog numbers. It can present the results to engineers through a user-friendly graphical user interface.[10] It can even make it easier to extract unstructured data from database text fields.

Using this tool, Tektronix deactivated 32,000 part numbers from an active base of 150,000. Bob Vance, Tektronix vice president

FIGURE 5–1

Examples of Part Type Listing Orders

Part Type	Listing Order
Threaded fasteners	Thread diameter, pitch, length, head type, material/coating, grade
Washers/spacers	O.D., I.D., thickness, material, finish
Gears	Pitch, number of teeth, face width, material
Gearboxes	Ratio, horsepower, shaft orientations, shaft diameters
Motors	Horsepower, voltage, phase, shaft diameter, mount
Pumps	Pressure, flow rate
Power supplies	Output voltage, wattage
Resistors	Ohms
Capacitors	Microfarad
Integrated circuits	Generic numbering system (e.g., 74F00)

and chief information officer, summarized the return on eliminating excess parts: "There are few areas where a manufacturing company can make such a significant impact to its bottom line with so little effort. We want to invest our resources in product innovation and customer services, not carrying an overburdened parts inventory."[11]

The Results of Part Proliferation

The net result of part proliferation is that most companies have thousands or even hundreds of thousands of different part types (unique part numbers). Such internal variety is rarely necessary and is usually the result of this careless proliferation of parts. The absence of any standardization goals or awareness allows designers to simply choose new parts for new designs, without any consideration of prior usage of similar parts.

Every company can investigate the extent of part proliferation by simply looking up the total number of active part numbers for all part categories. In many cases, the proliferation will seem obvious, even to the most casual observer. Another revealing investigation would be to summarize the "materials" budget for all the overhead expenses related to parts. It is hoped these investigations will provide the motivation to eliminate existing duplicate parts and to substantially reduce part types for new designs using the effective procedure presented next.

THE PART COMMONALITY APPROACH

The following methodology is an easy-to-apply approach that is more effective than *part type reduction* measures, which require tremendous efforts for their return. Reducing active part numbers, say from 20,000 to 15,000, will lower material overhead somewhat, but may not reach the threshold (eliminating part-related setup) that would enable the plant to build products flexibly without delays and setups to get the parts, kit the parts, or change the part bins.

Part commonality is a very effective technique to reduce the number of different parts (part types) by standardizing on certain *preferred* parts. This usually applies to purchased parts, but it could also apply to manufactured parts.

Part commonality methodology is based on a *zero-based* principle that asks the simple question: "What is the minimum list of part types we need to design new products?" Answering this question can be made easier by assuming that the company (or a new competitor) has just entered this product line and is deciding which parts will be needed for a whole new product line. One advantage of new competitors is the ability to "start fresh" without the old baggage: too many parts. Just imagine a competitor simultaneously designed the *entire* product line around common parts. Now imagine doing the same thing internally. This is called the *zero-based approach*.

The zero-based approach, literally, starts at zero and adds only what is needed, as opposed to reducing parts from a overwhelming list. An analogous situation would be cleaning out a cluttered desk drawer, a purse, or a glove compartment; removing unwanted pieces would take much effort and still not be very effective. The more effective zero-based approach would be to empty everything, and add back only the items that are essential. Where the "clutter" ends up is the difference in the approaches: in the drawer, purse, or glove compartment or in the garbage can. Similarly, parts reduction efforts have to work hard to remove the clutter (excess part variety) in the system, whereas zero-based approaches exclude the clutter from the beginning. The clutter is the unnecessary parts that would have not been needed if products were designed around common parts. Not only do these excess parts incur overhead costs to administer them, but they also lower plant efficiency and machine utilization because of the setup caused by products that are designed to have more parts than can be distributed at every point of use. Chapters 3 and 6 discuss the economic impact of part commonality.

The commonality approach determines the minimum list of parts needed for new designs and is not intended to eliminate parts used on existing products, except when the common parts are functionally equivalent in all respects. In this case the new common part may be substituted as an equivalent part or a "better-than" substitution, where a common part with a better tolerance can replace its lesser counterpart in existing products.

Even if part commonality efforts apply only to new products, remember that in these days of rapid product obsolescence and short product life cycles, all older products may be phased out in a few years.

The following description shows how to implement part commonality using the zero-based approach.

1. Determine Inherent Commonality

The first step in the commonality approach is to ascertain the company's *inherent* part commonality for each category of parts. It would be very unusual if all existing parts had identical usage histories. Every category of parts has some "high-runners" that are used far more often than others. Rather than choosing arbitrary values for new products, choose values that correspond to existing high usage parts as much as possible. One reason for this approach would be to avoid adding *new* common parts to a bloated list of parts already in use. Another reason is that the values already in widespread use probably were chosen for reasons that may apply to old and new products alike.

To determine the company's inherent commonality, first obtain prioritized lists of each part category:

a. *Parts used in the greatest total quantity per year or per month.* This can be obtained from purchasing or MRP (material requirements planning) data.

b. *Parts that are used on the most products.* This can be found by a "where used" report from most MRP systems. This list is useful if the company manufactures many products and may be especially important if parts used on many products need to be kept active for service and spare-parts kits.

c. *Parts with consistent usage over many years.* This may be an important list over time if older products in the field may still need service and spare-parts kits.

Then plot the above data, for each category of part type, in the format of Figure 5–2. The upper curve plots yearly usage volume for each part in Pareto order (greatest on the left, lowest usage on the right). Our experience suggests that these curves will almost always assume this exponential shape with a few parts used in great quantity and very many parts used in very low quantities.

The lower curve plots the "where used" data showing which parts are used in the greater number of products. Note that it

FIGURE 5–2

Inherent Commonality

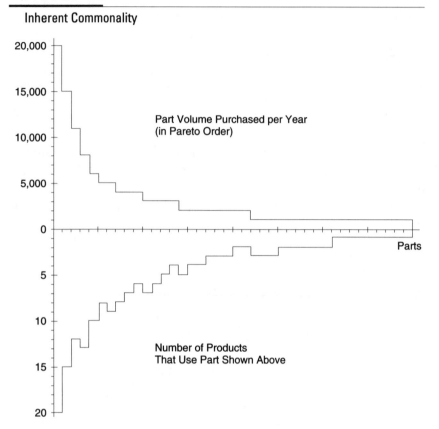

would be quite unusual for both curves to correspond exactly, that is, with the volume rank always corresponding to the product usage rank.

Thus, one curve lists parts in Pareto order. The other curve will be based on the same part number order, not necessarily in its own Pareto order (this explains the jagged lines in the lower curve in Figure 5–2). In this way, usage patterns for two criteria can be analyzed simultaneously. This will be helpful for the next step, which will be to apply judgment to the curves, to determine which existing parts should be candidates for the commonality list. Note that the first Pareto list (top curve) should be based on the most dominant criteria: either volume usage per year (as shown in

Figure 5–2) or the "where used" criterion. For product lines with very few products, part usage volume would be the dominant criterion. Conversely, for product lines with very many products, the dominant criterion may be the number of products that use each part. This will give the dominant criterion a preference in the selection procedure that will be discussed next.

2. Establish Baseline List

Investigate Existing Part Usage

The next step is to establish a *baseline list* that will be based on the inherent commonality of existing parts determined above. Obviously, the "high runners" on the left of the curves should be part of the baseline list and the low-usage parts on the right should not. Where to draw the line that separates common parts from the rest will require some judgment. This judgment should come from a consensus of all engineering groups, Manufacturing, Purchasing, and those who qualify parts and suppliers (Quality or Materials Engineering departments). The last function would be interested because minimizing the number of part types has a positive impact on procurement and quality activities, since fewer part types means that more attention can be focused on procurement, vendor qualifications, and quality issues for the common parts.

If the usage profile looked like the top curve of Figure 5–2, the left third of the parts might qualify for the baseline list. When parts proliferation has been more rampant, the low-usage and single use parts would extend much farther to the right. In such a case, the commonality parts may be only the top 5 or 10 percent of the parts.

Next, select appropriate parts from the secondary (bottom) curve. In some cases, there may be anomalies, such as parts used in low volume but used in very many products. The widespread use may qualify that part for the list, despite the low volume. In other cases, a part may be used on only one product, but in very high volume. This may require some investigation to determine if the design team has discovered a clever use for the part that may apply to future projects.

These parts become the baseline list, which would then be arranged in some appropriate order, as discussed earlier.

3. New Generation Parts

Add new generation parts (that have no usage history) to the baseline list. Again, this is a judgment that would best be done by consensus of engineers from "advanced" design groups, materials qualifying groups, Manufacturing, Purchasing, and Quality.

4. Consolidate Duplicates

As discussed before, many duplicates get into the system and good parts management can eliminate the exact duplicates. When companies start investigating duplications, they often discover slight differences between the duplicate parts. This presents an opportunity to select the part that could most likely replace the others. This may involve choosing the "better" part, using the procedure discussed next.

5. Consolidate Parallel Lines of Parts

Next, consolidate parallel lines of parts. If whole families of parts are available in multiple tolerances, quality levels, thread pitches, or material finishes, the team should consolidate them into one set of parts, even if it has to standardize on the more expensive parts. Usually, any increase in part cost, due to using the "better" parts, will be dwarfed by the savings from having fewer parts overall. If the company cost accounting system can not quantify the value of this, then the company must recognize the qualitative value to manufacturing flexibility and lowering material overhead costs (see discussion below on standardizing on expensive parts). For example, various grades of bolt strength or resistor tolerance could be consolidated, as indicated by the following example.

When the author was initiating a parts standardization program at Intel's Systems Group, there were two different families of resistors: 5 percent (tolerance) carbon resistors and 1 percent metal film resistors. He consolidated the line to exclusively 1 percent resistors, thus eliminating hundreds of part numbers for new designs. These parts were also substituted in existing products since this was considered a "better than" substitution. The higher order quantities resulting from making all resistor purchases the same tolerance (1 percent) may cancel out the perceived "extra" cost of raising the 5 percent parts to the 1 percent level, thus resulting in overall cost savings.

Note that consolidation based on higher-quality parts may, in reality, raise the quality of the products, even if the lower-quality parts were *theoretically* adequate.

6. Structure List

Structure the list into appropriate order, as shown in Figure 5–1, by values of diameter, pitch, ratio, power, flow rate, voltage, ohms, microfarads, and so on.

7. Review the Lists

Then review the tentative baseline lists for each type of part and feature by involving representatives of all relevant engineering departments for feedback and approval. This could be a formal process that is part of the procedures to generate commonality lists. Or it could be an informal process that would solicit informal feedback from some experienced engineers who could be assumed to be representative of their departments. Earlier participation of representatives of these departments on the task force should minimize surprises at this stage.

8. Circulate the Lists

Circulate the tentative lists to all engineers with a explanation of why the commonality is important to company goals, especially mass customization goals. Solicit feedback about whether the tentative baseline list has the right parts for new designs. Query reviewers if any part on the list is superfluous or if any important part was wrongly omitted.

9. Finalize the Lists

Review feedback from all those reviewing the list. Investigate promising suggestions and add or subtract appropriate items to or from the list. Finalize the list and prepare it for implementation.

Since commonality is a prerequisite for flexible manufacturing and build-to-order, which, in turn, are prerequisites for mass customization, the commonality program must be implemented decisively.

10. Determine Scope of Implementation

The scope of the commonality effort should be matched to implementation resources and the general company awareness of the importance and value of designing around common parts. Some companies may choose to start with the "low hanging fruit" first, say fasteners or resistors. Success here may then be leveraged to other types of parts. As companies embark on the mass customization of their products, strong commonality efforts for all parts become imperative.

11. Educate the Design Community

Before commonality lists are issued, the design community needs to be educated on the importance of using common parts in new designs. Point out how important this is to manufacturing flexibility and to lowering overhead costs. Another educational and motivational technique is the "embarrassing statistics" technique: Reveal the scope of past part proliferations, which are usually caused by designers who arbitrarily chose a low-usage part when a high-usage part would have worked. Design engineers need to realize that *no matter how simple a part appears, every part number incurs a material overhead burden* to document, procure, store, distribute, resupply, and, most significantly, to manufacture in low volume.

12. Determine the Strictness of Adherence

The strictness of adherence to the commonality list should reflect the company's need for manufacturing flexibility, automation utilization, overhead cost reduction, and ease of service. A high-volume, flexible plant with expensive automation might require 100 percent adherence to the commonality list so that the equipment would not have to stop to load noncommon parts. Mass customization environments may require 100 percent adherence, if manufacturing flexibility is essential. Companies contemplating adherence of less than 100 percent need to analyze the effect of this "un-commonality" on the flexibility of operations.

Many companies just want to reduce the active parts base and encourage engineers to use parts that are already in use. For instance, General Electric Lighting has established a goal of 90 percent parts reuse in all new designs.[12]

13. Issue the Commonality Lists

Designate the parts on the commonality lists officially as *common* parts or *preferred* parts and give them special emphasis with an asterisk or bold type on the larger approved part lists that may still be used for products that are not mass customized. A more effective method is to present the preferred common parts on a separate list, perhaps in the front of the section containing that category of parts. Intel's Systems Group presented preferred parts on a gold page, followed by the existing approved parts on white paper. When common parts are to be used exclusively, the commonality list would be the only parts list issued to engineers.

PART COMMONALITY RESULTS

This part commonality approach was implemented by the author at Intel Corporation's Systems Group. Starting with 20,000 parts for printed circuit boards and computers, this commonality approach generated a "preferred" parts list of 500 parts. For the categories of "axials" (resistors, capacitors, and diodes), 2,000 values were reduced to 35 values, one set for leaded axials and another set for their surface mount equivalents.

Fasteners for computer systems were standardized on one screw! This is how the commonality process worked: Service wanted a Phillips head so they could keep using the same tools; Quality wanted a captivated "crest cup" washer to protect surface finishes; Engineering wanted the 6-32 size screw to be only a quarter inch long; Manufacturing recommended that the screw be three-eighths of an inch long so that it would not tumble as it was fed to auto-feed screwdrivers. Previous designs had so many different screws that Manufacturing could not use the auto-feed screwdriver. The next design that used the standard screw in 40 locations. This, plus the correct screw geometry, made use of the more efficient auto-feed screwdriver practical. To make the screw one-eighth of an inch longer than needed, the screw would protrude beyond the fastener material. This violated a workmanship standard prohibiting such protrusions. The standard was modified to allow the protrusion as long as it did not pose a safety hazard or compromise product functionality in any way.

Intel's enforcement goal was not 100 percent, as might be required for an operation flexible enough to mass customize, but we felt that even 95 percent usage would result in significant material overhead savings.

TOOL COMMONALITY

A subject related to part commonality is tool commonality, which determines how many different tools are required for assembly, alignment, calibration, testing, repair, and service (fabrication tool commonality will be discussed next under *feature* commonality).

Tool commonality affects Mass Customization by eliminating the setup to locate and change tools needed in the manufacturing process. If customization is to be provided by dealers or users, ideally no tools should be required. But if tools are required, the product should be designed around common tools that are easy to use and would be available to dealers or users. A single customization tool, which performs all customizations, may be supplied with the product.

Some designs may require several lengths of screws, but if they have the same head geometry, then one screwdriver could be used for all of them. Tool commonality becomes even more important if service people have to be mobile or have to perform service in awkward situations such as clean rooms, crawl spaces, catwalks, utility poles, underwater, in space, and so on. Tool commonality can also help minimize the expense of providing repair tool kits with products (as provided with some automobiles) and enable the user to perform more repairs.

Tools should be standardized on *standard*, readily available tools. Often *special* tools are required because tool specification was not part of the design process. Sometimes special tools are required simply because tool access was not designed into products.

Companywide tool commonality can be determined as follows: First, analyze tools used for existing products. Prioritize usage histories to determine the most "common" of existing tools. Work with people in manufacturing and service, in addition to dealers and users, if appropriate, to determine tool preferences. Coordinate common tool selection with common part selection. Issue common tool lists with common parts lists.

FEATURE COMMONALITY

Features such as drilled holes, reamed holes, punched holes, and sheet metal bend radii require special tools, such as drills, reams, hole punch dies, and bending mandrels. Unless there is a dedicated machine for each tool, the tools will have to be changed, and this results in a setup change every time the tool needs to be changed. Some machines have automatic tool changing capabilities, but all are limited in the number of tools they can store.

Most sheet metal bends do not need to be any specific value within a reasonable range, but designers must enter a single bend radius value on the drawing to complete the drawing. Unfortunately, most designers specify an arbitrary bend radius, which often requires the shop to locate and change mandrels to bend the sheet metal to those arbitrary radii.

A more subtle, but still important, form of feature commonality is standardization around cutting tools used on machine tools such as lathes and milling machines. As with bend radii, many designers specify arbitrary fillet radii when a standard fillet radius might satisfy the needs of the entire product family. Multiple fillet radii may force the machinist to change cutting tools often.

When designing parts for CNC milling, designers should specify the same standard fillet radius throughout the product family so that a single cutter or "end mill" may be used. This ensures that all parts in the family can be milled without setup changes and, thus, ensures flexibility and high machine tool utilization on expensive equipment.

To implement feature commonality, standardize features around standard production tools, making sure not to exceed the tool storage capacity. Investigate the tools used by the plant and by key outside vendors (whether currently used or not). A safe approach is to choose only features that can be easily built by *all* potential production facilities and vendors. Based on the production tool availability and capabilities, compile a feature list and issue it with the commonality lists for parts, hand tools, and raw materials (discussed next).

RAW MATERIALS COMMONALITY

Mass Customization needs raw material commonality for products whose customization is accomplished by "cut-to-fit" operations. If the raw materials to be processed can be standardized, then the processes can be flexible enough to make different products without any setup to change materials, fixturing mechanisms, or cutting tools.

Bar Stock/Tubing

If raw materials can be standardized on size one bar stock or one size tubing, then computer-controlled machines can be programmed to cut off required lengths from the same stock. This flexibility may determine the feasibility of cut-to-fit customization. Although manual cut-off operations may be more adaptable, material standardization would simplify instructions to the length only. This would minimize the chances for mistakes related to picking the wrong material.

Sheet Metal

If sheet metal can be standardized on one thickness and alloy, then computer-controlled laser cutting machines can cut all the sheet metal parts needed without changing sheets. Automatic sheet feeders could reload the machine as needed. This is even more important if the parts are so small that many parts could be cut from the same sheet without having to change sheets.

Molding/Casting

Part of a mass customization strategy may involve offering a wide variety of molded or cast parts. Molding and casting operations will be more cost-effective if they can standardize on the same raw material, so that many different parts could be made in the same mold, thus sharing processing time and tooling expense. Standardizing materials avoids the setup of changing materials and cleaning the equipment. If molds are designed with *fixturing* commonality, they could be changed rapidly to minimize setup time. With casting material standardization, several molds could be filled with the same "pour" from a single "melt."

Protective Coatings

Standardizing on protective coatings simplifies processing and makes coating operations more flexible by eliminating the setup to change coating materials and clean equipment. As with parts commonality, coatings could be standardized on the "better" coating. Even if that coating appears to cost more, the net result may be overall cost savings, considering the process value of this standardization. The logic of this concept is discussed further in the section on standardization of expensive parts below. Coating standardization could also apply to paint if the purpose of the paint is purely functional with little aesthetic considerations, such as for industrial equipment or inside major appliances. In fact, many industrial and agricultural products enjoy brand recognition because of a standard paint color. For instance, farmers immediately recognize a green tractor or combine as a John Deere product.

Programmable Chips

Many integrated circuits (ICs) can be programmed separately or in the product. Programmable chip commonality standardizes on the fewest types of "blanks." This allows the flexibility to program these devices "on the fly" by on-line programming stations as they are assembled into the product. Ideally, each programming station would be dedicated to one blank device to avoid setup changes. Thus, programmable chip commonality minimizes the number of programming stations and, thus, may make it possible to program chips as they are inserted or placed onto circuit boards.

Linear Materials

Commonality can also be applied to material purchased by length: wire, rope, plastic tubing, cable, chain, and so on. Linear material variety can be reduced in the following ways:

- *Cut as needed.* Linear materials can be standardized by *type* only with the length cut as needed. Available equipment will even cut and strip the ends of wires. This approach would require a dispensing machine at each point of use.
- *Kanban system.* Alternatively, wire and tubing can be cut ahead of time, but, to keep overhead low, not be given individual part numbers. The following system was developed by MKS Instruments, Inc., makers of vacuum and flow measurement/control instrumentation. Instead of issuing part numbers and treating many cut lengths as many different parts, a predetermined amount (for instance, one day's worth) of wire or tubing can be cut to the needed lengths and placed in each of two adjacent Kanban bins at each point of use. The kanban bins are arranged one in front of the other. When the front bin is emptied, it is sent to a central dispensing machine. The label on the bin tells the machine operator the material type, length, quantity, and the bin's return destination in the factory. After filling the bin, it is returned to the point of use and placed behind its counterpart so it can be moved forward and used when the other bin is emptied. This simple approach can eliminate hundreds or thousands of part numbers from the plant, thus lowering costs, minimizing delays, improving flexibility, and encouraging mass customization.
- *Printing while dispensing.* The number of types of linear materials can be reduced further by using equipment that prints on wire and tubing as it is dispensed, so that many various colors of the material need not be stocked. Printing on wire and tubing can minimize mistakes in assembly and service, since workers do not have to memorize or refer to color codes. Using words, rather than color, also solves problems associated with color blindness. Examples of printing would be: Ground; +12 volts; Supply; Return; 1,000 psi; etc. For international products, these codes can be printed in multiple languages, which may reduce internal variety due to labeling differences. Such printing/dispensing equipment could be utilized either at each point of use or at a central location to feed dual kanban bins.

PROCESS STANDARDIZATION

Standardization of processes results from the concurrent engineering of products and processes to ensure that the processes are actually specified by the design team, rather than left to chance or "to be determined later." Processes must be coordinated and common enough to ensure that all parts and products in the mass customization family can be built without the setup changes that would undermine flexible manufacturing.

One of the processes affected by part standardization is mechanized screw fastening. Auto-feed screwdrivers (see Figure 5–3) are a very cost-effective mechanized tool that orients and feeds screws that are then blown down a tube to the screwdriver head, where it waits for the operator to activate the power drive by pushing down on the screwdriver handle. A preset torque-limited mechanism makes sure the screw is fastened consistently. This useful production tool can feed any style of screw (machine threads, self taping, etc.), but *only one size and type at a time*. Changing screw sizes is possible but would cause too much of a setup to be used in

FIGURE 5–3

Auto-Feed Screwdriver

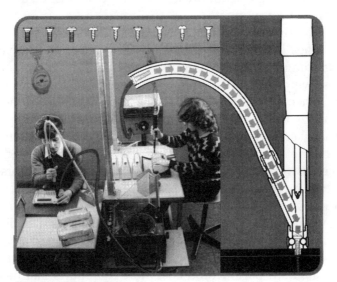

Photo courtesy of Deprag, Inc.; Lewisville, Texas

flexible operations. Thus, auto-feed screwdrivers can be utilized effectively only if there is fastener commonality.

Another concurrent engineering issue is that the screw specified must be longer than it is wide so that it will not tumble as it is blown down the feed tube. Each manufacturer has specific guidelines for specifying these dimensions.

Similar devices, based on the same principle, can fasten screws automatically when mounted on robots or on assembly mechanisms specifically designed to dispense screws, such as those used in Hewlett-Packard's DeskJet factory in Vancouver, Washington.

STANDARDIZATION OF EXPENSIVE PARTS

Usually, commonality programs for inexpensive parts, like fasteners, do not meet serious resistance, since the common parts cost about the same as nonstandard parts. But, as the cost of the parts increases, standardization efforts confront more resistance because of the *perception* that specifying the next larger (and more expensive) standard component would cost more than one that just satisfies its requirements in the product. However, considering the *total* cost of standardization can encourage standardization, even for expensive components.

The following experience illustrates the resistance and the opportunities involved in the standardization of expensive parts. While training a company that manufactured air conditioners and furnaces, we discovered the company used 152 different types of motors. When we challenged the designers, they insisted they needed every size to specify "just the right" motor for every application. Then we asked their supplier, GE Consumer Motor Division, "What would be the savings if those 152 motors could be reduced to 5 or 10?" The answer was "Massive!" Each of those 5 or 10 motors would be ordered in volumes that would be 10 times their current order volumes, resulting in greater economies of scale. Further, the 5 or 10 chosen would have been the most cost-effective in their line—the motors produced in high volume for other customers too.

The upper graph in Figure 5–4 shows the *apparent* implication that the standard parts would cost more than parts that have "just enough" performance for a given product. However, if *all* company products use company standard parts, the cost of those parts will be

FIGURE 5–4

Standardization of Expensive Parts

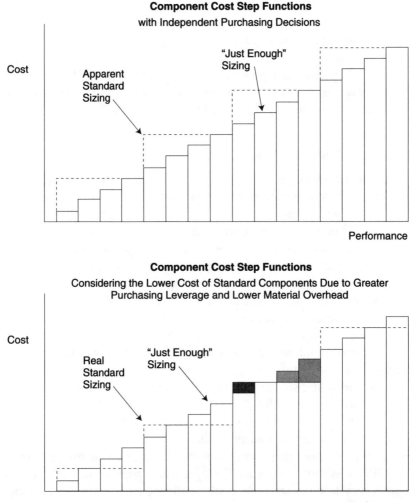

Component Cost Step Functions

with Independent Purchasing Decisions

Cost

Apparent
Standard
Sizing

"Just Enough"
Sizing

Performance

Component Cost Step Functions

Considering the Lower Cost of Standard Components Due to Greater
Purchasing Leverage and Lower Material Overhead

Cost

Real
Standard
Sizing

"Just Enough"
Sizing

Performance

less, due to purchasing leverage and material overhead savings. Thus, there would be a net company savings for expensive parts, as shown in the lower graph in Figure 5–4. Some products may be forced to use a more expensive part than is required (as shown for one size by black shading), but most products would be able to use less expensive standard parts (as shown by the crosshatch shading). The result is a net cost savings for the company plus the flexibility that is essential for Mass Customization.

Further, when a commonality task force standardizes on expensive parts, it can select the most cost-effective parts made in large enough quantities to take advantage of suppliers' economies of scale. These parts are usually the ones that have better availability and, possibly, better quality and reliability. Design engineers, however, may not be aware of these nonlinear relationships between performance, price, availability, and quality.

ENCOURAGING STANDARDIZATION

Given the importance of internal variety reduction to mass customization, it is imperative that mass customizers, or *potential* mass customizers, encourage standardization implementation as early as possible. This means encouraging design engineers to design around common parts (even ones that might appear too expensive), specify common design features, designate common tools, base designs on common materials, and concurrently design products to be built on common processes. The author's experience indicates that design engineers are not naturally committed to these goals. In fact, engineers may be actually pushed the other way by poorly conceived metrics, such as emphasizing parts' cost and low bids for single products instead of *total* costs for product families.

The following steps can be taken to encourage standardization. They involve "discounting" material overhead rates for common parts, prequalifying common parts, making samples and specifications of common parts readily available, and emphasizing total-cost thinking, preferably incorporated into total cost accounting systems. In addition to these procedural steps, managers should take every opportunity to emphasize in goals, policies, directives, "pep talks," and training the importance of commonality.

Material Overhead Rate

The procurement of common parts and their distribution through the plant will incur less overhead burden than with the usual excessive internal variety. Therefore, the material overhead rate for common parts should be less, to reflect the lower actual overhead.

In addition to being a more accurate reflection of overhead costs, lower material overhead rates for common parts should motivate engineers to specify common parts.

The simplest method is to establish a two-tiered overhead rate, as done at Intel's Systems Group: a general material overhead rate and a lower rate for common parts. This is a very logical approach since common parts really do consume less overhead expense, because of the reasons pointed out above. To compensate for a lower material overhead rate for common parts, the general material overhead rate may have to be raised from the previous single rate. It is also logical to assign a higher overhead rate to low-usage parts because of their higher overhead demands. Thus, if engineers choose common parts, their design will be "rewarded" with the lower material overhead rate. Conversely, if they choose noncommon parts, the overhead rate will be higher than even the previous single rate.

Another method of establishing overhead rates for commonality parts is a variable rate that would be inversely proportional to volume, so that a very high-usage part would have a very low material overhead rate and a very low-volume part would have a much higher overhead rate. This approach is used by the Portable Instruments Division of Tektronix as a "cost driver" to discourage engineers from using low-volume parts.13

Prequalified Commonality Parts

A company using common parts would be using many fewer types of parts for new designs than without commonality. Thus, these common parts can be more thoroughly evaluated and their suppliers can be more thoroughly scrutinized than possible with 10 times the number of parts in the system. The common parts can be prequalified for immediate use. This can accelerate product development, since design teams do not have to wait for this qualification.

Floor Stock

Usually, the list of common parts is small enough to allow a "floor stock" to be kept in the engineering area, so engineers can always have samples of the common parts available in the design area. Having floor stock samples can help the design team visualize concepts based on common parts and, thus, encourage common part usage. Floor stocks can make common parts readily available for engineers to evaluate parts, conduct experiments, and build breadboards. Floor stocks can also be mounted on display boards in prominent places near the design team.

Personal Display Boards

For small, inexpensive parts, such as fasteners, every engineer could be issued a personal display board with the common parts mounted with labels that list the generic value plus the company part number. Hewlett-Packard, at the author's recommendation, followed the above procedure and reduced the number of fasteners for large format plotters from dozens to only seven. Samples of these seven fasteners were mounted on an aluminum plate with values and part numbers printed on paper affixed to the plate. These personal display boards were issued to all engineers to remind them to use standard fasteners.

Spec Books

Part specifications for commonality parts could be reproduced and compiled into a single "spec book" or database. This would encourage engineers to use the commonality parts since they could find all specifications in a single reference.

Cost Metrics

If cost metrics are based on total cost for product families, they will encourage commonality. If they are based on parts' costs alone for single products, they may discourage commonality. If accounting systems cannot quantify total cost, then engineers should be encouraged to balance the costs that are reported with the qualitative benefits of commonality as addressed in the next section.

WHY REDUCING INTERNAL VARIETY IS SO IMPORTANT

Implementing commonality for parts, features, tools, and materials can benefit any company, even before it embarks on Mass Customization. Since commonality is a prerequisite for Mass Customization, commonality programs are one of the first steps to implement. Since commonality generally applies only to new products, the programs should be implemented as soon as possible in order to reap the benefits as soon as possible. The following discussion presents the benefits of commonality under four categories that are very important to Mass Customization: flexibility, responsiveness, cost reduction, and quality. The cost-reduction aspects of these benefits will be discussed in more detail in Chapter 6.

1. Flexibility

Eliminating Setup

If the number of parts used in manufacturing is small enough, those (commonality) parts can be permanently loaded on assembly machines or in the manual assembly pick bins. This allows all the products to be built by the same process without having to change the setup for different parts.

Inventory Reduction

Inventory can be significantly reduced with fewer types of parts to stock and distribute. This will reduce incoming or "raw" parts inventory. Parts commonality and setup elimination also encourage just-in-time operations that can drastically reduce work-in-process inventory expense and floor space.

Internal Material Logistics

The flow of parts within the plant will improve with fewer parts to order, receive, log in, stock, issue, load, assemble, test, and reorder. Having few enough parts to distribute at their points of use will avoid the space and expense of kitting parts.

Breadtruck Deliveries

High-usage, low-cost common parts can be delivered right to the point of use *without any overhead* costs for purchasing or internal distribution. Arrangements can be made with suppliers of low-cost parts who will simply keep the bins full of common parts at all the points of use, much like "breadtruck" deliveries keep the shelves stocked with bread in markets. The supplier simply bills the company for each month's usage. This is a very attractive approach for low-cost common parts such as fasteners, washers, resistors, and so on. In addition to the obvious cost savings, this procurement methodology is much less likely to cause part shortages, which can stop production, even for lack of a one-cent washer.

Flexible Manufacturing

Eliminating setup changes allows products to be built in any size lot. With setup reduced to zero, any quantity of any product in the family can be built. This flexibility is the key to building products to order that allows companies to mass customize orders.

2. Responsiveness

Build to Order

Flexible manufacturing, in turn, can eliminate finished goods inventory and let the plant build only the products that will ship immediately (for which it has orders). This is known as "build to order." Another important benefit of build-to-order manufacturing is that scarce parts are only consumed in products that go immediately to customers. Further, expensive parts are consumed closer to the time of the sale, thus lowering interest expenses.

Parts Availability

In general, fewer part types used in greater quantity will mean less chance of running out of parts and delaying production. There are special availability considerations when mass customized products are built to order. Consider, for a moment, the situation when products are built to forecast: The forecast provides the information that MRP systems use to order parts in advance, so they can be shipped to the plant before they are needed. Build-to-order environments have much less forecasting information to use for ordering parts. Stocking all parts for all possible orders would theoretically work but would incur too much inventory expense and space. This dilemma can be solved with parts commonality in one of three ways: Just-in-time deliveries can be arranged for the high-volume common parts. "Breadtruck" vendors can keep bins full for inexpensive high-usage parts. The remaining common parts could be stocked, since each stocked part could be used for many different order scenarios in a mass customization environment.

Quicker Deliveries from Vendors

Commonality of parts and materials can accelerate deliveries from vendors if they have fewer types of parts to order and stock. Parts designed around common raw material sizes will be quicker to order and may even be in the vendor's own raw materials stock. Vendors will not need to order special tools if products are designed around the common tools they already have.

3. Cost Reduction

Purchasing Costs

Common parts will incur much less procurement cost because fewer parts are being purchased in larger quantity. This not only results in fewer purchasing actions, but also results in better purchasing leverage that entitles the company to quantity discounts and better delivery. Ordering fewer types of standard parts in large quantities is the key to arranging just-in-time deliveries and may be crucial to Mass Customization.

Inventory Cost Reduction

Part commonality can, directly or indirectly, reduce all three categories of inventory and their significant carrying cost. Use of common parts and materials results in fewer types of parts in incoming parts inventory and fewer types of materials in raw materials inventory. Part and feature commonality help eliminate setup, which supports just-in-time programs, which reduce WIP inventory. Commonality makes parts available for build-to-order operations, which can reduce finished goods inventory.

Floor Space Reduction

Reducing inventory and eliminating kitting can significantly reduce floor space requirements. Floor space can also be saved by eliminating the forklift aisles needed to move large bins of parts, since just-in-time operations move single parts between workstations. Reducing floor space needs can be a very attractive alternative to adding new buildings or moving to larger facilities. This issue may be a real "sleeper" until the company needs to expand facilities or move to where more floor space will be available. If floor space reduction was part of a continuous improvement program, the need to expand facilities or to move may be postponed or averted.

Overhead Cost Reduction

In addition to purchasing, inventory reduction, and floor space reduction, commonality also reduces the other costs that constitute materials overhead, including the documentation, administration, qualification, and distribution of parts. Feature commonality lowers tooling costs by minimizing the number of tools needed to fabricate features like punched holes and sheet metal bends.

4. Quality

Product Quality

Having fewer part types in the plant means there will be less likelihood of using the wrong part. A manufacturer of semiconductor processing equipment had so many different screws that the wrong screw, one that was too long, was used to fasten the cover to a case that housed light-sensitive sensors. Since the screws were too long, they "bottomed out" in the blind tapped holes and, thus, did not adequately seal the case from extraneous light. This caused the equipment to malfunction when placed in service. The company and its customer wasted much time on the diagnostic effort, first checking the sensors and related circuitry before discovering the light leak caused by the wrong screws.

Continuous Improvement

In addition to the enormous cost savings of eliminating WIP inventory, discussed earlier, inventory reduction is also a key element to *continuous improvement* programs.[14] Inventory hides many problems; eliminating the inventory exposes the problems and, thus, forces solutions.[15]

Vendor Reduction

Commonality programs reduce the number of vendors because fewer parts usually come from fewer sources. Dealing with fewer vendors can strengthen ties with those vendors, thus resulting in the very desirable "vendor partnership" relationship. Fewer vendors means the company can do a better job qualifying each vendor and also do a better job evaluating each part.

The message to mass customizers or potential mass customizers is clear: act *now* to reduce internal variety, eliminate setup, and standardize on parts, features, tools, processes, and materials. This will help ensure that products designed around these standards will be able to be produced flexibly enough to make mass customization feasible and profitable. All departments will need to work together to reduce internal variety with these commonality methodologies. The payoff is great, even for a stand-alone commonality program. The payoff for mass customization will be even greater.

NOTES

1. Clay Chandler and Michael Williams, "A Slump in Car Sales Forces Nissan to Start Cutting Swollen Costs," *The Wall Street Journal*, March 3, 1993.

2. Brian H. Maskell, *Software and the Agile Manufacturer* (Portland, OR: Productivity Press, 1994), p. 335.

3. Robin Cooper and Peter B. B. Turney, "Internally Focused Activity-Based Cost Systems," in *Measures of Manufacturing Excellence*, ed. Robert S. Kaplan (Boston: Harvard Business School Press, 1990), p. 293.

4. Tim Stevens, "Prolific Parts Pilfer Profits," *Industry Week* 244, no. 11 (June 5, 1995), pp. 59-62.

5. Venkat Mohan, president and chief operating officer, CADIS Inc., Boulder, Colorado.

6. George Taninecz, "Faster in, Faster Out," *Industry Week* 224, no. 10 (May 15, 1995), pp. 27–30.

7. Michael R. Ostrenga, Terrence R. Ozan, Robert D. McIlhattan, Marcus D. Harwood, *The Ernst & Young Guide to Total Cost Management* (New York: John Wiley & Sons, 1992), p.150.

8. Marshall Fisher, Anjani Jain, and John Paul MacDuffie, *Strategies for Product Variety, Lessons from the Auto Industry* (Philadelphia: The Wharton School, University of Pennsylvania, October 9, 1992, revised January 16, 1994).

9. Eric Teicholz and Joel N. Orr, *Computer Integrated Manufacturing Handbook* (New York: McGraw-Hill, 1987), p. 96.

10. CADIS-PMX (Parts Management eXpert) is available from CADIS, Inc., 1909 26th Street, Boulder, Colorado 80302; (310) 440-4363.

11. Stevens, "Prolific Parts Pilfer Profits."

12. CADIS case study, CADIS, Inc., Boulder, Colorado.

13. Cooper and Turney, "Internally focused."

14. Kiyoshi Suzaki, *The New Manufacturing Challenge, Techniques for Continuous Improvement* (New York: The Free Press, 1987).

15. Richard J. Schonberger, *Japanese Manufacturing Techniques; Nine Hidden Lessons in Simplicity* (New York: The Free Press, 1982); *World Class Manufacturing; The Lessons of Simplicity Applied* (New York: The Free Press, 1986).

THE CHALLENGES OF MASS CUSTOMIZING PRODUCTS

Cost and Speed

CHAPTER

Putting the "Mass" in Mass Customization

THE CHALLENGES OF MASS CUSTOMIZATION

The challenge in mass customization is not just offering the customization, *per se*. Craft industries did that for centuries before the Industrial Revolution. Rather, the challenges are to:

1. Build customized products *quickly*. Being able to build to order quickly in a flexible manufacturing environment will accomplish this. The next chapter will discuss this.

2. Build customized products *at low cost*. This chapter shows how mass customized products can achieve low cost, "the mass in Mass Customization," *by design*.

Cost must be designed out of the product and production processes, as it is very difficult to remove cost through "cost-reduction" measures *after* the product has been designed. Cost "reduction" rarely even pays off the expense of the cost-reduction effort.

The key to achieving the lowest-cost product is to base all thinking and decisions on a total cost perspective. Unfortunately, the typical company cost system reports only material and labor costs. All other costs are called overhead, which is spread over all

corporate activities according to some arbitrary allocation algo-
rithm, such as proportional to material, labor, or processing cost.
And yet, all products do not have the same overhead demands. In
fact, much can be done to lower overhead costs by design.

This chapter will discuss two categories of cost: "reported
costs" such as labor and materials, and "unreported costs" such as
overhead costs. It will show how to use advanced design techniques to design low-cost products for the minimum labor and
materials costs and then build them very efficiently for the minimum overhead cost.

This chapter has two goals. One is to suggest several categories
of cost savings over more conventional operations. Using total cost
methodologies, presented at the end of the chapter, this cost savings
can be calculated. This will be especially important if mass customized products must share production facilities, and some of their
overhead, with noncustomized products. The lower overhead
demands of mass customized products, as pointed out below, will
need to be considered when overhead costs are allocated.

The second goal is to show all the monetary benefits to mass
customized production so the reader will be *motivated* to implement and support the programs that will generate these benefits:
advanced product development methodologies, parts commonality, modular design, setup reduction, just-in-time, flexible manufacturing, and build-to-order, which together will yield a production organization capable of Mass Customization.

HOW NOT TO ACHIEVE LOW COST

Before learning how to design low-cost products, it is important to
dispel some myths about cost. Low-cost products do *not* come
from volume alone; that is the Mass Production paradigm. With
proper design and flexible operations, mass customized parts can
be made at low cost virtually *independent* of volume.

Low-cost products do not come from cheap parts, which are
often chosen because they appear to lower the *reported* material
costs. However, cheap parts will usually explode other costs: for
quality, service, operations, and other overhead costs. Similarly, cutting corners in any manner will probably end up costing much more
later. Total cost accounting can help by quantifying all costs, but
until that arrives, product designers must rely on total cost *thinking*.

An unwise strategy to reduce cost may be to omit features. Although this may reduce cost, it also may reduce revenue and hamper product evolution.

In their haste to rush early production units to market, many companies defer cost concerns until later with "cost-reduction" efforts. The first problem with this strategy is that it probably will not happen because of competing priorities: thus, costs remain high for the life of the product. The second problem is that cost reduction simply cannot be very effective!

Cost is very difficult to remove after the product is designed. As will be shown below, 80 percent of the cost is designed into the product and is very difficult to remove later. Shaving cost off reported costs (such as parts) might explode other costs (such as quality). Changing the design to reduce costs may force other changes. Trying to significantly lower cost after production release is usually futile because of many early "cast-in-concrete" decisions, which limit opportunities. Finally, the *total cost* of doing the change may not be paid back by the cost savings within the expected life of the product. Few companies really keep track of the total costs of changing designs.

There are also intangible impacts of excessive focus on cost reduction: It absorbs effort and talent that could be applied to more productive activities, such as developing better *new* products. One division of a large international company did not have time for training on low-cost product development because employees were too busy with 31 cost-reduction efforts!

Low-cost products do not result from "saving" cost by cutting product development and continuous improvement efforts. This may not be a stated policy, but product development budgets can be impacted by corporate directives such as, "All departments will reduce their budgets by 15 percent."

Low-cost products do not result from manufacturing misconceptions like purchasing policies based on low-bidder or offshore manufacturing to lower labor costs, which too often raise many other overhead costs and lengthen delivery times.

MINIMIZING COST THROUGH DESIGN

As shown in Figure 6–1, 80 percent of the lifetime cumulative cost of a product is determined by the product's design.[1] Even more

FIGURE 6-1

When Cost Is Determined

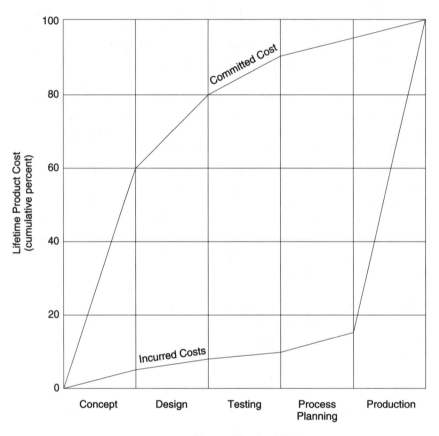

Product Cost versus Time

Phase of Product Life

important for mass customization is that 60 percent of a product's cost is determined by product *architecture*. Low-cost product design is based on the premise that cost is designed *into* the product, especially by early concept decisions.

Tools such as "design for manufacturability" can help design products that are easier, and thus less costly, to build. Concurrent engineering can ensure the lowest-cost processing since the processes were concurrently designed with the product. Quality can be designed into the product with "robust" design techniques

(Taguchi methods, design of experiments) and then built into the product with process controls instead of the more expensive inspection paradigm. Maximum utilization of catalog hardware can minimize part cost. Involving vendors early can result in lower-cost outsourced parts. All of these subjects will be discussed in Chapter 9. Total cost accounting data (see below) can lead to decisions that result in the lowest total cost.

Optimizing Architecture

The greatest leverage opportunities for minimizing cost are in the architecture stage, which generally determines 60 percent (or more) of a product's lifetime cumulative cost. And yet this high-leverage opportunity is virtually ignored in many product development projects, when designers assume the product will have the same architecture as previous or competitive products. The architecture phase of product development abounds with opportunities to greatly lower cost through creative concept simplifications. Some examples of this will be presented in Chapter 9.

For Mass Customization, the architecture phase will determine how products can actually be customized. This phase will determine the optimal balance of modularity, adjustability, and cutting-to-fit. Ultimately, the architecture phase will decide if products can be customized efficiently enough to be *mass* customized.

MEASURING TOTAL COST

Usual Definition of Cost

Traditional cost systems provide the cost breakdown shown in the top of Figure 6–2 and encourage product development teams to focus only on material, labor, and tooling costs. Considering only these costs gives a limited perspective and might lead to short-sighted conclusions that 80 percent of the product's cost is parts (and tooling). Therefore, "cost-reduction" measures often focus on minimizing parts costs, usually by buying cheaper parts.

Total Cost Definition of Cost

Total cost measurements provide the cost breakdown shown in the bottom of Figure 6–2 and make it possible for decisions to be based on total cost considerations. Designers must acknowledge overhead

FIGURE 6–2

Cost Breakdowns with and without Overhead

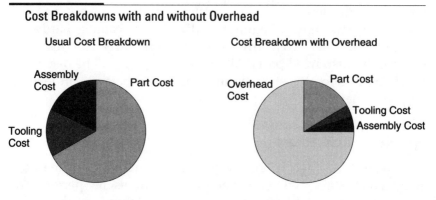

costs are significant (often more than labor and materials) and that designers really do have influence over overhead costs.

Some engineers think manufacturability is not important if labor cost is a small percentage of the total cost. However, manufacturability problems can cause significant overhead demands for problem solving, firefighting, engineering change orders (ECOs), documentation support, tooling changes, and penalties and missed opportunities caused by delays.

MINIMIZING OVERHEAD COSTS

Engineers, purchasing agents, and "cost-reduction" managers often spend much effort trying to reduce reported costs, such as labor and materials. They precisely calculate these costs, and *then multiply by four!* Yet they rarely challenge the overhead "burden" rate.

Product development can have significant effects on overhead costs by *designing* to minimize overhead costs. Overhead costs can be reduced by design by minimizing product development expense, the "cost of quality," inventory and other factory overhead costs, and materials overhead.

This approach can significantly lower overhead cost with concurrent product/process design, parts and processes standardization, reuse of engineering and software code, modular design, designing quality into the product, designing it "right the first time," and designing to optimize manufacturing flexibility. Since

Mass Customization depends on manufacturing flexibility, it will benefit from the cost savings inherent in flexible operations.

Product Development Expenses

Advanced product development methodologies, described in the next chapters, can significantly reduce product development and related expenses through the following activities.

Optimal Product Family Selection

The *very* first step in product development is deciding what to develop. For all the agile paradigms, this selection process should involve product families for products that share parts, modules, software, processes, engineering, and logistics support. Decisions should be made in terms of product families, or platforms, *and their evolution over time.*

Before deciding in which market segments to compete, companies should understand the *true* profitability of their existing products. As pointed out in Chapter 4, the *reported* profitability of existing products is only as meaningful as the *reported* costs. As will be discussed later in this chapter, typical cost reporting systems are too "aggregate" to distinguish the real cost differences between products, thus distorting product costing. Distorted product costing leads to distorted perceptions of profitability and, thus, to distorted decision making on which products to develop. Developing products for *truly* profitable market segments will result in the most efficient utilization of product development resources. Developing products for market segments that are *thought to be* making money but are really marginal or losing money is a waste of product development resources.

Decisions on which product families to develop must be based on a balance of customer/market needs and opportunities *and* corporate strengths, such as talent, technology, patents, reputation, and so forth. This will be discussed further in Chapter 8.

One final consideration for product development selection is to *make decisions rationally.* It is very easy to get sidetracked by exciting technology and enticing market opportunities. The rational approach would be to objectively assess potential technology, methodically define product specifications to satisfy the "voice of the customer" (as will be discussed in Chapter 10), and to base all decisions on *total* cost numbers (as will be discussed at the end of this chapter).

Multifunctional Design Teams

To minimize product development expense, product development teams must be efficient. They must do it right the first time because engineering change orders are expensive and redesigns are even more expensive. Designing products right the first time requires good product development methodologies, which will be the subject of Chapter 9.

Using multifunctional teams to raise and resolve issues early will save the considerable expense of trying to do this later, after things are "cast in several layers of concrete."

Multifunctional teams can concurrently design/select the optimal processes/vendors for the lowest total cost. With manufacturing and vendors involved, the team will be better able to make rational decisions regarding tooling and automation.

Product development expense can be minimized by utilizing the most efficient designers, which are not always in-house engineers working alone. The multifunctional team *with active manufacturing or vendor assistance* would be more efficient than an isolated group of designers. The vendors who make the parts may be the most efficient at designing them and will probably design lower-cost parts, too.

And remember, the most efficient part design effort is none at all! This is accomplished with optimal use of off-the-shelf hardware.

Methodical Product Definition

Similarly, product development expenses can also be minimized *by defining it right the first time* because it is very expensive to make product definition iterations at the prototype stage when the customer says, "That's not what I wanted." Designing in unwanted features wastes product development resources and causes the product to be overly expensive. Product definition, using QFD (quality function deployment), will be discussed in Chapter 10.

Total Cost Decision Making

All decisions must be consciously based on a total cost focus, *even if total cost cannot be quantified.* The product development culture must support decisions that "just make sense" from a total cost perspective, even if they cannot be justified by the current cost system.

Arbitrary decisions must be avoided; making arbitrary decisions assumes that all choices have the same cost impact, which is rarely the case.

On the other hand, cost concerns can have a counterproductive effect if decision makers are focusing too much on *reported costs*, such as labor and materials, and not enough on *total costs*. Sometimes product development teams limit their opportunities by making major decisions based on rough estimates of reported costs, instead of using good cost models based on *total* costs for *multiple approaches/ideas/scenarios*.

Efficient Design Techniques

"Reinventing the wheel" can be avoided on every product development with maximum use of reusable engineering and versatile modules. Product development projects tend to ignore previous work and completely start over, when they could be more efficient by leveraging previous work. This can be facilitated by proper CAD practices: A good "layer" convention will segregate designs into well-defined layers, so that subsequent development projects can easily find and reuse previous engineering. Modular design, a key component of Mass Customization, can allow new products to be derived from standard modules.

Basing designs on catalog parts can eliminate the cost of designing those parts and, at the same time, lower part cost and quality costs for those parts.

Product life can be extended through upgrades rather than redesigns. Products can be *designed* to be easy to extend the product life with upgrades. Modular design can facilitate upgrading if anticipated changes can be confined to the fewest number of modules. Many common functions of a product can be reused for an entire sequence of products.

Minimizing debugging cost can be accomplished by using existing modules that have already been debugged. Some companies believe this is the best way to produce bug-free software. With a high percentage of reuse, debugging efforts can focus on new aspects.

Diagnostic test development can be avoided by designing quality into the product and building it in with process controls. In such a "quality" environment, failures would be so low that diagnostic test development could not be justified.

Development expenses would be paid off sooner because of quicker product development cycles. This lowers the "interest" or "opportunity" cost of the money invested in product development. Similar logic applies to research expenses for technology development and to tooling expenses.

More Efficient Development Costs Less

Advanced product development methodologies are more efficient because the product is well defined and the architecture is simplified around optimal concepts. This thorough early development work means fewer false starts, less "looping back" to do things over, and fewer changes.

Faster Developments Have Less Obsolescence Risk

Shorter product development cycles result in less chance of market shifts and technical obsolescence by the time the product reaches the market, thus resulting in fewer redesigns.

Engineering Change Orders

Advanced product development methodologies result in more products designed right the first time and, thus, fewer engineering change orders (ECOs). Better product definition results in fewer changes to satisfy customers. Early changes (as practiced by Japanese product development teams) in the planning stage involve less expense than late changes at the hardware stage. Reused engineering and modules have fewer bugs because of their widespread usage over time and across many product lines.

Well-designed products can minimize a substantial overhead expense that is not always included in ECO cost reporting: "firefighting" or problem solving. This is the often-considerable effort expended to solve production problems, which is usually intense when a new product is launched.

The cost of changes rises drastically as the product progresses toward production. Figure 6–3 shows how the cost *for each change* escalates during the development of a major electronics product.

FIGURE 6–3

Cost of Engineering Changes

Time of Design Change	Cost
During design:	$1,000
During design testing:	10,000
During process planning:	100,000
During test production:	1,000,000
During final production:	10,000,000

Source: "A Smarter Way to Manufacture; How 'Concurrent Engineering' Can Reinvigorate American Industry," *Business Week*, April 30, 1990.

Cost of Quality

The "cost of quality" is really the cost of poor quality: the cost of finding and repairing defects. Companies without strong total quality management programs can have a cost of quality equal to 15 percent to 40 percent of revenue.[2] Advanced product development can *design in* quality. Concurrently engineered processes that are in control can *build in* quality. This dual approach to quality can substantially reduce both the internal and external cost of quality.

Internal cost of quality includes the cost of testing, diagnostics, rework, scrap, waste, and so on. It also includes the cost of test development, which for some products can exceed the cost of product development. Designing in quality and designing well-controlled processes can produce products with such a low failure rate that diagnostic test development would not be required. At IBM's Lexington, Kentucky, plant, printed circuit boards that were expected to have higher than a 98.5 percent first-pass-accept rate could avoid diagnostic testing. This eliminated time-consuming test development and the expensive ATE (Automatic Test Equipment) "bed-of-nails" testers, which can cost well over $1 million. Above this threshold, it was more cost-effective to discard defective printed circuit boards than to pay for the testers and test development.

External cost of quality includes the cost of field failures, warranty expenses, legal liabilities, and hard to quantify costs, such as bad publicity that damages a product's reputation.

Companies can have poor internal quality, but with a good "test screen" can keep defects within the factory and have high external quality. Achieving external quality totally by testing and rework is very expensive, and such a company would have a high cost of quality. Many "luxury" products, such as luxury automobiles, enjoy a quality reputation but are very expensive because quality is achieved at a high cost. Some luxury automobiles require several times more labor to fix than a well-designed car requires to build.[3]

Another cost of quality is the "pipeline" effect (recurring defects), as discussed in Chapter 3. Mass Customizers operate in a flexible manufacturing mode with little or no WIP inventory, so there should be very little chance of recurring defects being produced, as is so common in batch manufacturing with large lots. Coupling the low WIP inventory to the rapid quality feedback of JIT operations results in reduced quality costs because recurring defects are spotted immediately, rather than being discovered at assembly or test after thousands of defective parts have been built.

Continuous improvement is an effective technique to keep driving costs down with incremental improvements that can have significant cumulative effects. Continuous improvement can be performed spontaneously by in-house workers,[4] as a part of TQM programs,[5] or in cooperative efforts with suppliers.[6]

Factory Efficiency

Rapid product development can more quickly phase out older, more costly products with new generation cost-effective products. The older, less efficient products, in addition to having higher direct costs for labor and materials, have higher overhead demands for ECOs and firefighting. More efficient production, from better-designed products, can result in more output from existing plants and equipment. For growing companies, this extra output might spare the company, or at least defer, the expense of adding new equipment or expanding facilities.

Rational Selection of the Lowest-Cost Manufacturer

This decision encompasses both the make/buy decision and vendor selection. These decisions must be made rationally on a total cost basis. As discussed in Chapter 3 and at the end of this chapter, conventional cost systems can mislead decision makers if they report only labor and materials. Not quantifying and including all the overhead costs for in-house manufacture creates a bias toward that option, since purchases include all costs, by definition.

Regarding vendor selection, total costs can actually increase as a result of choosing the supposedly "low bidder" if purchase cost is emphasized over such subtle, but important, characteristics as quality, delivery, flexibility, and help with product development. Jordan Lewis, in his book about customer–supplier alliances, *The Connected Corporation*, commented about the effects of General Motor's 1992 demands for double-digit price cuts from suppliers:

> By emphasizing price alone with its suppliers GM won immediate savings—and ignored total cost. At GM's plant in Arlington, Texas, an ill-fitting ashtray from a new, substandard supplier caused a six-week shutdown of Buick Roadmaster production."[7]

Another GM plant saved 5 percent going with a low bidder; when the parts were delivered, half failed quality tests. The other supplier, who lost the bid, had to gear up production in four days and fly parts to GM by chartered plane. The second supplier commented, "My guess is that their 5 percent savings turned into a 15 percent loss."

By contrast, concludes Lewis, Chrysler has treated its suppliers like partners and the "cost savings *proposed* by suppliers helped Chrysler become the lowest-cost, highest-profit vehicle automaker in North America."[8]

Peter Drucker, writing in *Managing in a Time of Great Change*, encourages lowering total cost by minimizing "interstitial" costs between suppliers and manufacturers or between manufacturer and distributer:

> But the costs that matter are the costs of the entire economic process in which the individual manufacturer, bank, or hospital is only a link in a chain. The costs of the entire process are what the ultimate customers (or the taxpayer) pays and what determines whether a product, a service, an industry, or an economy is competitive.
> The cost advantage of the Japanese derives in considerable measure from their control of these costs within a *keiretsu*, the "family" of suppliers and distributors clustered around a manufacturer. Treating the *keiretsu* as one cost stream led, for instance, to "just-in-

time" parts delivery. It also enabled the *keiretsu* to shift operations to where they are most cost- effective.[9]

Flexibility

Flexibility can reduce overhead costs significantly and can put the "mass" in Mass Customization. There are some interesting parallels between flexibility and quality. Twenty years ago, it was commonly believed that quality cost more. Then Philip Crosby wrote the book *Quality is Free* and showed that the gains from lowering the cost of quality would pay for quality, thus making it free. Similarly, the financial gains derived from flexible operations can more than pay for the effort to make operations flexible. These gains will become a source of competitive advantage over competitors that do not embrace Mass Customization.

There is a lot of *working capital* tied up in various forms of inventory: raw materials and parts inventory; work-in-process inventory; and finished goods inventory in factory warehouses, at distributors, and at the dealers. *Fortune* magazine estimates that, for Fortune 500 companies, working capital averages an amount equal to 20 percent of sales.[10]

Ironically, inventory shows up on the balance sheet as an asset when, in fact, inventory is really a *liability* to the operation of any manufacturing plant, especially those needing to be flexible. This point was one of the revelations presented in Eli Goldratt's *The Goal* when managers of the fictional plant, faced with extinction, realized they had to focus on "the goal" (of making money) instead of letting their behavior be dictated by irrelevant cost accounting metrics.[11] One progressive materials manager of a processing equipment company told the author that after much successful work to reduce inventory, he got a call from the company controller, who was having trouble preparing the annual report because the inventory had been reduced so much it was "lowering company assets" according to their traditional accounting rules. Companies must make sure they are pursuing the real goal instead of irrelevant metrics.[12]

The following discussion presents several opportunities to lower the costs of inventory and other overhead costs by designing flexibility into products and plants.

Customization and Configuration Costs

As pointed out at the beginning of Chapter 3, many companies offer customized goods but do not do it cost-effectively. By *mass* customizing products, the customization process is built into the system—the product design and the manufacturing operation.

Thus, the mass customizer has a cost advantage over companies that are inefficient at customization and configuration. Two cost categories are shown on the "reactive" side of Figure 3–1: custom engineering and changing/modifying standard designs and processes. Both of these activities usually cost much more than is indicated by current cost systems. Many companies do not even keep track of engineering costs by project. Plus, engineers get a lot of help from many support people "on overhead."

The extra manufacturing cost to do ad hoc customization and configuration of "reactive" products is much more than it would be for mass customized products. These customization costs often include extra tooling, lengthy setups for small runs, inefficient production control, low equipment utilization, special programming, slow and frequent "learning curves," special tests and inspections, and lots of "fire drills" to shove customized products through a mass production factory. Further, these low-volume customized products may disrupt the manufacturer of the standard products, thus increasing their cost. Thus, in companies with traditional accounting systems, custom products are really being subsidized by the standard products.

Cost of Variety

A large part of working capital is tied up in the cost of variety, which was the title of Chapter 3. Eliminating setup and reducing the lot size to one eliminates most of the cost of variety. As shown in Figure 3–3, true one-piece flow can eliminate WIP inventory or reduce it to one piece between stations.

As discussed in Chapter 3, the key element to just-in-time operations and manufacturing flexibility is setup elimination. If setup can be eliminated, then operations are said to be flexible, meaning that every product could be different and still reap Mass Production efficiencies. In low-volume operations, setup could be caused by any effort to do something "different," including design, documentation, procurement, logistics, and so on.

Chapter 7 will discuss how to eliminate setup and implement flexible manufacturing. The following discusses many categories of cost-saving opportunities that are made possible by eliminating setup and operating flexibly in a just-in-time mode.

WIP Inventory

WIP inventory can be virtually eliminated by setup reduction, JIT, and design commonality of parts and processes. As shown in Figure 3–3, WIP inventory costs rise proportional to lot size, except when the lot size is one, in which case WIP inventory can be eliminated. As mentioned in Chapter 3, WIP inventory carrying cost could be 25 percent of its value per year. Thus, eliminating WIP inventory could result in substantial savings.

Floor Space

Floor space can be reduced because of reduced inventories, elimination of the forklift aisles necessary to move large batches of parts, elimination of kitting, and higher utilization of machinery and people. Appreciation of the cost or value of floor space varies according to the need to expand manufacturing. But floor space reduction should be constantly pursued. The cost of expanding manufacturing space may force a company to move away from an area that is too crowded or expensive. Floor space reduction can provide an attractive alternative to expansion or relocation. Further, floor space requirements can be reduced faster than new facilities can be built. The lead time for physical plant expansion is so large that such plans must be started well ahead of the anticipated need, often based on inaccurate long-range marketing projections. Between 1991 and 1994, Compaq Computer quintupled production without increasing factory space by implementing programs such as WIP inventory reduction.[13]

Internal Transportation

Internal transportation costs, such as forklift activity, can be reduced. This can be eliminated when parts and products flow individually, between adjacent workstations, instead of in large, heavy bins between distant workstations. Lot size n on Figure 3–3 indicates the threshold beyond which forklifts are required to move material through the plant.

Utilization

Utilization is improved with less setup, thus reducing equipment cost, a very big cost savings potential for expensive equipment, like CNC machining centers, surface-mount printed circuit assembly equipment, or expensive testers. Machine tool utilization can be as low as 10 percent, which means the equipment is producing parts only 10 percent of the time the machine is available for work; the remainder is setup or waiting. It is important to realize that *doubling the utilization rate will double output.* If production equipment had utilization of 30 percent, output could be *doubled* by raising the utilization to 60 percent. Utilization improvement is a cost-effective way to increase production, *and* it is quicker, considering the lead time to procure and install new production equipment.

The graph labeled "machinery" in Figure 3–4 plots machinery cost for a given volume of production. The variation is caused by the utilization. Note that the curve has two low points. The traditional approach to setup reduction is to minimize the number of setup changes with very large lots. But this practice incurs many other costs that were just discussed with Figure 3–3. If the lot size was one because setup had been eliminated, then machine utilization would approach 100 percent and the machinery cost would be at a minimum.

Setup Labor

Setup labor expenses can be eliminated including the labor cost to change machine setups and to retrieve parts, tools, and drawings.

Flexibility

Flexibility can improve the balance of labor and machinery utilization in sequential operations such as assembly lines. Products built in flexible lines can be optimally ordered to offset imbalances in the workloads of adjacent machinery or people, using a concept known as *product complementarity.*[14]

Adaptable Production

Production can quickly adapt to changing market conditions by building all the products on the same flexible line. Inflexible operations are always faced with a dilemma when the demand for "model A" has exceeded capacity while "model B" is having a sales slump. Manufacturing may have adequate overall capacity, but model A will not be able to satisfy demand while the model B line or plant is partly idle or laying off people. A slightly more flexible approach would be to move people from the A line to the B line, but that assumes adequate equipment capacity on line A. Flexible operations would simply pull more model A products and fewer model B products through the flexible line.

Kitting

Kitting cost and space can be eliminated. Without flexibility, there will be labor costs and space requirements to gather all the parts for a batch, "kit" them together and deliver them to manufacturing.

Operational flexibility can allow companies to transfer production from one flexible line or plant to another to respond to changing market conditions, rather than the more expensive alternatives of overtime, rapidly bringing contract labor up to speed, and spontaneous outsourcing to ease production bottlenecks for the product that is in demand. Similarly, by transferring production, companies can avoid layoffs at plants making products in low demand. Mazda resolved such a dilemma by moving production of the popular Miata from its Hiroshima plant to the Hofu plant, which was underutilized with Mazda 626 production. Because of manufacturing flexibility, Mazda could combine production of a niche sports car with a family sedan in the same plant to balance output at these two plants.[15]

Materials Management

Purchasing costs are reduced because there are fewer purchasing actions for fewer part types. Commonality parts will cost less because of the greater purchasing leverage of higher-volume parts. Further, the "breadtruck" concept can be used where a supplier is responsible for keeping the bins full for common inexpensive parts, much like a breadtruck keeps the shelves full in a grocery store.

Vendor fabrication and assembly is more feasible with the well-defined modules used in Mass Customization. The ability to outsource module fabrication, and even design, can save cost over in-house operations if the vendors are more efficient.

Fewer part numbers mean less material overhead for raw materials and parts inventories, documentation, controls, and so on. There will also be less expediting cost for seldom-used parts that are difficult to obtain. Pareto's law (the "80/20" rule) applied to inflexible plants would say that 80 percent of the material overhead costs would be consumed on low-usage parts that may represent only 20 percent of total part volume.

Spare parts logistics and field service are greatly simplified, and thus cost less, with part commonality and modular design. Products designed around common parts have smaller spare parts kits. This could lower the effective product price for customers, who add the cost of spare parts kits to the product's list price. Part commonality can also result in less downtime due to part shortages. Service costs can be reduced if failed modules can be quickly replaced and repaired in more efficient facilities.

Marketing Cost

The *learning relationships* discussed in Chapter 1 result in the ability to "keep customers forever," as reflected in the title of Joe Pine's article in the *Harvard Business Review*.[16] Not only is this good for generating revenue, but it also saves the considerable cost of acquiring new customers to meet growth objectives. Studies, such as one done by the Technical Assistance Resource Project for the U.S. Office of Consumer Affairs, show that the price of acquiring new customers is five time greater than the cost of keeping old ones.[17]

Sales/Distribution Costs

There are considerable cost-reduction opportunities in the warehousing and distribution of products. The physical distribution system accounted for 9.8 percent of the gross national product in 1994.[18]

Mass customizers have a cost advantage over their mass production competitors with respect to the way products are configured, packaged, shipped, distributed, and sold. Supply chain management, in general, has become a strategic competitive advantage for Hewlett-Packard.[19]

Peter Drucker points out the opportunities of minimizing cost in the supply chain: "Process-costing from the machine in the supplier's plant to the checkout counter in the store also underlies the phenomenal rise of Wal-Mart. It resulted in the elimination of a whole slew of warehouses and reams of paperwork, which slashed costs by a third."[20]

Mass customizers enjoy an even greater opportunity. One of the most effective cost-reduction tools of the mass customizer is to eliminate most of the distribution chain as we know it. Being able to build to order and ship from the plant eliminates warehousing and associated distribution costs from the plant to the customer.

In industries where product variety is considerable, such as blue jeans and shoes, this cost can be enormous, considering the number of sizes and styles. Sung Park, founder of Custom Clothing Technology Corporation in Newton, Massachusetts, which developed the technology that Levi Strauss is using for its customized Personal Pair line, said, "You've got to look at the whole value chain. Zero inventory. No markdown. No distribution-centered costs. The product doesn't sit in the warehouse."[21]

A Westport, Connecticut, company, Measurably Better, plans to use this principle to offer customized shoes, made in Italy for individual customers, at the cost of traditional Italian shoes. A 3D scanner measures the feet so a digital record of the size and exact shape can be sent by modem to the factory where programmable leather cutters cut custom pieces, which are then joined together to form truly custom shoes. By shipping each pair of shoes directly to the store, the company avoids the considerable cost of stocking and distributing all the sizes and styles.

Life Cycle Costs

An often-neglected part of total costs are life cycle costs, which are those costs that are incurred over time, such as service, repair, maintenance, field failures, warrantee claims, legal liabilities, changes over the life of the product, and subsequent product developments. Products can be designed to minimize life cycle costs. The cost of changes can be minimized by a methodical product definition and thorough product development. Change costs and subsequent product development costs can be minimized with modular product architecture, where many modules can remain unchanged as products are updated or redesigned.

Designing for reliability can minimize many costs related to product reliability. Several techniques that can be used to maximize reliability are presented in Chapter 9.

Build to Order

Mass customized products are built to order in flexible plants. This capability to build to order is a key to minimizing cost that will allow mass customized products to compete with mass produced products and yet provide the additional competitive advantage of exactly meeting the needs of individual customers.

Factory finished goods inventory can be eliminated by building products to order, instead of "building to forecast" and then holding products in a warehouse until ordered by distributors or customers. Like WIP inventory, finished goods inventory may cost the same to carry except that finished goods are completed and therefore are more valuable. Using 25 percent of value per year, $10 million worth of finished goods in inventory would cost $2.5 million per year to carry. Build to order methods can eliminate factory finished goods inventory and, thus, save its yearly inventory carrying cost.

Dealer finished goods inventory can be eliminated if customized orders can be quickly filled and delivered to the customer. As with factory inventory, dealer inventory has a carrying cost. Even if the dealer/distributor is separate from the manufacturer, the carrying cost will have to be paid, ultimately by the customer. For example, an automobile dealer with 200 vehicles in stock with an average value of $20,000 each would represent $4 million worth of inventory. Using a yearly carrying cost of 25 percent, the carrying cost would be $1 million per year.

When new car prices exceed customers' ability to afford them, customers buy more used cars as a cost-effective alternative.[22] Built-to-order new automobiles could compete well against used cars, with lower prices, since the new cars could avoid dealer inventory expenses, whereas used cars must be stocked in inventory.

Supply chain inventory can be minimized since build-to-order products do not need to be stocked at various warehouses along the supply chain: at distributors, consolidators, forwarders, and so on. Similarly, a build-to-order system "pulls" parts from suppliers on a just-in-time basis, thus eliminating parts inventory along the supply chain. Regardless of who "pays" for this inventory, the customer ultimately must pay a higher price. Eliminating excessive supply chain inventory costs will allow customers to pay less for equivalent products.

Companies known for rapid deliveries, like Federal Express, are providing companies with "inventory-less" direct deliveries of parts and products to and from factories. After National Semiconductor commissioned Federal Express to run National's storage, sorting, and shipping activities, delivery time was reduced from 45 days to 4 days with an ultimate goal of 72 hours. At the same time, distribution costs have been reduced from 2.6 percent of revenue to 1.9 percent.[23] Adding the value of increased sales from customer satisfaction would make inventory-less distribution even more attractive.

Less interest expense will be incurred for expensive components in products that sell sooner because of the quicker throughput of flexible plants and the elimination of finished goods inventory.

Inventory write-offs can be eliminated because there would be no products in inventory that could deteriorate or incur damage or become obsolete. If there is a substantial finished goods inventory of an expensive product at the end of that product's life, the obsolescence write-off can be enormous.

Quicker transitions to new technology are possible if there are no older technology products waiting in inventory that must be sold first. Rosendo G. Parra, group vice president of Dell Computer Corporation, summarized the advantage of built-to-order manufacturing for Dell: "We were probably the first vendor to transition into the new Pentium FPU processor, simply because we didn't have a hundred and some days of inventory out in distribution that we had to move first."[24]

BOM/MRP expenses could be minimized. Build-to-order methods could minimize overhead expenses for every custom order with respect to generating bills of materials (BOMs) and translating forecasts into materials ordering requirements with MRP (materials requirement planning) systems.

Realistic early production feedback can be obtained from "pilot" manufacturing runs in a real (flexible) manufacturing environment rather than in separate pilot manufacturing lines or plants. Mass Production plants do not have the capability or the patience to experiment with pilot builds. So pilot runs are built in pilot "plants" with special, not production, machinery by prototype technicians, who exercise more skill and perseverance than typical production line workers. Because of this, pilot runs in pilot plants can be successful, but the product can still have a difficult launch into the real production environment. The result of realistic feedback at the pilot stage is less introduction cost and quicker product introduction ramps.

REVENUE GAINS FROM MASS CUSTOMIZATION

In addition to the above cost savings, Mass Customization can also improve profits through increased revenue.

Customers' needs are satisfied better with customized products that are exactly what they want. The increase in sales would be the difference between customers that would be satisfied with "standard" products and customers that would be satisfied with custom products.

Price premiums will be possible for customized products, since they meet customers' needs better, and should be worth more to customers. The customized product, in the form the customer wants, may have little or no competition and, thus, may enjoy somewhat of a monopoly with all the ensuing pricing advantages. As mentioned in Chapter 1, price premiums often range from 10 percent to 50 percent.

Mass Customization is a paradigm shift that will forever change customers' expectations. Today, customers may be reluctantly buying the product that comes "closest" to meeting their needs. Offer them exactly what they want at an attractive price and they will no longer be content with "close." They will now expect exactly what they want. And that is worth something to the customer.

Mass customizers will have the pleasant decision of whether to apply cost savings and premium pricing opportunities to the bottom line or pass these savings on to the customers to compete better on price and expand market share.

Broader markets can be served by versatile designs and flexible plants. Even if products are not customized for individual customers, flexible operations can efficiently produce products for many small niche markets that might otherwise be ignored. Common modules can still enjoy economies of scale even if the products compete in many low-volume markets. Mass customizers will be able to compete better in niche markets than less flexible competitors.

Mass customizing is good market research. Customizing *some* products can predict customer preferences for related mass produced products. Standard products will be quicker to market because customized products will be predicting markets better. National Bicycle's mass customized bicycle operation offers an almost infinite variety of colors to its customers. The mass customization operation records the most popular colors ordered and feeds this information next door to the larger mass production operation, which offers those colors on standard models.

Mass customizers can offer a progression of "new" products. Flexibility in design and manufacturing can enable all companies to efficiently launch a continuous stream of product improvements that are "new" to customers. New products need not be totally new because they will be based on modules and previous engineering. A steady stream of new "standard" products could be accomplished much like the literal mass customization scenario of a different product for each customer.

Product lives can be extended for quasistandard products if only certain modules need to be changed, and manufacturing can quickly integrate the extended products into flexible manufacturing environments. This "upgrade-ability" is especially valuable when a product is firmly entrenched in its operating environment, such as equipment in remote sites or semiconductor processing equipment installed in clean rooms. A strength of flexible manufacturing is the ability to continue to efficiently produce products as demand continues to decrease. Combining the capability to easily upgrade designs with the capability to produce products efficiently independent of volume can extend products' lives and potentially generate high profits for those products whose development and tooling expenditures have already been paid off.

Mass customizers can quickly adjust to changes in markets, technology, standards, trends, and so on. Operational flexibility can rapidly shift production to products in demand. Mass customizers can use many standard modules to quickly create new products to satisfy changing environments.

Fewer orders will be lost since mass customization can always, within overall capacity limits, build the products in demand, unlike mass production "focused factories" that each have their own capacity limitations, which cannot be offset by excess capacity elsewhere in the company. Flexible plants can adapt quickly internally and "share capacity" with other plants to ensure that orders are not lost or delayed for lack of capacity. Further, inventory-less distribution from a build-to-order factory, as mentioned earlier, can prevent shortages caused in distribution channels. The result is fewer "opportunity" losses. Compaq Computer estimates that it lost between $500 million and $1 billion in sales in 1994 because of product availability problems.[25]

Scarce parts and capacity are utilized wisely in build-to-order. Without build-to-order methods, scarce components could be built into products that sit in the warehouse unsold while the company turns down other business because of the lack of the same scarce components, for instance, microprocessors or memory chips. A build-to-order factory consumes only parts that are going immediately to customers. Similar logic applies to "scarce" production operations. If plant capacity is limited by one bottleneck machine, it would be inadvisable to use that scarce capacity to build products that sit unsold in a warehouse or dealers' inventory.

Orders can be filled quicker on custom orders, enabling order fulfillment time to be a competitive advantage. Efficient mass customization operations can ship built-to-order custom products faster than competitors who have to customize products "the hard way."

Quicker delivery may command quicker payments. Rapid product delivery can be used as a basis for expecting prompt payments from customers. This saves interest expense on the money invested in producing products.

Customers save money if they avoid buying unwanted options. Because customized products can be ordered with only the options customers want, they will not be forced to buy a "bundled" option package to get the one option they really want. Even with a premium price, customers may still save money by avoiding unwanted options. This is a real "win/win" situation, if manufacturers can charge a premium and customers still pay less for exactly what they want.

REVENUE GAINS FROM QUICKER TIME TO MARKET

Advanced product development coupled with the improved market feedback of Mass Customization will allow companies to be first to market, thus resulting in the following sales benefits:

■ Market availability for product releases will be sooner because new product releases can be based on previous engineering and modules. Further, the improved market feedback from *any* mass customization offerings will help subsequent products satisfy customers needs more quickly and accurately.

■ Market share is 100 percent for the first to market. The earlier a product can be introduced before competitors, the longer the "reign" at 100 percent. Mass customizers will be able to take full advantage of this opportunity because their flexible operations will be able to quickly respond to rapidly growing demand.

■ The first "mass customizer" gets good, free publicity. Offering a custom product quickly at a competitive price is news, especially if it is the first one in a certain market or industry. That, in itself, is news. A newsworthy product introduction has much potential for positive publicity.

■ The first to market is perceived to be a leader. Market perception of leadership is of value in generating early sales and commanding price premiums. A steady stream of product improvements or a broader range of mass customized offerings can ensure a continued reputation of leadership.

■ The first to market can set standards, either de facto or official. Customers become committed to using a company's products by training, operating system, language, protocol, and so on.

■ The first to market can acquire attractive distribution channels. This may be especially important for mass customization, which may depend on good distributors to perform some of the customization at the point of sale.

■ Rapid developers take better advantage of windows of opportunity, with respect to both markets and technology. Unless technology is developed internally, competitors are in a race to be the first to develop technology into products. A mass customizer can incorporate new technology into existing platforms using existing modules and previous engineering and software code.

TOTAL COST ACCOUNTING

To appreciate all the above cost savings and revenue enhancements, it would be advantageous to be able to *quantify all costs*. If costs were tracked on a *total cost* basis, then the cost saving potential of mass customized products could be known, and products could be given an appropriate and competitive price.

Most companies have such inadequate cost systems that it actually hinders good product development and distorts product development decisions. Merely reporting labor and material costs encourages (sometimes forces) engineers to specify cheap parts and low bidders to achieve "cost targets" and move manufacturing off-shore, away from engineering, which thwarts Concurrent Engineering. Products with too much setup, inventory, "firefighting," engineering change orders, excessive parts variety, low equipment utilization, and high quality costs should have a higher overhead rate. Products that are designed, using the methodologies presented herein, for quick and easy manufacture and customization should have a much lower overhead rate. Overhead rates should be proportional to overhead demands, which vary by product.

The new paradigm for total cost accounting is Activity-Based Costing (ABC), sometimes referred to as Activity-Based Cost Management. The ability to quantify total cost is an important infrastructure for Mass Customization.

As in Chapter 3, let us consider the proverbial "Model T plant," a plant with only one product and no variations. *The Ernst & Young Guide to Total Cost Management* discusses the cost management implications of a single-product plant:

> If product variety were absent, the business environment would be simple . . . In a world like this, you could do product costing literally on the back of an envelope. You would simply divide the total production costs by the total production volume to calculate a unit cost."[26]

However, as Cooper and Kaplan pointed out in an article with the profound title, "How Cost Accounting Distorts Product Costs," overhead costs "vary with the diversity and complexity of the product line."[27] As pointed out in Chapter 3, product diversity and complexity are increasing because of market pressures and perceived opportunities. Thus, it is important to quantify overhead costs, since they can be several times more than the typically reported costs of labor and materials.

QUANTIFYING OVERHEAD

Four steps are involved in quantifying overhead. The first is to acknowledge deficiencies in current product costing practices. The second step is to estimate the degree of cost distortions. The third step is to understand the value of total cost measurements. The final step is to implement total cost measurements.

Deficiencies of Traditional Accounting

The first step in quantifying overhead is to acknowledge the deficiencies in the current cost system, which is the central theme of Johnson and Kaplan's pivotal book, *Relevance Lost, The Rise and Fall of Management Accounting*.[28] Traditional cost accounting systems were designed to present operational results and the financial position of the organization *as a whole* for investors and for agencies that tax or regulate. On the other hand, managers and engineers need *relevant* cost information to make good decisions. Typical problems caused by conventional cost systems include the following.

Distortions in Product Costing
Distortions in product costing are discussed at length in the Cooper and Kaplan reference cited above. Johnson and Kaplan concur:

> The management accounting system fails to provide accurate product costs. Costs get distributed to products by simplistic measures, usually direct-labor based, that do not represent the demands made by each product on the firm's resources.[29]

The *Guide to Total Cost Management* asserts that product costs "are distorted because each product typically includes an assignment of overhead that was allocated on some arbitrary basis such as direct labor, sales dollars, machine hours, material cost, units of production, or some other volume measure."[30]

Distorted product costing results in distorted pricing, which can underprice some products so low that they lose money and overprice other products to the point where they are uncompetitive.[31] Distorted product costing results in a distorted perception of the profitability of all the company's products, as pointed out in Chapter 4. This distorted view of profitability can cause managers to "feed the problems and starve the opportunities" with detrimental effects on product development priorities. Understanding *the real* profitability will allow companies to drop unprofitable products, as prescribed in Chapter 4, and focus on profitable products.

Cross-Subsidies

Cross-subsidies occur when high-volume products subsidize low-volume products and standard products subsidize custom products. A Johnson and Kaplan quote cited in Chapter 4 will be repeated here for emphasis:

> The standard product cost systems, which are typical of most organizations, usually lead to enormous cross-subsidies across products."[32]

Cooper, Kaplan, et al., in their Institute of Management Accountants-sponsored study, summarized what their eight case-study manufacturing organizations discovered after they implemented Activity-Based Costing:

> The manufacturing companies generally found, as expected, that low-volume, complex products tended to be much more expensive than had been calculated by the existing standard cost system.[33]

Relevant Decision Making

Good decisions are the key to success in any business venture, and this especially applies to product development. Unfortunately, many managers and engineers try to make decisions by the numbers, when the numbers are misleading or even irrelevant. Again quoting Johnson and Kaplan:

> Ironically, as management accounting systems became less relevant and less representative of the organization's operations and strategy, many companies became dominated by senior executives who believed they could run the firm "by the numbers."[34]

Again quoting the *Ernst & Young Guide:*

> If the costs are wrong, then all decisions about pricing, product mix, and promotion could be undermining long-term profitability.[35]

Johnson and Kaplan state that accurate, relevant numbers, based on total cost, can lead to much better decision making:

> The management accounting system also needs to report accurate product costs so that pricing decisions, introductions of new products, abandonments of obsolete products, and responses to the appearance of rival products can be made with the best possible information on product resource demands... An ineffective management accounting system can undermine even the best efforts in product development, process improvement, and marketing policy."[36]

Cost Management

Since one of the major challenges of Mass Customization is to produce products at low cost despite the other challenges of speed and customization, cost management takes on a new level of importance. But conventional cost management systems are of little help here:

> Management accounting reports are of little help to operating managers attempting to reduce cost and improve productivity.[37]

Downward Spirals

Cost accounting distortions can cause "reinforcing" behavior (reinforcing loops) that can cause a business to "spiral down." The concept of reinforcing loops was presented by Peter Senge in his book, *The Fifth Discipline*.[38] If overhead is spread "like peanut butter," then the following spiral will occur:

- High-volume products are overpriced because low-volume products are subsidized.
- Sales of the subsidized low-volume products rise; sales of the overpriced high-volume products decrease.
- *Real* overhead demands increase because of the higher proportion now of low-volume products.
- The higher overhead is now spread over all products as is customary.
- Costs go up further; sales go down further . . .

Thus, the loop reinforces and the company continues to "spiral down." This may drag a company down to the point of unprofitability or weaken an otherwise strong company.

Estimate the Degree of Cost Distortions

The second step in quantifying overhead is to estimate the degree of cost distortions. This can be accomplished by:

- Subjectively drawing conclusions about how much cost distortion is probably occurring when overhead is "spread like peanut butter."
- Conducting a pilot investigation to quantify one worst case product cost distortion. Choose the most likely product suggested by the rationalization Pareto plots presented in Chapter 4. Using polls and surveys (criteria 6 in Chapter 4) may narrow the search by asking manufacturing people to vote on a candidate. The list of factory processing incompatibilities (criteria 7 in Chapter 4) may help identify a candidate.

Understand the Value of Total Cost Measurements

Total cost measurements can be extremely valuable for the following decisions:

1. Knowing the *relative* profitability of *existing* products to see if the *current* most profitable products are:

High tech	versus	low tech.
Custom	versus	standard.
High volume	versus	low volume.
Private label	versus	name brand.

2. Rationalizing / consolidating product lines (Chapter 4).
3. Prioritizing product development and resource allocations.
4. Redesigning a product to lower cost.
5. Justifying high-quality parts and good vendors.
6. Designing parts or buying them off the shelf.
7. Integrating silicon (VLSI, ASICs) and structures (part combinations).
8. Eliminating "cost-reduction" ECOs that will not pay off their implementation cost during the life of the product.

This can free valuable resources for higher-leverage activities like helping new product development teams.

9. Justifying design tools, training, overhead reduction programs, and programs to improve quality, productivity, and flexibility.

10. Colocating or separating Engineering/Manufacturing.

11. Handling variety, configuration, and customization.

12. Investing now in the development of hardware and software modules that will benefit future product developments.

13. Identifying products that are losing money or have very low margins (criterion 5 in Chapter 4).

Implementing Total Cost Accounting

There are three approaches to implement total cost accounting. The first can be applied before any cost accounting changes are implemented: This is the subjective approach where decisions are based on *total cost thinking*. The second is the "low-hanging fruit" approach where *cost drivers* are introduced that quantify important metrics that can affect costing decisions and influence behavior. The third is the implementation of Activity-Based Cost (ABC) Management or Total Cost Management systems.

1. Total Cost Thinking

Even before any formal total cost accounting programs are implemented, companies can improve some decisions subjectively by using total cost thinking. The principles presented in this book can help individuals make better subjective decisions by correcting many misconceptions about cost and instilling the proper attitudes and beliefs.

But, for this to happen, the culture must encourage this. Management policies can either encourage or discourage this. If all proposals must meet strict criteria for payback and return on investment, this will govern the decision-making process. If the criteria are based on traditional cost accounting, then the decisions will tend to be governed by irrelevant numbers (mentioned above) and many truly good proposals will fail to win approval because much of their benefit comes from benefits that are not quantifiable by the current system. If companies rigidly adhere to criteria based on incomplete costs, then attempts to inject subjective total cost decision making will fail, even if it is in the best interest of the company and its customers.

One subjective approach to this dilemma was proposed by Robert Kaplan in the article about justifying Computer Integrated Manufacture (CIM): "Must CIM be Justified by Faith Alone?"[39] Kaplan's technique to "work around" deficiencies in accounting systems was to:

1. Compute how much the proposal fell short of the objective criteria: the *shortfall.*
2. Summarize the "intangible" benefits (all the benefits that could not be quantified).
3. Pose the question, "Is it worth the shortfall to gain all these intangible benefits?"

Sometimes decisions are just based on the proverbial "leap of faith." One of the best examples of Mass Customization is the Ross/Flex Division of Ross Controls, as mentioned in Chapter 1. Ross/Flex manufactures special and prototype valves for special customer applications.[40] Custom valves are designed jointly by customers and Ross integrators, who are engineers and veteran machinists. They have established a CAD "components" (blocks, symbols) library and proprietary CAD software based on dual-screen Integraph Corp. CAD systems.[41] Once a system is designed to solve a customer's initial problems, Ross continues to get feedback from the customer and make continuous upgrades to the designs.[42] The integrator then develops tool-path programs for the CNC machine tools and digitally transfers the custom programs to manufacturing. After the new program is downloaded, the CNC equipment machines the custom valve bodies and other parts. There are no paper drawings, manufacturing engineers, machinists, or inspectors.[43]

To accomplish this, Ross invested $30 million in sophisticated CAD systems and automated product equipment over seven years. Regarding the justification, Ross Chief Operating Officer, Henry Duignan noted that traditional return-on-investment analysis would never have justified the strategy, adding, "You have to make a leap of faith."[44]

But the results seem to justify the faith. Cost has dropped an order of magnitude and delivery time is one-hundredth of the conventional time.[45] The quick-turn Ross/Flex operation has grown from 5 percent to 20 percent of revenue in the past four years[46] and in 1995 was growing at 400 percent per year.

One example of part standardization, cited in Chapter 5, was the author's efforts to standardize all resistors to 1 percent tolerance to replace the previous duplication of resistors in both 1 percent and 5 percent tolerance versions. No numbers were available to justify the change, but it "just made sense" to cut in half the number of resistors in all three factories. Subsequently, the author has learned of people who did the same part consolidation and realized that the purchasing power of the combined orders offset the "cost" of the higher tolerance. Thus, all the variety cost savings, as discussed in Chapter 3, would go straight to the bottom line.

Sometimes, subjective decisions must be made *despite the numbers*. One of the author's clients, who makes water meters, consolidated seven raw castings into three by adding extra brass (for test ports) to every product, whether or not they needed the optional tapped holes. This added extra material cost to half the raw castings because of the extra brass on versions that did not need the test ports. In fact, the person who did the change thought he would be "beat up" for raising the standard cost. But company management supported the change, knowing subjectively that it would lower the cost of variety enough to be a net gain and make operations more flexible.

Management policies can encourage total cost thinking by *empowering* product development team leaders to make the best decisions, in their judgment, instead of trying to *limit bad decisions* by making them pass some predetermined threshold. Empowerment is part of the team approach to product development and will be discussed further in Chapter 9.

Mass Customization encourages the manufacture of products in very low volume—down to volumes of one! But the rationalizing procedures of Chapter 4 may determine that some "cash cows" may remain in the high-volume mass production mode. Therefore, in these mixed environments, it is extremely important to assign overhead costs rationally in proportion to their overhead demands.

2. Cost Drivers

In any change process, there is always some "low-hanging fruit," which is always a good place to start to get some early results with little effort. Success in these high-leverage areas can then generate more interest and support for more ambitious efforts. The low-hanging fruit approach is also a good way to start the change process if there is a lack of widespread support.

In ABC implementation, the low-hanging fruit is the identification and implementation of simple *cost drivers* that make cost accounting more accurate and relevant and encourage behavior to lower these costs. Cost drivers are defined as the *root cause* of a cost—the things that "drive" cost.

The cost driver approach identifies key drivers of cost that should be quantified instead of lumped in with all other overhead. The cost driver approach is easy to implement and starts with the most important overhead costs that need to be quantified. New data collection efforts are focused on only a few key cost drivers. Cost drivers can be based on estimates, as long as there is universal consensus. Cost drivers can provide a more rational basis for performance measures.

The *activities* that incur the following costs could be analyzed for significant ranges beyond the averages that usually are the basis for overhead allocation.

- Material overhead.
- Quality costs, scrap, rework, and other nonvalue activities.
- Inventory costs and inventory related costs.
- Setup costs.
- Equipment utilization.
- Process yields.
- Engineering change order costs.
- Costs of field service, repairs, warrantees', claims, litigation, etc.

The activities that cause these costs should be analyzed to find out what is causing the variation. Experienced managers will probably be able to identify the key cost drivers that are the driving difference in these activities, for instance:

- Volume: high volume or low volume.
- Degree of customization: standard or custom.
- Part standardization: approved or preferred.
- Part destination: for production products or spare parts for products that are out of production.
- Distribution costs: direct or through channels.
- Product age: launching, stabilized, or aging (experiencing processing incompatibilities with newer products and/or availability challenges for parts and raw materials).
- Market niches: commercial, OEM, military, medical, and nuclear markets have varying demands for quality, paperwork, proposals, reports, certifications, traceability, etc.

Those activities that incur difference costs from the variations in these cost drivers should be investigated. The costs of these activities should be charged accordingly. For instance, if low-volume products incur more cost than high-volume products, then this should be reflected in the allocation. If standard, preferred parts incur less material overhead, then they should be charged a lower overhead, as will be shown in the next examples. If certain operations incur more overhead than others, then the cost drivers should reflect this, as will be shown in the following examples.

Intel's Systems Group When the author implemented a parts standardization effort, using the procedure described in Chapter 5, the result was that 500 "commonality" parts were identified as being preferred for new designs. These common parts really did deserve lower material overhead than the 13,000 remaining "approved" parts because they were purchased in higher quantities. And the standardization program wanted to encourage engineers to use these parts. To accomplish both these goals, the Accounting Department structured material overhead into a two-tiered system: one rate for the 13,000 approved parts and a lower rate for the 500 commonality parts. This reflected greater "material world" efficiencies and encouraged usage.

Tektronix Portable Instruments Division To encourage part commonality and assign accurate material overhead, Tektronix assigned a material rate that was inversely proportional to volume. Thus, a high-volume part had a very low overhead rate; conversely, a "low runner" was assigned a very high rate.[47]

HP Roseville Network Division (RND) HP RND formerly had only two cost drivers for its printed circuit board assembly: direct labor hours and the number of insertions. A special survey showed that axial insertions were about one-third the cost of DIP insertions; manual insertion was three times as expensive as automation; and "low availability" parts had an additional cost of 10 times their materials cost. So they implemented the following nine unit-based cost drivers.[48]

1. Number of axial insertions.
2. Number of radial insertions.
3. Number of DIP insertions.
4. Number of manual insertions.
5. Number of test hours.
6. Number of solder joints.
7. Number of boards.
8. Number of parts.
9. Number of slots.

HP Boise Surface Mount Center (BSMC) HP BSMC implemented the following 10 cost drivers for surface-mount printed circuit board manufacture.[49] Note driver 7, which encourages part commonality.

Cost Pools	Drivers
1. Panel operations	Percent of a whole panel; if one panel contains four individual boards, then each board is charged 25% of the panel rate
2. Small component placement	Number of "small" components placed
3. Medium component placement	Number of "medium" components placed
4. Large component placement	Number of "large" components placed
5. Through-hole component insertion	Number of leaded components inserted
6. Hand load component placement	Minutes required to place all components that must be hand loaded rather than automatically placed on the board
7. Material procurement and handling	Number of unique parts in the board
8. Scheduling	Number of scheduling hours during a six-month period
9. Assembly setup	Number of minutes of setup time during a six-month period
10. Test and rework	Number of "yielded" minutes of test and rework time per board

3. Implement Total Cost Accounting

Programs to implement total cost accounting are usually called Activity-Based Costing (ABC), Activity-Based Cost Management, Total Cost Management,[50] or the earlier "transaction- based" costing. Activity-Based Costing is a system that focuses on the *activities* performed to produce products. Costs are assigned directly to products or to activities, which are then assigned to products based on how much of these activity costs were incurred by each product.

Cost Systems ABC is not intended to replace the existing finance system. In most cases, ABC implementations create independent decision-making models. In the study that Cooper, Kaplan, et al., did for the Institute of Management Accountants, this was the case:

> No modifications to existing financial systems were required, and companies continued to run all their existing systems in parallel with their new ABC model. . . . The activity-based model was treated as a management information system, not as part of the accounting system.[51]

The numbers from this model were more useful than that available from the existing cost system:

> Managers found the numbers generated from the activity-based analysis more credible and relevant than the numbers generated from the official costing system.

Resistance to ABC Despite the deficiencies pointed out earlier about traditional cost systems and case study testimonials, like the one cited above, many managers resist companywide ABC implementation. This stems from a general resistance to change based on these misperceptions. Many managers:

1. Do not accept the deficiencies in the current system. This was the topic of the first section of this discussion on total cost accounting. Many of the books referenced in this section make thorough arguments about this point, especially Johnson and Kaplan's *Relevance Lost, The Rise and Fall of Management Accounting.*[52]

2. Underestimate the benefit. This book reinforces the value of relevant cost numbers as a basis for good decision making, in general, and specifically for decisions governing product line rationalization, standardization efforts,

implementing manufacturing flexibility, and many
aspects of product development.

3. Overestimate the effort to make any improvements. In
   fact, much of the information is already in some computer! The Ernst & Young guide states that ABC can draw
   much information from MRP-II files: "In fact, the very
   existence of rich databases is precisely what makes the
   actual implementation of ABC systems feasible."[53]

Implementation Effort for ABC Most companies do not need a
system as complex as would be needed for the multinational
megacorporation, despite misconceptions to the contrary.
Implementing some degree of activity-based costing can be
achieved with modest resources. Of the eight companies that
implemented ABC in the Institute of Management Accountants
study, the companies that used "medium involvement" of outside
consultants took an average 6.5 months by 2.1 full-time equivalent
workers (FTEs) to implement the ABC model. Companies that
used "active involvement" of consultants took an average of 3
months by 1.6 FTEs.[54]

One practitioner reported that efforts to implement basic ABC
have "ranged from 80 hours for a small commercial printer to 500
hours for a large automotive supplier with very poor historical
financial and operating records."[55]

Tracking Product Development Expenses Some companies fail to
collect important information, such as tracking product development expense, since they believe they cannot ask engineers to keep
track of which projects they work on. Many engineers do, in fact,
resist such rigor. But such information is extremely important for
making good decisions about product development and product
costing. In fact, engineering labor accountability may be the
biggest "hole" in the activity-based accounting program. The solution to this apparent dilemma is as follows:

1. Emphasize the importance of the information, using all
   the reasoning presented herein and in the references.
   Some experts in the field argue that "an organization's
   cost accounting system can actually make or break an otherwise sound business."[56]

2. Make it easy to keep track of engineering time. It is better to have an approximate accountability than nothing at all. One division of Hewlett-Packard used the "bowling score" method to track engineering effort. The engineers are provided a form with lines for all the projects they may be working on. At the right of each line, there is a square box. An engineer who worked all day on one project would enter the bowling mark for a strike. An engineer who worked on two or more projects would enter the symbol for spare on each of them. Here is how the system worked in practice: Engineers agreed to cooperate because the system was easy. But since engineers are inherently precise, they eventually "corrected" the impreciseness of the system and voluntarily began to fill in more precise entries like hours or percent time worked.

3. Make it required. Activity-Based Costing depends on adequate data input. If senior management decides this is an important initiative, then everyone in the company will have to participate. Emphasizing the importance and making it easy will certainly make any mandates more easily implemented and ultimately more effective.

Implementing "abc" for Smaller Companies An excellent "how-to" book oriented toward cost- effective ABC implementations is Douglas Hick's *Activity-Based Costing for Small and Mid-Sized Businesses*. It is based on the valid premise that *it is better to be approximately correct than to be precisely wrong; accuracy is preferable to precision.*[57] Knowing that a product has a negative profit margin between –55 percent and –65 percent is more valuable than *thinking* it has a positive profit margin of exactly 10.89 percent (these are real numbers from product 3 in the Schrader-Bellows case study cited in Chapter 4). Hicks claims the false pursuit of precision in product costing is unrealistic: "No cost accounting system provides an organization with precision. *All* product costing is approximate. *All* cost systems contain too many estimates and allocations to be precise."[58]

With this focus on relevancy over precision, it is easier to implement Activity-Based Costing than the "full-blown" version, especially for smaller companies. Hicks calls this "activity-based costing" with the lower case acronym, "abc."

> In abc, activities are defined as groups of related processes or procedures that together meet a particular work need of the organization. Under this definition, the activities of the accounts payable department would most likely be accounts payable. Period.[59]

Hicks makes similar arguments for treating the entire purchasing function as an activity, instead of identifying all the activities in purchasing. For Mass Customization, it may be wise to segregate purchasing and other "material world" functions into two activities: those supporting conventional forecast-based production and those supporting JIT production. As pointed out in Chapter 3, many purchasing costs are avoided by *kanban* and "breadtruck" deliveries. Plus ordering fewer types of parts in larger quantities reduces purchasing costs and increases purchasing leverage. The study published in *Just-in-Time Purchasing* reported that JIT users expected to cut expediting effort by a factor of three.[60]

If good quantitative data are lacking, it would be preferable to implement some of the following shortcuts than to continue with grossly inaccurate allocations. One of these shortcuts is to *estimate* the percentage of an activity's cost caused by a particular cost driver, for instance, high-volume products compared to low-volume products. Thus, instead of averaging the cost allocation where all products get the same charge, the low-volume products would be charged, say, 80 percent and the high-volume products 20 percent (if the typical Pareto effect was in effect).

Hicks presents a simplified approach to implementing abc, with the emphasis on accuracy and relevance rather than precision. He proposes an abc model in a format suitable for spreadsheets, such as Lotus 1-2-3™ and Excel™.

An alternative to creating a model on a spreadsheet would be software specifically developed for ABC analysis. The eight case studies, cited in the Institute of Management Accountants ABC study, all used such software packages on PCs.[61]

Typical Results of ABC Implementations   When ABC is implemented, companies start to see the real picture about product cost, which is often surprising. Cooper, Kaplan, et al., refer to the "typical ABC pattern," where several offerings are shown to be highly profitable, most at or near break-even profitability, and a few highly unprofitable.[62] The Schrader-Bellows case study,[63] cited in Chapter 4, showed that, out of seven products originally thought to be profitable, three actually were, one was barely breaking even, and three were unprofitable, with one highly unprofitable.

Total cost analyses often adjust manufacturing costs up for most products, while lowering them only for a few "deserving" products. When Hewlett-Packard implemented ABC at its Boise Surface Mount Center, it analyzed 57 products (printed circuit boards) for true manufacturing costs.[64] After implementing the nine cost drivers cited above, it found that 72 percent of the products were really costing more than assumed. Cost adjustments ranged from slightly lower to double! The actual percent adjustments were shown in Figure 4–4.

NOTES

1. David M. Anderson, *Design for Manufacturability, Optimizing Cost, Quality, and Time-to-Market* (Lafayette, CA: CIM Press, 1990).

2. Phillip Crosby, *Quality is Free* (New York: Mentor Books, 1979).

3. James Womak, Daniel Jones, and Daniel Roos, *The Machine That Changed the World* (New York: Rawson Associates, 1990; paperback: New York: Harper Perennial, 1991)

4. Kiyoshi Suzaki, *The New Manufacturing Challenge, Techniques for Continuous Improvement* (New York: Free Press, 1987).

5. James H. Saylor, *TQM Field Manual* (New York: McGraw-Hill, 1992), chaps. 3 and 4.

6. Jordan D. Lewis, *The Connected Corporation, How Leading Companies Win Through Customer–Supplier Alliances* (New York: Free Press, 1995), chap. 8; and Womack et al., *The Machine That Changed the World*, chap. 6.

7. Lewis, *The Connected Corporation*, p. 38.

8. Ibid.

9. Peter F. Drucker, *Managing in a Time of Great Change* (New York: Truman Talley Books/Dutton, 1995), p. 117.

10. Shawn Tully, "Raiding a Company's Hidden Cash," *Fortune*, August 22, 1994, p. 82.

11. Eliyahu M. Goldratt, *The Goal* (New York: North River Press, 2nd rev. ed., 1992), p. 268.

12. Eli Goldratt's *The Goal* makes this point often about the need to do "what makes sense" to achieve "the goal" rather than basing decisions and actions on attempts to satisfy arbitrary performance metrics and cost measurements that only make a small part of the system appear to look productive or cost-effective.

13. Ronald Henkoff, "Delivering the Goods," *Fortune,* November 28, 1994, p. 62.

14. Marshall Fisher, Anjani Jain, and John Paul MacDuffie, *Strategies for Product Variety: Lessons From the Automobile Industry* (Philadelphia: Wharton School, University of Pennsylvania, January 16, 1994), p. 26.

15. Ibid., p. 31.

16. B. Joseph Pine, II, Don Peppers, and Martha Rogers, "Do You Want to Keep Your Customers Forever," *Harvard Business Review,* March–April 1995, p. 103.

17. Wilton Woods, "After All You've Done for Your Customers, Why Are They Still Not Happy," *Fortune,* December 11, 1995, p. 180.

18. Robert V. Delaney, *Sixth Annual State of Logistics Report* (St. Louis, MO: Cass Information Systems, June 5, 1995), Figure 8.

19. Dr. Corey Billington, "Strategic Supply Chain Management," *OR/MS Today,* April 1994 (published jointly by the Operations Research Society of America and the Institute of Management Sciences), pp. 20–27.

20. Drucker, *Managing in a Time of Great Change.*

21. Niklas von Daehne, "Database Revolution," *Success* 42, no. 4 (May 1995), pp. 38–42.

22. Douglas Lavin, "Stiff Showroom Prices Drive More Americans to Purchase Used Cars," *The Wall Street Journal,* November 1, 1994, p. 1.

23. Henkoff, "Delivering the Goods," p. 64.

24. Von Daehne, "Database Revolution."

25. Henkoff, "Delivering the Goods," p. 62.

26. Michael R. Ostrenga, Terrence R. Ozan, Robert D. McIlhattan, Marcus D. Harwood, *The Ernst & Young Guide to Total Cost Management* (New York: John Wiley & Sons, 1992).

27. Robin Cooper and Robert S. Kaplan, "How Cost Accounting Distorts Product Costs," *Management Accounting,* April 1988.

28. H. Thomas Johnson and Robert Kaplan, *Relevance Lost, The Rise and Fall of Management Accounting* (Boston: Harvard Business School, 1991).

29. Ibid.

30. Ostrenga et al., *Total Cost Management,* p. 27.

31. Douglas T. Hicks, *Activity-Based Costing for Small and Mid-Sized Businesses, An Implementation Guide* (New York: John Wiley & Sons, 1992), p. 20.

32. Johnson and Kaplan, *Relevance Lost.*

33. Robin Cooper, Robert S. Kaplan, Lawrence S. Maisel, Eileen Morrissey, Ronald M. Oehm, *Implementing Activity-Based Cost Management* (Montvale, NJ: Institute of Management Accountants, 1992), p 4.

34. Johnson and Kaplan, *Relevance Lost.*

35. Ostrenga, et al., *Total Cost Management*, p. 146.

36. Johnson and Kaplan, *Relevance Lost.*

37. Ibid.

38. Peter M. Senge, *The Fifth Discipline, The Art and Practice of The Learning Organization* (New York: Doubleday/Currency, 1990).

39. Robert S. Kaplan, "Must CIM Be Justified by Faith Alone?" *Harvard Business Review*, March–April, 1986, p. 87.

40. Steven L. Goldman, Roger N. Nagel, and Kenneth Preiss, *Agile Competitors and Virtual Organizations; Strategies for Enriching the Customer* (New York: Van Nostrand Reinhold, 1995), pp. 18, 170.

41. Mary Brandel, "One Pneumatic Valve to Go," *Computerworld*, November 22, 1993, p. 95.

42. Pine et al., "Do You Want to Keep Your Customers Forever?"

43. "Creating a 21st Century Business," *Industry Week*, April 19, 1993, p. 38.

44. Ibid.

45. Otis Port, "Custom-Made, Direct from the Plant," *Business Week*, 21st Century Capitalism issue, 1994, p. 158.

46. Pine et al., "Do You Want to Keep Your Customers Forever?"

47. Robin Cooper and Peter B. B. Turney, "Internally Focused Activity-Based Costing Systems," *Measures of Manufacturing Excellence*, ed. Robert S. Kaplan (Boston: Harvard Business School, 1990) pp. 292–93.

48. Ibid., 294–96.

49. Mike Merz and Arlene Harding, "ABC Puts Accountants on Design Team at HP," *Management Accounting*, September 1993, pp. 22–27.

50. Ostrenga et al., *Total Cost Management.*

51. Cooper et al., *Implementing Activity-Based Cost Management* p.7.

52. Johnson and Kaplan, *Relevance Lost.*

53. Ostrenga et al., *Total Cost Management*, p. 32.

54. Cooper et al., *Implementing Activity-Based Cost Management*, p. 296.

55. Douglas T. Hicks, *Activity-Based Costing for Small and Mid-Sized Businesses, An Implementation Guide* (New York: John Wiley & Sons, 1992), p. 9.

56. Ibid., p. 14.

57. Ibid., p. 7.

58. Ibid., p. 8

59. Ibid., p. 35.

60. A. Ansari and B. Modarress, *Just-In-Time Purchasing,* (New York: Free Press, 1990), p. 44.

61. Cooper et al., *Implementing Activity-Based Cost Management*, pp. 6, 25, 256.

62. Ibid., p. 5.

63. The Schrader-Bellows case study is described in Harvard Business School Case Series 9-186-272; a summary of the findings appears in Robin Cooper and Robert S. Kaplan, "How Cost Accounting Distorts Product Costs," *Management Accounting,* April, 1988.

64. "ABC Puts Accountants on Design Team at HP," Merz and Hardy.

CHAPTER

Building Products Quickly with Agile Manufacturing

To be able to mass customize products, build them to order, or excel in niche markets, products must be built flexibly. This means being able to *efficiently* and *quickly* build products that may be different from the one before or the one after.

Manufacturing agility is not that hard to accomplish when products are designed right, using the principles of this book. It is not necessarily expensive to accomplish and does not depend on extensive automation or elaborate information systems. Manufacturing agility can even be achieved in manual assembly as shown in Figure 2–1. Agile manufacturing capability is one of the key process infrastructures needed for Mass Customization.

Implementation can be achieved primarily through "soft" programs such as setup reduction, just-in-time (JIT), flexible manufacturing, continuous flow manufacturing, demand flow manufacturing, build-to-order, and the various initiatives under the label of *agility*. Of the top 25 candidates in *Industry Week's* 1994 "Best Plants" survey, 72 percent utilized flexible manufacturing systems, 64 percent used flexible assembly systems, and 48 percent had flexible machining centers.[1]

A Coopers & Lybrand study of 10 clients that it had helped to implement JIT showed an average lead time improvement of 83.1 percent.[2] A JIT study of 1,165 companies, reported in the APICS journal, *Production & Inventory Management Journal*, showed throughput time decreased an average of 59.4 percent as a result of implementing JIT.[3]

EARLY STEPS AND PREREQUISITES

Chapter 5 discussed the importance of standardization of parts, tooling, fixturing geometries, processes, procedures, and raw materials. Standardization is the first prerequisite for manufacturing agility.

Parts must be common enough to be distributed at all points of use without the setup of changing parts. Tools must be common enough to avoid setup delays to change them. Tooling and dies must be designed with standard interfaces so they can be changed quickly. Fixturing geometries must be common enough to avoid setups related to fixturing work pieces. Processes and procedures must be standardized to avoid setup related to changes and learning between successive products. Raw materials must be common enough to avoid the setup of finding different raw materials or the setup of changing the raw materials being fed into cut-off saws, screw machines, and other machine tools.

Many standardization efforts can only be fully realized as new products and processes are introduced into production. Part standardization, as discussed in Chapter 5, generally applies to new products. However, efforts to eliminate duplicates can immediately improve the flexibility of operations. Similarly, "better than" substitutions (e.g., 1 percent tolerance parts for 5 percent parts) can immediately reduce part variety of existing products and possibly improve product quality at the same time.

SETUP AND BATCH SIZE REDUCTION

Mass Customization strives to produce different products in the same plant with virtually zero changeover time. This requires that the factory be *flexible* or *agile*. If successive products are to be unique and different, there cannot be significant delays to get parts, change dies and fixtures, download programs, find instructions, or make any kind of manual measurement, adjust settings, or position parts or fixtures. The wasted time of these delays is called setup. Setup makes the factory inflexible and discourages mass customization.

The usual approach to dealing with setup is to accept it as a necessary evil and then spread it over as many products as possible in *batches* or *lots* to minimize the setup "charge" per part. Industrial engineers have developed formulas for the "economic order quantity" (EOQ) that determines the "optimal" batch size based on the setup time. The higher the setup, the higher the batch size and the less flexible the plant. Setup reduction efforts are aimed at reducing the setup and, thus, the batch size. As setup goes to zero, the economic order quantity goes to one, which is true flexible manufacturing.

Lot size reduction is an important step that many leading companies are taking. *Industry Week's* "Best Plant" 1994 survey of the 25 top performing candidates indicated that 92 percent of plants manufacture or assemble components in small lot sizes. Their lot size reduction programs resulted in a median component lot size reduction of 75 percent.[4]

To achieve this agility, which is a prerequisite for Mass Customization, *all* forms of setup must be driven to zero. If part variety is too excessive to allow distribution at all points of use, then enough parts for a *batch* must be assembled into a *kit*, which is put together in the raw materials warehouse, delivered to the assembly area, and then distributed to part bins or automation machines. This *kitting* is a setup that will inhibit flexible manufacturing and mass customization.

The design implications to eliminate kitting are that all parts in a mass customization family must be able to be distributed to all points of use. This should be the focus of *concurrent engineering* efforts to coordinate the design of the product and the processes so that this becomes a reality, using the standardization techniques presented in Chapter 5.

The product must also be designed to eliminate the need for tooling changes for dies, molds, tool plates, and fixtures or to make the changes as quickly as possible. Parts needing dies for molding or casting should be designed to be versatile enough to accommodate all products in the mass customization family. For instance, if castings for water meters or gas regulators need to accommodate various combinations of test ports and other options, all those features could be molded or cast into a common casting.

Tool plates and fixtures can be designed to be versatile enough to accept a common *blank,* which then can be customized by computer-controlled machine tools or robots. The blank must quickly be positioned in the fixture without any need for measuring and manual positioning. Thus, the blank must be designed with common fixturing geometries. Examples of this include the common faceplate blank shown in the instrument example in Figure 2–2. Another example involved designing all circuit boards in the same "form factor" (size and shape) with the same tooling holes so all of them use the same tooling plate, pallet, or material handling devices.

Single tooling fixtures can be cleverly designed to accommodate more than one blank or printed circuit board. To improve the flexibility of Intel's Systems Group operations, the author developed a single tool plate that accommodated seven different circuit board form factors. Pairs of tooling pins were permanently mounted around the central opening of the tool plate. Adjustable support arms could swing out to hold up boards that were too small to span the opening. Common tool plates can thus eliminate the setup usually required to change tool plates.

Programs from computer-controlled production equipment can be changed quickly with all programs stored in a *file server* that can download programs almost instantaneously based on identification of the part by some means, such as a bar code.

In manual assembly, even taking the time to find assembly instructions or drawings is a setup. To be flexible enough for Mass Customization, this setup should be eliminated by making the processes identical. A small number of choices in assembly could be displayed on a chart in front of the worker. More complex and varied instructions could be changed instantaneously on a computer monitor, as shown in Figure 2–1. If graphical images, say from drawings or illustrations, are needed, these can also be displayed on computer monitors, as is done for the assembly of Compaq computers in Houston, Texas.[5] Apple Computer has even made animated assembly instructions that are displayed on their own Macintosh computers.[6] As with the automation programs, the manual instructions can be changed by input from a bar code wand.

The importance of setup reduction/elimination depends on factors like the volume of production. High-volume mass customization will absolutely require setup elimination and true agile manufacturing. Low-volume production may tolerate somewhat greater setups, but the cumulative cost and time of such setups must be considered. Remember, the goal is to make mass customized production of a variety of products as efficiently as the mass production of one product.

INVENTORY REDUCTION/JUST-IN-TIME

Just as standardization is the prerequisite to setup reduction, setup reduction is the prerequisite to inventory reduction and just-in-time programs. Like many innovative programs, the "just-in-time" label generates its share of misunderstanding. Critics and many people who do not understand the concept think that just-in-time only consists of delivery trucks skidding up to the loading docks with parts delivered "just in the nick of time" before production halts. Further, they also think that incoming inventory has been simply shifted from the assembly plant floor to the suppliers' warehouses. The latter perception is sometimes true when suppliers want to do business with Just-in-Time customers but are not, themselves, "with the program."

However, the real goals of Just-in-Time programs are inventory reduction, throughput reduction, flexibility improvement, and the continuous improvements forced by the elimination of "just-in-case" inventory. It is the flexibility improvement that is of interest to companies implementing agile paradigms like Mass Customization, Build-to-Order, and niche markets. But being able to build customized products in "lots of one" requires the virtual *elimination* of setup and inventories rather than just their *reduction.*

America's leading companies are implementing JIT as part of a general improvement strategy. *Industry Week's* 1994 "Best Plant" survey of the 25 top candidate plants showed that 96 percent of these companies had JIT/continuous-flow production.[7]

However, many companies have had varying degrees of success attempting or implementing JIT/inventory reduction programs. The degree of success will be largely proportional to how well the products are designed for this environment, which is the overall purpose of this book. If products are designed around too many types of parts to distribute at all points of use, then parts will have to be kitted and JIT will not be possible. Too many setups in manufacturing can inhibit and frustrate JIT and inventory reduction programs. Thus, manufacturing agility is ultimately dependent on product development—the *concurrent* development of products *and* flexible processes.

EFFECTS OF PRODUCT LINE RATIONALIZATION ON AGILITY

In most cases, factories can make significant improvements in agility before a new generation of products arrives. The first step would to be to rationalize the product line using the techniques presented in Chapter 4. Most likely, products that are eliminated or outsourced are those that have the least "fit" with the flexible factory. Thus, their removal from operations will probably eliminate most of the oddball parts and the longest setups. In fact, programs to improve manufacturing agility may be one of the driving forces for product rationalization. The rationalization effort will be even more effective toward this goal if manufacturing agility, and its contribution to Mass Customization and Build-to-Order, is identified as a core competency that is a cornerstone of corporate strategy.

With the oddballs gone or outsourced, the factory can start focusing on improving the flexibility of the products that remain. Since the rationalization effort may have created some major changes in a factory's remaining product lines, the next step would be to regroup in both the figurative and literal meanings. Plant management should use this opportunity to take a new, objective look at the operation's big picture and question and challenge everything from plant layout to the flow of parts and products. Maybe the rationalized product line now will permit improvements that were not considered possible before.

Manufacturing management should ask the following questions, ordered with the most global first, about the product lines that remain after the rationalization:

- *Multiplant strategies.* How does this rationalization affect existing or proposed multiplant strategies? Can one or more plants be focused on certain groups of compatible products?

- *Production line consolidation.* Can the new product mix be built on one production line? Or how can they be grouped for the minimum number of lines that would be needed? What would be required to consolidate manufacturing lines?
- *Make/buy strategy.* What is the optimal make/buy strategy now? Are there opportunities with the "virtual corporation"[8] or "virtual organizations"[9] where an agile network, or *keiretsu,* of suppliers delivers parts as part of a just-in-time *kanban* parts resupply system? Conversely, are there some critical processes whose outsourcing causes delays that inhibit flexibility? Do vendor/partner relationships need to be developed? There are occasions when some processes must be brought in-house for agility. For instance, a water meter company brought in-house the printing of the dial faceplates, despite the fact that this was not a core competency, because it had one of the largest lead times of any part in its otherwise flexible manufacturing operations.
- *Scope of early improvements.* Are there opportunities to focus on a particular group of products or one plant for a "pilot" implementation?
- *Plant layout.* Are machine tools and other product activities arranged by departments or functions? Is there a milling room, a lathe room, and an assembly area with parts forced to move in large batches as they work their way from room to room? Does this product line rationalization permit more efficient plant layout possibilities?
- *Trends.* What trends affect the above issues? Will there be further, more ambitious rationalization efforts in the future? What new products are planned and how will their introduction affect operations? Are there any new products to be added through mergers or acquisitions?

SCOPE OF IMPROVEMENTS

The scope of any improvement effort is affected by the potential returns. It would help in planning and motivating improvement efforts to know how inefficient the current operations really are by quantifying all the variety costs discussed in Chapter 3. Knowing the numbers can help justify programs with projections for return on investment (ROI) and payback periods. Even without that, there may be a corporate subjective feeling that there is too much inefficiency and that something needs to be done about it.

The other side of the subjective motivations would be the opportunity side: how manufacturing agility can help companies achieve their goals of excelling in niche markets, building products to order, or mass customizing products.

It is important to identify, and it is hoped quantify, the upside of such improvements, since implementing the changes may involve some expense or may have to change many "old ways." If enough "buy-in" is achieved, the implementation can be *revolutionary* and shift operations from a slow batch-oriented Mass Production paradigm to the rapid build-to-order world of Mass Customization. If there is limited buy-in, then the change will be more *evolutionary* with work beginning with the "low hanging fruit" and implementation starting with some pilot activity.

Implementations may be limited to that part of the product line with a potential for Mass Customization. The "cash cow" products, determined with the methodologies of Chapter 4, may be able to remain in the mass production mode.

Training and education may be necessary to help change the culture, shift paradigms, and implement the following steps, which are ordered with the low-hanging fruit first.

IMPROVING MANUFACTURING AGILITY

1. Standardization

All parts must be able to be *easily* distributed to all points of use. This requires aggressive part standardization for new designs using the procedure described in the last section. Some improvements can be made for the production of existing products.

Eliminate duplicate parts with parts management tools presented in Chapter 5. Substitute "better than" parts and material grades whenever feasible. Devise standard tool plates and fixturing devices that can accept entire families of parts.

Consider minor design changes that will enhance standardization, such as changing raw materials to more common "better than" materials; changing fasteners to the same head so common tools can be used; changing unusual fasteners to the next larger common part; and standardizing fixturing geometries on parts to correspond to versatile tooling.

2. Rationalization/Consolidation

Use the techniques of Chapter 4 to rationalize the product line and eliminate products from in-house manufacturing operations products that don't fit into a flexible environment, have low sales, have excessive overhead demands, are not really appreciated by customers, have limited future potential, or may really be losing money.

3. Addition of Part Bins

After the number of parts has been minimized through standardization and rationalization, adding part bins on assembly machines and manual work stations may improve flexibility. If there are more part types than bins, then someone will have to setup the machine twice, first with the first "half" of parts and then the second half.

As mentioned in Chapter 2, more part bins could be added to the manual assembly station shown in Figure 2–1. However, too many part bins may be confusing and may require lights on the bins that would signal when a part would be used.

Part bins can sometimes be added to automatic assembly machines, such as printed circuit board placement or insertion equipment. A semiflexible but easier approach is to change part cartridges or magazines (each of which may hold several part bins) for various product families. This is, in fact, a setup but it may occur infrequently.

Even though adding part bins does involve some expense and effort, it may be necessary to achieve flexibility with the current product line. However, it may *not* be needed later as older products are dropped and new generation products go into production, it is hoped with much better part standardization, if the lessons of Chapter 5 are applied. Thus, plans to add part bins should be coordinated with product line rationalization and new product development. Feedback from manufacturing on this subject may make product line rationalization more aggressive and new product development more serious about part standardization.

4. Pilot Activities

After rationalizing the product line, select the *easiest* product line or family of products for a pilot. Focus activities on that group of products and implement as many of these steps as are practical.

Document the "before" condition for inventory costs, setup costs, recurring quality costs, the real equipment utilization, the real throughput, and so forth. See Chapter 3 for a complete list of these variety costs. Compare these metrics to the "after" condition and use these results to summarize improvements. Use these success stories to justify subsequent activities.

5. Setup Elimination and Batch Size Reduction

The "optimal" batch sizes that are calculated using economic order quantity formulas *do not take into account all overhead costs related to inventory and agility.* The result is inflexible operations and high overhead costs for setup and inventory.

Several steps can be taken to eliminate setup. Identify setup activities and relate them to their total resultant costs: setup costs themselves; inventory caused by the setup, inefficient use of equipment; and all the related costs cited under "Cost of Variety" in Chapter 3. Prioritize setup elimination opportunities, like the ones below, keeping in mind that a coordinated effort may be necessary to eliminate several setups to make a production line flexible.

- *Kitting elimination.* Use part standardization or add part bins to eliminate the setup of gathering all the parts needed for a batch of products and delivering them to the assembly area.
- *Part shape consolidation.* Parts needing dies for molding or casting should be designed to be versatile enough to accommodate all products in the mass customization family. For instance, if castings for water meters or gas regulators need to accommodate various combinations of test

ports and other options, all those features could be molded or cast into a common casting.

- *Rapid die change.* There has been much progress and much written about rapid die changes.[10] Shigeo Shingo developed the methodology called "Single Minute Exchange of Dies" (SMED) for Toyota.[11] Clever die and mold mounting geometries have been developed to facilitate quick changeovers.[12] Conveyors and carousels that were first applied to moving parts and products are now being applied to moving dies quickly in and out of presses and molding machines.[13]

- *Versatile tool plates and fixtures.* Ideally, tool plates and fixtures should have to accept only one "blank" (e.g., bar stock, casting, bare circuit board, etc.) The blank must quickly be positioned in the fixture without any need for measuring and manual positioning. Versatile tooling fixtures can be cleverly designed to accommodate more than one blank. All the blanks must be designed with common fixturing geometries.

- *Instant CNC program changes.* Programs from computer-controlled production equipment can be changed instantly with all programs stored in a file server that can download programs almost instantaneously based on identification of the part by some means such as a bar code.

- *Manual instructions.* For manual assembly, even taking the time to find assembly instructions or drawings is a setup. To be flexible enough for Mass Customization, this setup should be eliminated with the on-line display of instructions, as discussed earlier.

6. Remove WIP Inventory

Most JIT scholars agree on the need to reduce inventory. Schonberger puts it bluntly: "Inventory is the root of all evil."[14]

But there are two schools of thought on how to approach inventory reduction. One school advocates eliminating problems and then reducing inventory.[15] The steps cited above would help eliminate problems. Another major category of problems that need to be eliminated is machine maintenance. One reason traditional manufacturing people like having WIP inventory is to have a buffer "just in case" a machine goes down. Several books have been written about equipment maintenance[16] and *Total Productive Maintenance,* which may be required as a supporting program to a JIT effort.[17]

The other JIT camp proposes to first withdraw buffer inventories to expose problems[18] and to focus attention on resolving the problems.[19] This may expose problems and focus attention on their resolution, but if inventory reduction is used to put pressure on people, it may place stress on workers.[20] It is probably not entirely within the production line workers' scope of influence to solve these problems.

As with any set of extremes, the best path is often to use the best of both. All the obvious problems should be solved first. Machine maintenance should be converted to a preventative basis from an ad hoc fix-it-when-it-breaks basis. Part variety should be reduced by standardization efforts. Product and part variety should be reduced by product rationalization efforts. Setup reduction should be implemented as much as possible for the remaining products. Then inventory can be reduced gradually to a level appropriate to setup times and problem occurrence. Inventory levels and "optimal" lot sizes should not be set blindly by EOQ formulas. As more problems are uncovered and solved, the WIP inventory can be reduced, not necessarily to zero but to a level that allows efficient manufacture in lots of one.

Reducing WIP inventories is a learning process and will probably have a learning curve. Consequently, inventory reduction should not be attempted when there are peak demands on production. Periods of low demand might be a good time for such an improvement activity, although inventory reduction should not be put off for the proverbial "rainy day."

Management should be supportive of this continuous improvement and view it as an *investment.* It should not be *imposed* on the workers, or they might resent the challenges and resist the change. All production workers should be *involved* in planning and executing continuous improvement activities. Often the workers themselves have the best ideas and suggestions.

7. Plant Layout Optimization

Removing WIP inventory will free a lot of space. As pointed out in Chapter 3, many JIT implementations have reduced floor space requirements by 50 percent or more.[21] When Omark Industries implemented JIT in Guelph, Ontario, for the production of chain saw chain, the "flow distance" went from 2,620 feet to 173 feet, an order-of-magnitude reduction.[22] Its Portland, Oregon, plant cut floor space 40 percent. GE's Philadelphia plant, which makes vacuum circuit breakers, reduced space from 2 million to 600,000 square feet, a 70 percent reduction. Westinghouse's Fayetteville, North Carolina, motor-control center plant reduced space 40 percent. Burlington Industries' custom-length drapery factory in Reidsville, North Carolina, cut floor space form 13,000 to 4,300 square feet, a 67 percent reduction. The defense weapons systems division of Texas Instruments in Sherman, Texas, cut floor space 40 percent.[23]

This saved space can and should be put to good use. Just leaving empty space where the inventory used to be wastes valuable floor space and, according to Parkinson's Law, will just fill up again, probably with inventory. Thus, to take advantage of the floor space savings, machines and workstations will have to move.

Plant managers may resist a new layout, even for a small part of a plant. But there are several compelling reasons to do so.

- *Growth.* Physically consolidating operations can make valuable floor space available for growth or to allow design engineers to be "co-located" close to the action. Such consolidations can even defer moving the plant to get more space for growth.
- *Support for agility programs* like Build-to-Order and Mass Customization.
- *Part flow.* The flow of incoming parts and materials may now flow directly to the line instead of from central warehouses (as discussed in the next section), and this may affect plant layout.
- *Throughput.* Moving operations closer together can result in enormous benefits in throughput, which may in itself be worth the cost of the move.

- *Quality.* If workstations are moved together, plants will reap the benefits of the rapid feedback that occurs when an operator hands off something to the next operator, who will be able to give instant feedback if anything is wrong with that part. Many companies have adopted the U-shaped line, which is arranged in the shape of a U to make each production line even closer together.[24]

- *Group technology layouts.* As lot sizes approach one, there are vast opportunities to improve the plant layout and the flow of parts and products. The traditional plant layout groups operations by function, for instance, with a room for milling machines, another room for lathes, and another room for assembly, and so forth. Since the machines are general purpose in nature, each job (lot) must be set up. To minimize the setup charge per part, the setup charge is amortized over large lots, which flow from room to room. This large WIP inventory causes all the problems discussed herein, such as slow throughput, poor quality, inefficient utilization of space and machinery.

  In contrast, agile plants are laid out according to part similarities and product families. Instead of parts flowing slowly in large bins from operation to operation, they flow quickly from operation to operation in very small lots or individually, which is called "one piece flow."[25]

- *Overhead cost reduction* from the above. Plant re-layout may pay for itself as a freestanding program, if the overhead cost reductions could be measured.

8. Breadtruck Deliveries

The "lowest-hanging fruit" in material logistics is the *breadtruck* delivery system for small, inexpensive parts. Instead of counting on sales forecasts to trigger an MRP system to generate purchase orders, all the small, inexpensive parts can be made available in bins at all the points of use. A local supplier is contracted to simply keep the bins full and bill the company monthly for what has been used, much like the way bread is resupplied by the breadtruck in a small market.

All the MRP/purchasing expense is eliminated, and this type of delivery can assure a constant supply of parts, thus avoiding work stoppages. Being off the forecast/MRP system, the supply of these parts can be assured for "forecast-less" operations such as Build-to-Order. Typical parts suitable for breadtruck deliveries are fasteners, resistors, capacitors, and almost any small, inexpensive part.

As companies become more agile, they may move slightly more expensive and slightly larger parts into the breadtruck system. The more expensive parts may incur some inventory carrying cost, but that should be outweighed by savings in purchasing, materials overhead, expediting, and avoiding work stoppages.

The criteria for breadtruck deliveries are:

- A reliable supplier can be contracted. Many suppliers welcome such business and want to perform well, since they usually get all the business for their categories of parts and raw materials.

- Parts can be distributed at *all* points of use. Of course, part standardization helps here.

- Parts are small enough and cheap enough so that sufficient parts will always be on hand. Bin count can be set high enough to preclude any chance of ever running out.

- Parts are not likely to go obsolete or deteriorate while waiting to be used.

- The breadtruck parts are not so attractive as to create a significant pilferage problem, since, generally, companies do not correlate part consumption with product sales. However, making breadtruck parts freely available for R&D prototypes and factory improvements may encourage innovation.

- Manual reorders are not anticipated to occur. The supplier should be in a continuous improvement mode and be constantly adjusting bin count to correspond to prevailing demand. The factory could alert the supplier about any anticipated spikes in demand.

9. Kanban Parts Resupply

Whereas the breadtruck system keeps parts bins full with periodic deliveries, the kanban system refills bins according to usage. Part usage itself *pulls* more parts into the system; hence this type of operation is known as a "pull system."

Figure 7-1 shows two rows of part bins that are set up for resupply by the two-bin *kanban* system. Initial assembly starts with all bins full of parts. When the part bin nearest the worker is depleted, the full bin behind moves forward, as shown by the empty opening on the table. The empty part bin then is returned to its source, which could be the machine that made the part, a sub-assembly workstation that assembled the part, or a supplier. The source fills the bin and returns it to this assembly workstation behind its counterpart, which is now dispensing parts.

Bin size can vary from the small tabletop bins shown in Figure 7–1 to pairs of truck trailers, where parts are drawn from one trailer while the other goes back to the source for more parts. Bins too large for a tabletop can be placed in one of two *kanban squares* marked on the floor.[26]

Alternately, instead of sending the empty bin back to the source, the two-card kanban systems[27] can be used where the "empty" card is physically sent back, faxed, or transmitted electronically. The source may be internal, like a machine shop or assembly cell, or external, like a supplier. In both cases, kanban parts must flow directly to the line, or *dock-to-stock*, without inspections (see next section).

Another kanban, suitable for raw materials such as sheet metal and bar stock, reorders material when the stack gets down to the *order point,* usually a mark on the wall.

In all kanban systems, the bin "size" needs to be established to balance the competing needs of minimizing the chance of running out with minimum bin space and inventory carrying costs. Variables include the size of the parts, the space available for the bins, the part cost, and the frequency of delivery. Kanban bin size can be determined by formulas[28] or empirically.[29]

Conventional wisdom discourages kanban usage for expensive parts or low usage parts, which should be resupplied by traditional techniques such as MRP.[30] However, a build-to-order environment may be running without MRP and be driven by demand from the customer. In this case, kanban may be used for all parts. Large or expensive parts can use smaller bin quantities and more frequent deliveries to minimize space and inventory carrying costs.

FIGURE 7–1

Kanban Parts Resupply

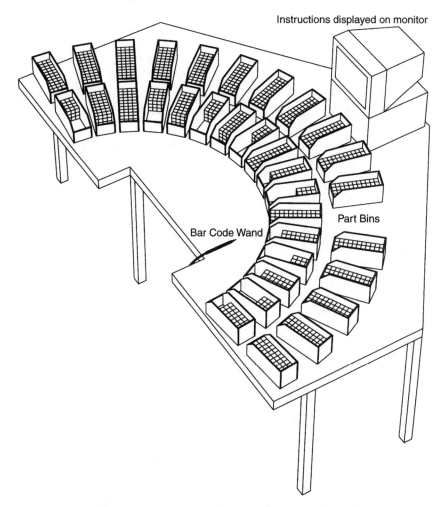

If the kanban supply is unexpectedly depleted by unusual demand, a defective part, or a down machine, *express* or *emergency* kanbans can be generated to quickly remedy the situation.[31]

Yasuhiro Monden, in an updated version of his classic *Toyota Production System*, states, "The kanban system's most remarkable feature [is] its adaptability to sudden demand changes or exigencies [urgencies] of production."[32] This is exactly what is needed for build-to-order environments, which are based on demand, not on planned production schedules.

The beauty of kanban part resupply is that the system ensures an uninterrupted supply of parts *without forecasts or complicated ordering procedures, like MRP procurement cycles.* This is especially important for built-to-order operations, because, by definition, forecasts are vague or unavailable. The number of parts in a bin can be based on estimates of the highest expected usage rate and the longest resupply time. The size of the bins is determined by the bin quantity and size of the parts.

For kanban systems to work, there must be enough room to dispense all parts at the point of use. Too many different parts may make kanban not feasible. This, again, emphasizes the importance of part commonality.

10. Dock-to-Stock Deliveries

As pointed out earlier, agile operations cannot tolerate any major setups. Kitting is a major setup. So, to be truly agile, incoming parts and materials must flow directly to the points of use, instead of being kitted together in some central receiving warehouse.

This may be easier to implement after part standardization, product line rationalization, breadtruck deliveries of all the "jelly-bean" parts, and kanban resupply of appropriate parts. Freeing up floor space by inventory reduction efforts will make room for this. However, JIT environments require much lower raw materials inventory than batch-oriented operations, so there will still be a net reduction in floor space requirements after implementing JIT.

When parts and raw materials flow directly to the point of use, it is called *dock-to-stock* delivery. These deliveries can be either triggered by purchase orders that come from MRP systems or they could be automatic kanban deliveries.

The big paradigm shift required for dock-to-stock deliveries is the elimination of incoming inspections of parts and raw materials. Incoming inspections are impractical for two reasons: time and effort. Just-in-time deliveries, as the name suggests, should be *just in time.* Going through incoming inspections, usually at central receiving stations, would cause too many delays for the fast-moving JIT environment. JIT deliveries may be smaller and occur more often than the traditional large order that is delivered infrequently. Consequently, inspecting many small orders would be very inefficient because of the inspection setup: getting up to speed on quality standards and procedures; setting up and calibrating test and inspection equipment; dealing with problems via MRB (material review boards).

But incoming inspections cannot simply cease without some way of assuring that the incoming parts and raw materials will have adequate quality. If a manufacturer simply dictates new standards for incoming part quality from suppliers, the suppliers may respond by shifting inspection from the manufacturer's receiving to the end of their process. This may screen out bad parts but at great cost in money and agility.

Suppliers, internal and external, need to adopt the TQM philosophy of assuring quality *at the source*. If part manufacturing and raw material processing is sufficiently *in control*, quality will be assured by the process, not by subsequent inspections. Statistical Process Control (SPC) is a proven tool for assuring quality by process controls.[33] Even though SPC is firmly founded on statistical principles, its implementation does not require the proverbial Ph.D. in statistics. Control charts, available from the American Society of Quality Control (ASQC), have the statistics built into the charts so that factory workers can use them by literally filling in the blanks and performing some simple arithmetic computations.

Suppliers that can prove that their processes are in control and, thus, can deliver good parts directly to the line are *certified* by the manufacturer. Similar certifications may also be applicable for raw materials suppliers to allow them to ship metals, plastics, and chemicals directly to the points of use without incoming inspections.

Dock-to-stock deliveries can be an essential part of a JIT program or may be instituted primarily to save cost and improve throughput. *Industry Week's* 1994 "Best Plant" survey of the 25 top-performing candidates indicated that 68 percent of suppliers deliver parts to the point of use in the plant.[34]

11. Soft Tooling

Physical "hard" tooling, such as dies, molds, and tool plates, may be causing setup delays to change them. One approach to eliminate these setups is to eliminate the hard tooling in favor of "soft" tooling, which involves no physical tooling but relies on computer numerically controlled (CNC) machine tools to perform the required operations.

This is especially applicable for low-volume parts where there would be a high proportion of setup to run time. In such situations, there might be less total cost from "hogging" (with a milling machine) a shape out of a standard block, compared to the total cost involved in building and maintaining all the various tooling, their recurring setup costs, and the variety costs (as cited in Chapter 3) of ordering and stocking several unique blanks, such as raw castings.

The blank blocks would be fixtured in some standardized way, for instance, on tooling pins or clamped into a corner (the intersection of three mutually perpendicular planes). This would eliminate locating and clamping setup. All cuts would use the same tool (like an end mill) or tools resident in the machine's tool changer. Similarly, for sheet metal, CNC laser cutters could perform all the functions of shears and punch presses in one machine without setup changes.

A commitment to agile operations may encourage this approach for many parts, since the delays caused by the traditional tooling setup may be enough to inhibit agile manufacturing.

12. Making Automation Flexible

Many plants have "islands of automation" where automated equipment is scattered throughout the plant and isolated from any information network. Programs often reside on floppy disks, magnetic tape, or punched tapes. Loading the programs for every different part is a setup that would have to be eliminated if it was slowing down the line.

Automation equipment could be controlled by a central controller as part of the Computer Integrated Manufacturing paradigm. Automated machines in a pull system could be isolated from central computer control as long as they could quickly, and maybe automatically, change their own programs. Each machine would have all programs stored in its own memory or a file server, which could be dedicated or serve several machines. The program could be changed by the following methods (in order of increasing flexibility):

a. An operator correlates the work order with the desired program and enters the program request manually on a keyboard or mouse-driven menu.

b. An operator enters the work order manually and the central computer finds the appropriate program.

c. An operator uses a bar code "wand" to read the bar code on the part or on the "traveler" paperwork that accompanies the part.

d. A bar code reader automatically reads the bar code of the next part and automatically loads the program. Tektronix in its Wilsonville, Oregon, plant has a flexible circuit board line where a stationary bar-code reader automatically reads the bar on each circuit board as it passes by on the material handling tracks.

e. The program automatically loads from a central computer based on the planned sequence of parts coming down the line.

Options *a*, *c*, and *d* could work for stand-alone machines with their own file servers operating in a pull system. Options *b* and *e* require a central computer to correlate work orders to programs or to correlate the sequence parts with the right programs. Options *c* and *d* could work with isolated or connected machines.

Loading parts on automatic machines may involve a setup that must be eliminated, for instance, positioning parts horizontally with calipers and vertically with blocks. Ideally, all parts in a family should load quickly and consistently, for instance, on tooling pins or some standard fixturing geometry on the part and fixture. This is a result of concurrent engineering where the parts and fixtures are concurrently designed for whole families of parts.

13. CAD/CAM Links

In a true mass customization operation, unique products can be generated by parametric CAD programs that can vary certain dimensions according to individual customer requirements. This was discussed in the context of the overall information flow in Chapter 2 and will be discussed in more detail in Chapter 8.

The product data file, or the electronic "drawing," is then used to generate the CNC machine tool program. This is the "link" between computer-aided design (CAD) and computer aided manufacture (CAM). It may be possible to automatically generate CNC programs from CAD/CAM systems based on customer requirement input.

14. Manual Processing Instructions

As pointed out before, finding drawings or instructions is a setup. Taking any time to study or search through these documents makes the setup even more time consuming.

The flexible answer to this problem is to put the drawings and instructions on computer monitors, as shown in Figure 2–1. The operation is described in Chapter 2 and the installation is described in Chapter 8.

15. Integration of the Information Flow

The last step to achieve manufacturing agility, and probably the most ambitious, would be to integrate the flow of information, as shown in Figure 2–2 and described in the last major section of Chapter 2. This need not require the ultimate computer integrated manufacturing system. The minimum elements are shown in Figure 2–2 for that type of product. Chapter 8 will discuss the information flow starting with customer input.

NOTES

1. *Industry Week,* "The Complete Guide to America's Best Plants" (Cleveland, OH: Penton Publishing, 1995).
2. William A. Wheeler, III, *JIT Client Engagement Results,* (Burlington, MA: Coopers & Lybrand Center for Manufacturing Technology, 1988).
3. Richard E. White, "An Empirical Assessment of JIT in U.S. Manufacturers," *Production & Inventory Management Journal* 34, no. 2 (Second Quarter 1993), pp. 38–42.
4. *Industry Week,* "The Complete Guide to America's Best Plants."

5. Association of Manufacturing Excellence plant tour, Compaq Computer, Houston Texas, February 2–3, 1989.

6. Kiyoshi Suzaki, *The New Manufacturing Challenge; Techniques for Continuous Improvement,* video program.

7. *Industry Week,* "The Complete Guide to America's Best Plants."

8. William H. Davidow and Michael S. Malone, *The Virtual Corporation, Structuring and Revitalizing the Corporation for the 21st Century* (New York: Edward Burlingame Books/HarperBusiness unit of HarperCollins, 1992).

9. Steven L. Goldman, Roger N. Nagel, and Kenneth Preiss, *Agile Competitors and Virtual Organizations, Strategies for Enriching the Customer* (New York: Van Nostrand Reinhold, 1995), chap. 6.

10. Hall, *Zero Inventories.*

11. Shingo, *A Revolution in Manufacturing.*

12. Suzaki, *The New Manufacturing Challenge, Techniques for Continuous Improvement,* chap. 3.

13. Suzaki, *The New Manufacturing Challenge, Techniques for Continuous Improvement,* video program.

14. Richard J. Schonberger, *Just in Time: A Comparison of Japanese and American Manufacturing Techniques* (Norcross, GA: Industrial Engineering & Management Press, 1984), p. 29.

15. Edward J. Hay, *The Just-in-Time Breakthrough* (New York: John Wiley & Sons, 1988), p. 33; and Shigeo Shingo, *A Study of the Toyota Production System from an Industrial Engineering Viewpoint* (Portland, OR: Productivity Press, 1989).

16. Several books on maintenance are published by the American Institute of Plant Engineers, Cincinnati, Ohio.

17. Several books on Total Productive Maintenance are published by Productivity Press of Portland, Oregon, and the Society of Manufacturing Engineers in Dearborn, Michigan.

18. Schonberger, *Just in Time: A Comparison of Japanese and American Manufacturing Techniques.*

19. Hall, *Zero Inventories,* pp. 4, 11.

20. Robert A. Inman and L. D. Brandon, "An Undesirable Effect of JIT," *Production and Inventory Management Journal* 33, no. 1 (1992), pp. 55–58.

21. Daniel J. Jones, "JIT & the EOQ Model: Odd Couples No More!" *Management Accounting* 72, no. 8 (February 1991), pp. 54–57.

22. Richard J. Schonberger, *World Class Manufacturing, The Lessons of Simplicity Applied* (New York: Free Press, 1986), p. 83.

23. Ibid., pp. 229–36.

24. Suzaki, *The New Manufacturing Challenge, Techniques for Continuous Improvement,* chap. 6.

25. Kenichi Sekine, *One Piece Flow, Cell Design for Transforming the Production Process* (Portland, OR: Productivity Press, 1992).

26. Hall, *Zero Inventories,* p. 46.

27. Richard J. Schonberger, *Japanese Manufacturing Techniques, Nine Hidden Lessons in Simplicity* New York: Free Press, 1982), p. 223.

28. Yasuhiro Monden, *Toyota Production System, An Integrated Approach to Just-in-Time,* 2nd ed. (Norcross, GA: Industrial Engineering and Management Press, 1993), chap. 18.

29. In an interview, Charles F. Sawhill, a Lake Oswego, Oregon, JIT consultant who taught JIT at Portland State University, said that when he was implementing JIT at Leupold & Stevens, he always used empirical (trial and error) methods to determine the optimal kanban bin sizes.

30. Schonberger, *Japanese Manufacturing Techniques,* p. 227.

31. Monden, *Toyota Production System, An Integrated Approach to Just-in-Time,* pp. 29–30.

32. Ibid., p. 27.

33. Robert Amsden, Howard Butler, and Davida Amsden, *SPC Simplified* (New York: Quality Resources, 1989).

34. *Industry Week,* "The Complete Guide to America's Best Plants."

PART FOUR

DEVELOPING MASS CUSTOMIZED PRODUCTS

CHAPTER

Product Planning and Order Fulfillment

The earliest actions in product development are crucial to ultimate success and exert significant influence on cost and time to market. Unfortunately, despite the importance of these early steps, far too many product developers almost bypass these early steps by making snap decisions based on whims, limited customer exposure, intracompany politics, competitive precedents, or the excitement of new technology or paradigm shifts. Not making a conscious decision is, nevertheless, a decision to pursue the status quo or blindly accept some "default" choices.

PRODUCT PLANNING

The first step in any product development is to *methodically determine which product to develop.* Companies must realize that this is an important step and deserves significant effort proportional to its ultimate effect.

Charles Nuese's book, *Building the Right Things Right,* describes two goals for any product development: It should be the *right prod-*

uct and it *should be built right.*[1] Before *doing it right,* companies must choose the right product to develop. Classic business failures, like the Ford Edsel, which lost $350 million, were caused by decisions to develop the *wrong product.*

Thus, even before product development teams start listening to the "voice of the customer," it is important to decide which "voices" to listen to, which market segments to compete in.

The very first step in deciding which market segments in which to compete is to *understand the true profitability of existing products* based on total cost accounting. Chapters 4 and 6 pointed out that distorted product costing results in a distorted perception of the profitability of all the company's products. Thus, there is a danger, as pointed out by Cooper and Kaplan, that "the firm might choose to compete in segments that are actually unprofitable."[2] Total cost accounting can reveal which products and market segments are currently the most profitable. It can also assign the real overhead cost allocation to current custom operations, which are traditionally subsidized by standard products. Knowing these results can provide a clear perspective of current profitability that will be quite helpful in mass customization product line planning.

For Mass Customization, the decision about what products to develop must be rationally based on *opportunities and strengths* in engineering, manufacturing, and marketing and distribution. There must be market opportunities to satisfy customers with custom products and the strengths in marketing and distribution to reach customers, efficiently take orders, and quickly deliver products. There must be opportunities and strengths in engineering to apply the principles presented herein to develop customized products and corresponding flexible processes. There also must be opportunities and strengths in manufacturing to quickly and flexibly build custom products in response to customer demand.

If companies are equally strong in all these areas, then a broader range of market opportunities can be addressed. If not, they should strengthen needed areas as soon as possible. Until then, they should focus on market opportunities that capitalize on existing strengths.

In contrast to the development of a discrete product, developing products for Mass Customization focuses on product *families/platforms* or many product families and their *evolution over time.*

To do this, strong multifunctional teams will have to work together *starting at the product planning stage* so that decisions regarding which products to develop are made jointly by all specialties who know their strengths. All these specialties should work together to devise a plan that is workable and then commit to the plan.

Companies need to thoroughly understand customers and how customers use existing products. A section in a *Fortune* magazine article, labeled "To understand your customers, walk in their shoes," cited the example of Weyerhaeuser's employees working *for* the customer for a week.[3]

The same article cited John Deere's policy: "Construction and agricultural equipment manufacturer Deere & Co. sends its engineers into the fields for 10 days or more to watch customers put prototypes to work." Tom Peters, writing in *Liberation Management,* had similar comments: "The multidisciplinary teams return to the field to test each prototype—*and even its operating manual* (Amen!)—under real-world conditions . . . "If a prototype breaks down in the field, the team services it . . . . Very quickly, boundaries between the disciplines start blurring. Today, understanding the use of the product and the needs of the user is as important for the purchasing guys as for the designers."[4]

According to Gemini Consulting's Francis Gouillart, this kind of deep, personalized research can be a better guide to strategy than simply sizing up your competitors or taking routine surveys of your customers. "If you work with one customer at a time, you can invent recipes that escape the commodity trap."[5]

The focus should be on *customers* instead of *competitors.* Again quoting Francis Gouillart: "If you define yourself in relation to your competition, you are commoditizing your product. You are already in a copycat mode." Focus on customers' needs, not on the company programs, competition, or technology.

In product planning, companies need to obtain *early* customer feedback on pivotal aspects of potential products with *multiple* proposals. New computer technologies can help with rendered 3-D drawings and illustrations; laptop displays of 3-D solid models; drawn (nonfunctional) software user-interfaces on monitors; computer simulations; and physical models and mock-ups made with "rapid prototype" techniques that can make models of parts or products in any scale from 3-D CAD input.[6] Remember, *it is much easier and faster to make many iterations at this time than at the proto-type stage.*

Finally, companies should methodically *define* product families to satisfy the "voice of the customer." This results in product speci-fications that the design team will use as design targets and resource prioritization for optimal resource allocation. Techniques for methodically defining products will be discussed in Chapter 10.

Mass Customization offers some powerful marketing opportu-nities. Joe Pine, in his *Harvard Business Review* article about keeping customers forever, concludes that by collaborating with customers, mass customizers develop *learning relationships* with customers:

> In learning relationships, individual customers teach the company more and more about their preferences and needs, giving the com-pany an immense competitive advantage. The more customers teach the company, the better it becomes at providing exactly what they want—exactly how they want it—and the more difficult it will be for a competitor to entice them away."[7]

ORDER FULFILLMENT

The Reactive Process

A key element in the mass customization process is the *dialog* between the customer and the company. In the reactive customiza-tion attempts, the customer expresses preferences, which triggers an inquiry, usually through the salesperson. The customer will say something like this: "This is what I want. When can I get it? How much will it cost?" In the reactive mode, the salesperson can only answer: "I don't know. I'll check with the plant and get back to you on that." Then begins several rounds of communication between the customer and the plant going through the salesperson.

Each question to the plant will begin an investigation to find out if the customization can be done, how long it will take, and how much it will cost. Usually, there is not single person or database that can answer the questions, so many people may become involved, with the usual delays associated with such inquiry "streams."

If the customer's first wishes cannot be fulfilled, then the plant informs the salesperson, who tells the customer: "No we can't do that, but how about this?" After some discussion, the customer and salesperson converge on a plan B, and this request is sent to the plant. This iterative process may happen several more times, sometimes taking weeks or months. When there is a consensus of everyone involved at the plant, a quote is generated for price and delivery.

The way these "custom" orders are filled can generate many other problems in the plant. Often, each custom version is treated like a unique "product" and given a unique product number with a unique bill of materials. The result is a proliferation of "products" and a paperwork explosion to process and build different versions of the same product. One of the author's clients has 1,700 bills of materials for one product, which it recognized as an excessive overhead burden.

The BOM situation can be simplified with *modular* bills of materials, in which every subassembly or option has its own BOM. The product would cite each subassembly needed and specify each BOM needed. Thus, a personal computer might have a BOM that consisted only of 10 other BOMs: one for the motherboard, one for each daughterboard, and so forth. However, modular BOMs would only be able to solve all the above problems for fairly simple products.

The Mass Customization Process

In the mass customization mode, the above dialog, including the price and delivery quoting, occurs in a matter of minutes, not weeks. The products and processes have been concurrently designed for broad ranges of customizations. Information about what is possible is well defined and quickly available to the salesperson, facilitator, integrator, or actual customer. The cost and delivery can be determined quickly by standard algorithms.

This capability is a key attribute to Mass Customization and Build-to-Order, since the reactive process is too slow and expensive. For simple products with limited ranges of options or customizations, it might be possible to present the necessary information on a printed specification sheet or computer spreadsheet or database.

However, the information must be complete enough to confirm the configuration and quote price and delivery on the spot without the lengthy "back and forth" dialogs as discussed above.

The available features and options would be presented. However, certain "rules" may have to be taken into account because certain options may be incompatible with other options. For instance, specifying a large automobile engine may require suitably large power-train elements such as the transmission and differential. A computer loaded with options may require a larger power supply. A computer with a more powerful microprocessor may require a larger fan.

Most mass customized products will have too many possible configurations and too many rules to keep track of on paper. The relationships between configurations and rules may be too complicated to easily set up on a spreadsheet and database.

Configurators

Fortunately, recent developments in information systems can help. Configuration software, called "configurators," has been developed to keep track of all the options and features and all the rules that apply to their use. In essence, configurators are *expert systems* that "know" all the things that had to be determined in the lengthy back and forth scenario used in the reactive process described above. The *knowledge* of the company "experts" is captured in the software and is readily available through a user-friendly interface. However, unlike many expert systems, configurators can be quickly updated, even over modems to units in the field.

All the features and options, and their prices, are embedded in the system. Also contained in the configurator are all the rules that govern dependencies, conflicts, constraints, and resources. The configuration "engine" can do the calculations to resolve complex relationships quickly. The customer is able to request multiple "what if" scenarios.

As mentioned in Chapter 1, window manufacturer Andersen Corporation developed its own configurator, the Window of Knowledge™, to let distributors work with customers to design their windows on a computer and interactively view prospective designs immediately.

There are four types of configurators: features and options, rules-based, knowledge-based, and constraints and resources. The May 1994 edition of the *AMR Report* describes each type, cites industry applications, discusses strengths and weaknesses, and lists vendors of each type.[8] Figure 8–1 presents a summary table that shows the type of configuration, the purpose of the configuration, and examples of which type of configurators are applicable.

Configurators are available from the following sources: Antalys of Golden, Colorado;[9] Calico Technology of San Jose, California;[10] Concentra of Burlington, Massachusetts;[11] CWC of Mankato, Minnesota;[12] Logia of Barrington, Illinois;[13] and Trilogy Development Group in Austin Texas.[14]

Some advanced configurators can display solid models and advanced graphics that show the customer what the contemplated product will actually look like. For example, for an automobile, the configurator could show a side view of the automobile in the color of choice and with the wheels selected. It could also show the inte-

FIGURE 8–1

Value Chain of Configuration

Type of Configuration	Example	Purpose of Configuration
Marketing configuration	Features and Options	Checks orders Constrains illegal combinations of features and options
Engineering configuration	Rules	Above plus physical simulation for assembly level from components Can drive manufacturing
Physical placement configuration	Rules Knowledge	Above plus checks engineering conditions and places components (builds assembly instructions)
Upgrade/add-on configuration	Knowledge	Above plus aftermarket addition to installed base of configurations Modifies and computes changes to system
Enterprise configuration	Knowledge Resources and constraints	Above plus multisystem configuration where components are themselves systems configured for communications compatibility
Solution configuration	Resources and constraints	Above plus abstracts solutions from customer requirements
Multivendor configuration	Resources and constraints	Above plus vendors work together to network with a database that creates multivendor configurations that optimize price or performance

Source: "Configurators Provide a Tool for Cycle Time Reduction." *AMR Report*, May 1994, p. 4.

rior view with the selected steering wheel and all the dashboard options, exactly like the order car will appear. These images, along with pricing, can be printed out on a color printer and given to the customer—in essence, a custom brochure for a custom product. For very new products, this visualization capability can help customers understand and comprehend new concepts and approaches. This can help get early feedback from customers.

THE INFORMATION FLOW

Figure 2–2 shows the flow of information through a mass customization operation. Note that, in contrast to the reactive process discussed above, the dialog between customer and the laptop configuration software is the *only* back and forth dialog in the whole system. The remainder of the information flow is one way and, thus, can be done quickly and cost-effectively.

The model shown in Figure 2–2, utilizes a configurator running on a laptop computer. Typically, configurators are used by salespeople. Alternatively, customers may use the configurator directly if the user interface is user friendly, and if the product configuration process is not too complex. Examples of this are Hallmark's Touch-Screen Greetings and MusicWriter, mentioned in Chapter 1.

At the Ross/Flex unit of Ross Operating Valve, employees, called integrators, receive customer orders, often over the telephone. The integrator works with the customer to "design" the custom valve in parametric CAD (see below) with standard designs, modules, and parts. In this case the CAD system serves as configurator and order entry database. Sometime down the road, Ross plans to give customers modem access to its CAD system so they can actually design their own values, which Ross would then manufacturer.[15]

The "order entry database" function, shown in Figure 2–2, could be performed by a configurator, such as Trilogy's SalesBuilder. It could be embedded within the CAD system, as done by Ross/Flex. This function could be performed by special-purpose proprietary databases or aided by product information management (PIM) or product data management (PDM) systems. EDS Unigraphics' PDM system, Information Manager, is integrated with its CAD system. Hewlett-Packard offers a PDM system called WorkManager. AutoCAD offers a technical documentation and work flow management system called WorkCenter.[16]

Parametric CAD

Parametric computer-aided design (CAD) is a powerful tool for Mass Customization that can make "drawings" easy to customize. To replace fixed dimensions, parametric CAD allows dimensions to "float" as *parameters*. The actual dimensions of a part can then be inserted, based on a customer's needs, to customize the drawing by changing the shape of the part and update dimension numbers. Customizing the part can, in turn, customize the assembly, since assembly drawings are based on part drawings.

These parametric CAD capabilities can be provided by leading software applications, such as Parametric Technology Corporation's Pro/ENGINEER[17] and Synthesis,[18] which run with AutoCAD,[19] to provide parametric capabilities. Synthesis consists of a spreadsheet, called a "SpecSheet," that links cells to dimensions in AutoCAD drawings.[20] These cells can be entered or computed from spreadsheet formulas, which could be governed by rules, such as A cannot be greater than B.

Parametric drawing customization can also automatically update analysis, such as stress analysis using finite element analysis, if the finite element "mesh" is set up properly. Parametric Technology's Pro/MECHANICA software enables engineers to quickly analyze structural behavior as well as motion, vibrations, and thermal behavior.[21]

Parametric dimensions can be entered manually or imported from databases, spreadsheets, or other applications. Intergraph's Windows-based Solid Edge[22] software uses OLE Automation to link engineering equations in a spreadsheet, for instance, with dimensions or parameters of designs created in Solid Edge. Parametric dimensions can be imported directly from configurators. One of Trilogy's modules is the "CAD Pack," which integrates the SalesBuilder configurator with commercial CAD systems.[23]

CAD/CAM

Linking CAD and CAM (computer-aided manufacture) is a key step in the mass customization information flow. Fortunately, much progress has been made developing proprietary in-house systems and off-the-shelf software solutions.

Ross/Flex has developed proprietary CAD software[24] that the integrator uses to develop tool-path programs for the CNC machine tools and digitally transfer the custom programs to manufacturing. After the new program is downloaded, the CNC equipment machines the custom valve bodies and other parts. There are no paper drawings, manufacturing engineers, machinists, or inspectors.[25]

The major off-the-shelf CAD applications either have their own CAD/CAM links, like Parametric Technology, or have many third-party "add-ins," such as for AutoCAD. Parametric Technology's Pro/MANUFACTURE application can generate tool paths for CNC machine tools.

A major supplier of CAD/CAM software is Camax Manufacturing Technologies,[26] which offers 30 modules that run under the Windows NT operating system. Bridgeport Machines of Shrewsbury, Massachusetts, has developed several CAD/CAM programs. EZ-Surf, used for 3-D milling operations, can be generated from DXF[27] files imported from CAD systems. EZ-Mill, used for up to 3-axis milling operations, imports geometry from CAD via DXF or the IGES[28] file transfer format.[29]

Some inexpensive CAD/CAM software is available from Surfware Inc. in San Fernando, California, which offers the SurfCAM two- and three-axis surface machining systems that provide basic machining, milling, EDM, and flame cutting. The "Plus" version has parametric design capabilities and can generate swept surfaces. The SurfCAM 3-Axis software can automatically create optimized tool paths based on user-defined tolerances. MasterCAM, from CNC Software Inc. in Tolland, Connecticut., provides a low-cost package for milling, drilling, and EDM that runs on Intel-based computers. The CAD/CAM software supports up to five-axes; CAD data can be imported via DXF and IGES or created in MasterCAM.[30] New file transfer opportunities for CAD/CAM include Microsoft's OLE (Object Linking and Embedding)[31] and STEP.[32]

CAD/CAM software for specific processes is available. Hewlett-Packard offers Sheet Metal Advisor and MetalSoft offers FabriWin, a Windows-based product, for "unfolding" 3-D sheet metal drawings into two-dimensional shapes that can be used to program sheet metal CNC equipment such as punch presses and laser cutters. Parametric Technologies offers the Pro/WELDING module for its Pro/ENGINEER product.[33]

Manual Assembly Instructions

Finding assembly instructions or a drawing is a setup, which would inhibit the flexible manufacturing of mass customized products. To eliminate that setup, manual assembly instructions can be displayed on a computer monitor as shown in Figure 2–1 and described in Chapter 2.

Displays for manual assembly instructions can be generated from two-dimensional CAD drawings, 3-D CAD solid models, drawn illustrations, or digital photographs that can be touched up to emphasize certain points. At the very minimum, the monitor can display text instructions that could be exported from appropriate documents in word processing or database applications. Instructions can be made available in multiple languages for multilingual workforces or to ease the transition when pilot production is transferred to the plant in another country.

If graphical representations are important, the monitors can show selected "views" from CAD drawings. They can be displayed on CAD "viewer" programs, like Autodesk View, which sell for a tenth of the cost of AutoCAD itself. Current "multimedia" tools could even animate important processing sequences, if needed.

The view would be advanced to the next instruction when the worker presses a "next" or "page down" button on an input device. The input device could be a foot pedal to keep hands free for assembly work. Keeping track of the timing of these steps can provide good statistical data for subsequent task analysis.

Instructions related to printed circuit boards can use the CAD view of the board in the appropriate level of assembly. Components being inserted could be highlighted in yellow on the color monitor.

Documentation

On-line instructions, similar to the manual assembly instructions, direct documentation workers to bundle specific documentation with the product. There are two types of documentation. Standard modular documentation is preprinted and available for the most frequent needs. Different versions of standard documentation would be preprinted to accommodate different languages, countries, regulatory compliance agencies, and various product options.

Custom documentation is printed on a nearby laser printer and then bundled with the standard documentation. The printing starts well ahead of the arrival of the product, so that printing is completed just in time to be bundled with the product.

Packaging and Shipping

The product and documentation bundle then go to Packaging where they are packaged along with the appropriate power cord and any other accessories. On-line instructions are again displayed on monitors. Reading the product bar code calls up shipping information, which is then printed on a label printer and affixed to the package. The labeled package is then picked up by local courier or next-day air service.

In smaller operations, documentation, packaging, and shipping could be performed at the same area using one computer monitor for on-line instructions.

NOTES

1. Charles J. Nuese, *Building the Right Things Right, A New Model for Product and Technology Development* (New York: Quality Resources, distributed by AMACOM book, American Management Association, 1995).
2. Robin Cooper and Robert Kaplan, "How Cost Accounting Distorts Product Costs," *Management Accounting,* April 1988.
3. Rahul Jacob, "Why Some Customers Are More Equal Than Others," *Fortune* 130, no. 6 (September 19, 1994), pp. 215–24.
4. Tom Peters, Alfred A. Knopf, *Liberation Management,* (New York: 1992), pp. 124, 728.
5. Jacob, "Why Some Customers Are More Equal Than Others," p. 222.
6. For more information on rapid prototyping, see the book, *Stereolithography and Other RP&M Technologies,* by Paul F. Jacobs (Dearborn, MI: Society of Manufacturing Engineers, 1995) or the videos "Rapid Tooling, Rapid Parts" (1994) and "Rapid Prototyping for DFM" (1991) also available from SME. Equipment supplier 3D

Systems, of Valencia, CA, manufacturers the Stereolithography Apparatus (SLA) product.

7. B. Joseph Pine, II, Don Peppers, and Martha Rogers, "Do You Want to Keep Your Customers Forever," *Harvard Business Review,* March–April 1995, p. 103.

8. "Configurators Provide a Tool for Cycle Time Reduction," *AMR Report,* May, 1994, pp. 1–12.

9. Antalys, 1697 Cole Blvd., Golden, CO 80401; (303) 274-3000.

10. Calico Technology, 4 North Second Street, San Jose, CA 95113; (408) 975-7400.

11. Concentra, 21 North Avenue, Burlington, MA 01803; (617) 868-2800.

12. CWC, 1983 Premier Drive, Mankato, MN 56002; (507) 388-5000.

13. Logia, 290 Deer Trail Court, Barrington, IL 60010; (847) 382-0680.

14. Trilogy Development Group, 6034 West Courtyard Drive, Suite 130, Austin, TX 78730; (512) 794-5900.

15. "Creating a 21st Century Business," *Industry Week,* April 19, 1993, p. 38.

16. Sidney Hill, "Manufacturing Systems Software Top 50—CAD/CAM," *Manufacturing Systems* 13, no. 7 (July 1995), pp. 84–99.

17. Parametric Technology Corporation, 128 Technology Drive, Waltham, MA 02154; (617) 894-7111.

18. The Synthesis Company, 2120 Ellis St., Bellingham, WA 98225; (206) 671-0417.

19. Autodesk, Inc., 111 McInnis Parkway, San Rafael, CA 94903; (800) 964-6432.

20. Chris Cummings, "Inexpensive Knowledge Base Makes Drawings Fast," *Machine Design* 67, no. 10 (May 25, 1995), p. 106.

21. Dan Deitz, "Customer-Driven Product Delivery," *Machine Design* 117, no. 12 (December 1995), p. 74.

22. Intergraph Corporation, Huntsville, AL, (800) 345-4856.

23. Trilogy Development Group, 6034 West Courtyard Drive, Suite 130, Austin, TX 78730; (512) 794-5900.

24. Mary Brandel, "One Pneumatic Valve to Go," *Computerworld,* November 22, 1993, p. 95.

25. "Creating a 21st Century Business," p. 38.

26. "CAD/CAM Industry Report 1995; Editors' Choice Awards for 1995," *Machine Design* 67, no. 10 (May 25, 1995), pp. 82–96.

27. DXF is a standard CAD file transfer format, developed for AutoCAD by Autodesk of San Rafael, CA.

28. IGES (Intermediate Graphic Exchange Standard) is a universal file transfer format for CAD drawings.

29. Michael Puttre, "CAD/CAM on a Budget," *Mechanical Engineering* 116, no. 12 (December 1994), pp. 66–67.

30. Ibid.

31. Dan Deitz, "CAD/CAM Vendors Adopt OLE Standard," *Mechanical Engineering* 117, no. 6 (June 1995), p. 24.

32. Davie Mattei, "CAD/CAM/CAE Vendors Get in STEP," *Computer-Aided Engineering* 14, no. 10 (October 1995), pp. 88–90.

33. Dan Deitz, "PTC Adds Data-Transfer and Welding Modules," *Mechanical Engineering* 117, no. 11 (November 1995), p. 24.

CHAPTER

Agile Product Development for Mass Customization

The phrase *agile product development* can be interpreted in two ways, both of which are correct and applicable to a wide range of products and industries:

1. An *agile product development process* that can rapidly introduce a steady succession of incremental product improvements—which can be called "new" products—that are really planned "variations on a theme," based on common parts and modular product architecture. This capability results in *ultrafast* time to market, much faster than possible with independent products that do not benefit from product-family synergies in design and manufacture.

2. *Development of agile products* that can be manufactured in the following agile environments: Agile/Flexible/Continuous-Flow Manufacturing, Just-in-Time, Build-to-Order, and Mass Customization.

Mass Customization requires a strong product development methodology infrastructure. Designing products that can be customized at mass production efficiency is one of the most challenging and rewarding product development endeavors. Therefore, companies embarking on Mass Customization must establish the most effective product development methodologies possible.

ADVANCED PARADIGMS FOR PRODUCT DEVELOPMENT

Leading-edge product development comes from a *whole company synergy.* Products must be developed by *multifunctional* teams that use *concurrent engineering* to concurrently design *families* of products and *flexible* processes. This is even more important for Mass Customization because of the demands that customization places on factory processes.

But leading-edge product development is more than having *engineers* concurrently designing products and processes. Multifunctional product development teams must include Marketing to ensure that the product will respond to the "voice of the customer." Purchasing must move away from "low-bidder" thinking and nurture *vendor/partner relationships* so that vendors will be willing to help design the product. This is an extremely valuable resource that will be available *only* if the vendor is confident there will be some return from this investment.

Finance should be a key part of the whole company synergy by providing relevant cost information that quantifies the *total cost* of products and by encouraging decision making based on *total cost.* Further, more relevant cost accounting can be the basis for better compensation systems.

Human Resources' role is to use relevant cost measures to structure compensation and reward systems to reward teamwork and "big picture" goals. Human Resources has several other important roles in leading-edge product development: hiring and developing strong team leaders and team players; training in advanced product development methodologies; encouraging job rotation; and retaining talent, information, and complete teams during downturns.

Most important, management needs to create a culture that supports this whole company synergy. Management must look on product development as an *investment* that can provide the *return* generated by a potent competitive advantage. This investment includes adequate resource availability to ensure that *multifunctional teams are complete and active early.*

Specifically, management must encourage thorough up-front work and ensure resource availability so that product development teams can commence with a complete complement of multifunctional specialities. Management needs to *empower* project team leaders, who, in turn, empower their teams rather than relying on *inspecting* the design process with design reviews.

Leading-edge product development does not come from any single "tool" or program. Success does not come from *adopting* tools or programs but from *implementing* new tools and programs in *all* corporate endeavors to achieve this *whole company synergy.*

Good product development practices can significantly reduce product development time. *Industry Week's* "Best Plant" 1994 survey of the 25 top-performing candidates indicated that 76 percent of companies surveyed had significantly reduced the product development cycle. The median reduction in the product development cycle was 45 percent.

PRODUCT DEVELOPMENT AS AN INVESTMENT

The most effective product development comes from the perspective of viewing product development as an *investment.* As with any investment, money invested in product development should pay back expected returns. Product development, done properly, can significantly impact total cost, marketability, and, thus, profits. The better the product development effort (the investment), the better will be the results (the return): time to market, total cost, quality, and customer satisfaction.

For Mass Customization, it is imperative that product development be viewed as an investment. The whole product line will have to be designed consistently around common modules and processes. It may be unrealistic to expect a single product development project, with the usual funding constraints and deadlines, to design a set of modules to be used by many products in the product line.

Therefore, companies should invest in the development of modules to be used by many subsequent product developments. A more synergistic approach would be to commission a mass customization project to simultaneously develop the entire product line with the necessary modules and flexible processing.

CONCURRENT ENGINEERING

Product development teams will be successful *to the degree* that they practice Concurrent Engineering principles. Concurrent Engineering means much more than sending a manufacturing engineer to the design release review, which, of course, is too late to influence the design.

Multifunctional design teams are the essence of Concurrent Engineering. The most successful product development teams are the ones with the most *complete* teams that have *all specialties present at the beginning of the project.* Much of the success of Japanese product development can be attributed to this, as illustrated by a quote from the $5 million MIT study that compared Japanese "lean" manufacturers to old paradigm "mass production" companies:

> In the best Japanese "lean" projects, the numbers of people involved are highest at the very outset. All the relevant specialties are present, and the [project leader's] job is to force the group to confront all the difficult trade-offs they'll have to make to agree on the project.
>
> By contrast, in many mass-produced design exercises, the number of people involved is very small at the outset but grows to a peak very close to the time of launch, as hundreds or even thousands of extra bodies are brought in to resolve problems that should have been cleared up in the beginning.[1]

Leading-edge product development derives much of its effectiveness from strong team leadership to maximize the effectiveness of multifunctional design teams. Another MIT study, *Made in America, Regaining the Productive Edge,* gave additional insight into Japanese product development project management:

> In the Japanese auto companies, each new product is assigned a program manager who acts as the product's champion, carries great authority with the firm, and along with his staff, stays with the product from conception until well past the production launch.[2]

One of the most important early tasks of the product development team leader is to make sure all the issues are raised and resolved. It is so much quicker and less expensive to resolve issues earlier rather than later on, even though the act of resolving these issues earlier may take some effort, as pointed out by the same reference:

A key task of the manager is to make sure that all disagreements are aired and resolved at the outset. Achieving consensus takes a great deal of effort, but by skillful management at this point it is possible to gain the full commitment of all members of the program team so that subsequent progress is very rapid.

The disagreements or issues include, but are not limited to, technical feasibility. Other key issues are identifying, and then eliminating early, the potential problems in product development, introduction into the factory, production, distribution, use, and service. Issues also involve minimizing risk and the effects of changing markets, customers, competitors, and regulations.

MULTIFUNCTIONAL DESIGN TEAMS

Design teams should consist of design engineering, manufacturing engineers, service representatives, marketing managers, customers, dealers, finance representatives, industrial designers, quality and testing personnel, purchasing representatives, vendors, regulation compliance experts, factory workers, specialized talent, and representatives from other projects. First, this helps to ensure that all the design considerations will be covered. Second, such diversity can lead to a better design because of contributions from many perspectives. This synergy results in a better design than could result from a homogeneous team consisting only of design engineers or scientists.

It is very important that all team members are present and active early so that they will make meaningful contributions to the design team. Team members need not all be full time, but they should not be so preoccupied with other tasks that they cannot make meaningful contributions. All team members should actively participate in the product development, not waiting for "designers" to design something and then reacting to their designs. Some key team members are discussed below.

Manufacturing, Service, and Vendors

Their input is crucial to ensure that the product development team designs manufacturability and serviceability into the product. Manufacturing engineers and vendors have the responsibility of making sure products are being designed for stable processes that are already in use or for new processes that will be concurrently designed as the product is designed. Manufacturing and service representatives must not wait until there are drawings to mark up. Their role is to constantly influence the design to ensure manufacturability and serviceability. Manufacturing representatives must be isolated from the daily "emergencies" that occur in manufacturing, since "urgent" matters usually take precedence over "important" matters. The author has seen problems when manufacturing engineers view team participation as a career opportunity to migrate into Engineering, designing one portion of the product very well for manufacturability, while the remainder of the product has manufacturability ignored.

Vendors and Purchasing

Vendors will participate in the design process only if they are reasonably sure those efforts will bring in some revenue downstream. Thus, it is Purchasing's role to narrow down the vendor base and qualify selected vendor/partners who, as *The Machine That Changed the World* reported in Japan, "are not selected on the basis of bids, but on the basis of *past relationships and a proven record of performance.*" If vendor/partner relationships cannot be established, vendors' representatives could be hired as consultants to help the design team design for their processes.

Industry Week's "Best Plant" 1994 survey of the 25 top-performing candidates found that 92 percent emphasize early supplier involvement in product development.[3]

Marketing

Marketing is the link to the customer and must help define the product so that it listens to the "voice of the customer." This is even more important for Mass Customization than it is for Mass Production. Product definition will be introduced later in this chapter and discussed in depth in the next chapter.

Customers

It is becoming more common to have customers actually participate on product development teams. When Boeing developed the

777, it invited representatives of its customers, the airlines, to help design the product. At first Boeing engineers were apprehensive, but they soon learned the value of hearing detailed customer input in the design stage.[4] For instance, the Boeing design team learned that its customers were having a hard time reading information displays on instruments mounted on the walls in a room below the floor of the airplanes. The body of the person trying to read the instruments was always blocking the only light, which was mounted on the ceiling. Once alerted by the customers, the engineers could easily solve the problem with a light bulb in each corner of the room. An added value to involving customers in the design process is that it bonds them to the product and tends to make them loyal customers.

Industry Week's "Best Plant" 1994 survey of the 25 top-performing candidates indicated that 96 percent of companies surveyed had customers participate in product development efforts.[5]

Industrial Designers

These creative people need to be part of the design team so that product styling is not "thrown over the wall" to Engineering, which must try to fit everything into a pretty enclosure. It is an encouraging trend that the leading industrial design firms are evolving away from a styling emphasis to include engineering, manufacturability, and usability.[6]

Quality and Test

The need for diagnostic testing is dependent on the quality culture of the company. If quality is *designed into* the product and then *built in* by processes that are in control, then the "fallout" will be so low that diagnostic tests may not be needed. At IBM's Lexington, Kentucky, plant, products that were expected to have higher than a 98.5 percent first-pass-accept rate could avoid diagnostic test development and the expensive Automatic Test Equipment (ATE) "bed-of-nails" testers. Above this threshold, it was more cost effective to discard defective printed circuit boards than to pay for the testers and test development. ATE testers can cost up to $1.5 million. For some printed circuit boards, test development can exceed the cost and the calendar time of product development!

Finance

Finance representatives can help decision making by providing relevant cost data, which does not automatically come from most accounting systems. Implementing Activity-Based Cost Management, as discussed in Chapter 6, can provide data based on *total cost* considerations, which will lead to much more rational decision making, for example, for trade-off analysis of quality/diagnostics, for make/buy decisions, for itemizing cost of quality, and for quantifying overhead cost savings resulting from standardization, commonality, and modularity.

Regulatory Compliance

Every design team needs representatives who can ensure that all applicable regulations are satisfied by the *initial* product design, not by costly and time-consuming rework. Future regulations must also be considered, since regulations can change faster than most manufacturers can respond with another product development cycle. Some companies have legislative or environmental lawyers on the design teams to anticipate future regulations. Efficiently producing regional product variations, for instance, for every country, is one promising application of Mass Customization. This requires that the design team incorporate every country's regulations into the design process.

Factory Workers

Factory Workers can be a valuable source of input, either from surveys or actual participation on the design team. Factory workers usually have no feedback channel for their vast amount of information on past manufacturability issues. Factory-worker participation in the design process may have the added benefit of improving labor relations and making the new product more easily accepted as it is launched into manufacturing.

Specialized Talent

Design teams may need help from specialized talent for automation, simulation, heat flow analysis, solid modeling, rapid prototyping, design of experiments, "robust" tolerancing, lab testing, safety, product liability, patent law, and so forth.

Other Projects

Coordinating multiple product development projects is important for Mass Customization because it is necessary to use common parts, modules, tooling, and processes. Coordinating multiple development projects within the same mass customization family is even more important.

THE TEAM LEADER

Early formation of a complete multifunctional team sets the stage for advanced product development. Success will depend on how well the team is led. The team leader's responsibility is to ensure that the team benefits from the knowledge and experience of the team members. As pointed out earlier, in Japanese development projects, the team leader makes sure all issues are raised and resolved early so that *subsequent progress is very rapid.*

Managing multifunctional teams will require strong team leadership, with a leader who understands the advanced product development methodologies summarized above and has the support of management to do the thorough up-front work that will guarantee success downstream.

The team leader needs to focus the team on a methodical product definition, a balance of design considerations (rather than the common temptation to design primarily for functionality), concept simplification, architecture optimization, and strategies for modularity and customizability.

Thus, the team leader must have proven abilities to lead the team and inspire team members to develop products in ways that may be different, unfamiliar, and possibly uncomfortable: working together early, resolving issues early, optimizing architecture before designing parts, focusing on total cost and true time to market.

The team leader also needs to have a balance of technical, marketing, and managerial proficiency. The team leader must have the respect of management and the ability to successfully secure the resources, tools, and empowerment necessary for success.

The trend in product development team leader selection is evolving from seniority to a new breed of experienced leaders that are savvy in advanced product development methodologies and have a balanced comprehension of technical *and* marketing issues.

ORGANIZATIONAL STRUCTURES

Organizational structures have evolved from the old functional model where Marketing threw a requirements document "over the wall" to Engineering, which designed the product and then threw the drawings over the wall to the Manufacturing Department, which in turn threw products over the wall to Distribution, Service, and eventually to the customer.

To break down the walls, multifunctional teams need to be formed with representatives from the various functional departments. Initially, this was accomplished by the "matrix" structure where engineers in the Engineering Department worked on various product development teams.

As the organizational evolution continued, team members were borrowed for a product development project, temporarily reporting to the team leader, but still administered by the functional departments. The latest step in this evolution is for the team members to actually be transferred to and from a succession of product development teams.[7] The traditional functional organizations may evolve into "personnel agencies," whose main functions are to hire, train, and maintain a reservoir of talent for product development teams. Some companies, such as Apple Computer, even have computer databases that correlate expertise, skill levels and availability.

As functional organizations decrease in importance or even disappear, the former functional managers may evolve into team leaders. This is becoming the trend at Ford Motor Company.

EMPOWERMENT

Advanced manufacturing environments have successfully evolved from the old paradigm of assuring quality by *inspections* to the new paradigm of *process controls* that minimize the need for inspections. A parallel trend is occurring in product development, which is evolving away from the "inspection" paradigm, which manifests as design reviews. Design reviews are periodic inspections of the design process that often cause calendar delays as well as consume many hours of work to prepare design review presentations.

The alternative to inspections in product development is *empowerment,* in which senior management *empowers* the project leader to lead the design team. After conveying expectations on product performance, product cost, quality, and development time and cost, management then empowers the project team leader to accomplish those goals. The team leader may, in turn, empower subteam leaders, who may empower team members.

The deadlines for the reviews and other milestones have traditionally been set by management, usually as part of a very early proposal, estimating or planning stage. Granted, product introduction dates are often determined by trade show introductions or seasonal constraints such as summer vacation or Christmas, and this may create a fixed deadline for the end of product development. But the empowerment approach encourages the *team* to set intermediate milestones based on the team's ability to meet all the expectations. This approach is superior to having intermediate deadlines imposed by management, because the team will be able to apportion the workload to the various phases that correspond to the importance of those tasks and the team's abilities to complete the tasks. Advanced product development places more importance on thorough up-front work to methodically define the product, raise and resolve issues, simplify the concept, and optimize the architecture. Further, the team will probably respect the intermediate milestones if they have set them themselves.

Development of the 1994 Ford Mustang is a good example of empowerment: The demands on product development were challenging: a three-year development time, 25 percent less than any new car program in Ford's recent history; and a budget of $700 million, 30 percent less than typical. The project team leader, William W. Boddie, negotiated a "contract" with Ford's CEO, Harold "Red" Poling, specifying performance, quality, cost, and development time expectations. Mr. Boddie could spend the $700 million as he saw fit! Instead of the usual lengthy reviews accompanied with mountains of paperwork, there was a single five-minute "review" that included a videotape and a five-page report presented to the CEO. After the go-ahead was given, the CEO told the team leader not to come back unless there was a problem. As it turned out, that was not necessary and, thus, no more reviews were scheduled. Management made no attempt to influence the design. The team determined the intermediate milestones. Personnel were transferred from functional organizations and reported to the team leader exclusively. A high-level manufacturing manager was on the team to coordinate the maximum utilization of existing tooling and to tell the designers how far they could go and still use existing tooling. The 400 people on the team were "co-located" in a refurbished furniture warehouse. The team had senior management "sponsors" who worked with team counterparts (for example, in Purchasing) to quickly overcome bureaucratic obstacles and resolve issues. The development project met all its goals and even finished one month early.[8]

DEVELOPMENT PHASES

For advanced product development, a minimum of the following phases are recommended. Each phase emphasizes a clear focus with important deliverables. The first two phases represent the all-important thorough up-front work that will ensure that subsequent progress will be rapid and that all design goals will be accomplished right the first time. Resolution of issues should start early and be continuously emphasized, especially in the early phases when issues are easier to resolve.

Some "phase/gate" methodologies recommend "breadboard" and "prototype" phases without really having a "design" phase. This places too much emphasis on building breadboards and prototypes instead of on thorough product design. Similarly, rapid production ramp-up should be emphasized instead of pilot activities. Introducing new products into a flexible manufacturing environment should be easier because the "new" products may really be "variations of a theme" if the products were designed around common parts, modules and processes.

Finally, the lessons learned from every product development should be captured, documented, and applied to all future product developments.

Phase	Deliverables
1. **Product definition**	Product specifications and resource prioritization
2. **Architecture**	Simplified concept and optimized architecture including modularity and customization strategies
3. **Design**	Product/process design so thorough that the need for prototype testing and pilot production is minimized or eliminated
4. **Ramp-up**	Smooth introduction into production with rapid volume ramp-up
5. **Follow-up**	Postmortem to capture lessons learned that can be applied to future projects

PRODUCT DEFINITION

The very first step of the design team is to *define* the product so that it satisfies the "voice of the customer." Good product definition is important enough for product development, in general, but is even more important for mass customizing products. Noncustomized products are defined so that a single product will satisfy "enough" customers to be competitive. Mass customized products must be defined so that a planned range of variations will be able to satisfy many individual customers, or at least niche markets. The next chapter will describe how to generate product definitions for Mass Customization.

Given the logical importance of defining the product well before launching into development, it is surprising how many product development projects leap right into design with sketchy product definitions, often quickly dispatched by people who *believe* they know what customers want. Sometimes the product definition is further distorted by product designers who believe the customer wants what *they* would want or think that customers automatically want all the latest exciting technology for its own sake.

After the product has been well defined, the design team should then list all the applicable design considerations.

DESIGN CONSIDERATIONS

The point of using multifunctional design teams is to design the product for a complete balance of design considerations, not just product functionality, as might be the temptation with a "team" of only design engineers. Despite a common misconception in engineering circles, very few products can compete on functionality alone. This is especially true for Mass Customization where the design and manufacture of the customization must be considered as a primary design consideration.

The following provides a list of design considerations that *all* need to be considered by product development teams:

Traditional

    Function

    Cost

Marketing

    Customers' needs

    Customization

    Time to market

    Breadth of product line

    Expansion/upgrading

    Future designs

    Competition

Factory

    Ease of fabrication and assembly

    Ability to customize products in the plant

    Quality and reliability

    Ease of service and repair

    Shipping/delivery

Social

    Human factors and usability

    Appearance/style

    Safety

Environmental

    Product pollution

    Processing pollution

    Ease of recycling product

    Energy efficiency

    Regulation

DESIGN PHILOSOPHY

It is very important that the design team has *early* representation of all the specialties and that the design proceeds with a *balanced* emphasis of all these design considerations. For Mass Customization, the design team must design the product to satisfy a balance of all these considerations *and* the additional considerations necessary to be able to efficiently build and market customized products.

An important axiom of advanced product development is: *The further one progresses into a design, the harder it will be to start satisfying additional needs.* Some designers may resist an early balance of these considerations if they think it limits their "design freedom." But, in reality, too few constraints may lead to the design equivalent of writer's block. If every design decision has many open choices, the whole design will represent an overwhelming array of choices that can lead to *design paralysis.*

So the designer breaks the impasse by making arbitrary decisions. Every arbitrary decision will probably make it difficult to incorporate other considerations later, unless the designer is incredibly lucky. And the further the design progresses (the more arbitrary decisions that are made), the harder it will be to satisfy additional considerations.

The most common delays in product development are caused by omitting important design considerations early in the design, such as manufacturability, and regulatory compliance, and adequately addressing customer needs. Omitting any considerations means they will have to be incorporated later, probably with much difficulty.

An all-to-common product development scenario starts with a feasibility study, a breadboard, or a proof of principle exercise that considers only functionality. This is justified since the goal was just to "see if we can get it to work." Once a single breadboard "works," there is great pressure to rush "it" (the breadboard) into production without really *designing* the product for manufacturability, serviceability, customizability, and so forth. Problems surface later because of the design considerations omitted and because feasibility was based on one example, hardly a statistically significant sampling of basic functional issues, manufacturing processes, or part/supplier combinations.

IMPORTANCE OF GOOD PRODUCT ARCHITECTURE

Optimizing product architecture starts with an early balance of all design considerations by a complete multifunctional team. This is the highest leverage activity in product development and has the greatest potential for ensuring success. But, as with product definition, the importance of this stage is often ignored by merely assuming that the product architecture will be the same as previous or competitive products.

As shown earlier, 60 percent of a product's lifetime cumulative cost is determined by the concept or architecture phase of a project (see Figure 6–1). By the time design is completed, 80 percent of the lifetime cumulative cost is determined. By the time the product reaches production, only 5 percent of the total cost can be influenced. This is why cost-reduction efforts can be so futile, because cost is really determined by the design itself and is very difficult to remove later.

Similarly, other important design goals, such as quality, reliability, serviceability, flexibility, customizability, and regulatory compliance, are most easily achieved by optimizing the product's architecture.

Time to market is heavily affected by early optimization of the early conceptual phase as shown by the Mentor Graphics model in Figure 9–1. The projected 40 percent savings in the *real* time to market is due to early conceptual optimization minimizing the need for revisions and iterations and making the manufacturing ramp-up several times faster. Note that the architectural phase, labeled "concept design," went from 3 percent in the old model to 33 percent (of the total development time) in the new model, *an order of magnitude increase!* The more thorough up-front work decreased the postde-

FIGURE 9–1

Mentor Graphics Model for Time-to-Market Improvements

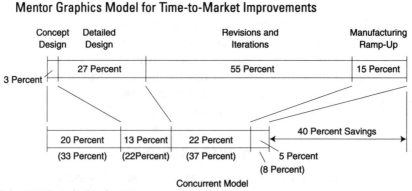

sign activities (the revisions, iterations, and ramp-up) from 70 percent to 27 percent of the product development cycle. It is more efficient to incorporate a balance of design considerations early than to implement them later with changes, revisions, and iterations.

The usual question that managers ask on seeing the order-of-magnitude increase in conceptual design in Figure 9–1, is "What do product development teams really do in that extra time?" or "What types of activities could really reduce the tail-end activities that much?" The key elements of an optimal architecture phase are the following:

1. *Product definition,* which defines what the customer really wants and minimizes the chance that the product will have to change to reflect "new" customer needs that were not anticipated in the beginning.

2. *Issues resolution,* which raises all the issues and then resolves them before proceeding further, thus minimizing the chances that these issues will have to be resolved later when each change is harder to implement and when each change may, in turn, induce yet more changes.

3. *Conceptual simplification,* which simplifies the overall product architecture with clever, elegant concepts, fewer parts, combinations of parts, higher levels of silicon integration, modular opportunities, and so forth.

4. *Architectural optimization,* which optimizes the architecture for minimum total cost, for designed-in quality and reliability, for manufacturability and serviceability, and for flexibility and customizability.

Concept simplification can be accomplished by creatively simplifying product architecture at the concept stage. Some examples include the following:

> *Automobiles.* Passenger cars used to be built by bolting sheet metal bodies onto heavy metal frames. Most cars now have combined automobile frames and bodies to form the integral "unit body" construction, in which the sheet metal body panels carry structural loads, so that the frame can be eliminated. This greatly lowers cost by simplifying assembly and lowering the weight of the car, which, in turn, lowers materials and operating costs.

Electronic systems. Electronic systems can be greatly simplified when all the circuitry can be placed on a single circuit board, instead of using multiple circuit boards that require interboard wiring operations or card cages to connect them.

Personal Computers. Early DOS personal computers required a "chip set" of 170 individual integrated circuits, not counting memory. Present PCs have consolidated that functionality, plus even more, into just a few VLSI (very large scale integrated) or ASIC (application specific integrated circuit) chips. High levels of this integration can greatly simplify electronic systems, making it possible to combine the functionality of several printed circuit boards onto one, thus eliminating interboard wiring and card cages.

Gable-top milk carton. The gable-top milk carton uses clever folds in a one-piece rectangular cardboard blank to form an entire milk carton with a resealable pour spout. This was much easier to manufacture than the previous multipiece cardboard "pop-top" carton and performed better too.

Automotive sheet metal simplification. Thirty years ago, passenger cars had a complex piece of sheet metal between the hood and the windshield. This part was hard to fabricate because of the many louvers for the ventilation system, plus the holes and dimples for the windshield wipers and washers. It was hard to handle because, before it was welded to the body, it was quite flimsy. It had to fit well with the hood, which created a very visible alignment problem. Most modern cars have simply eliminated that part and presented "hidden" windshield wipers, a desirable feature. Further, eliminating the alignment issue with the hood is surely welcome in an age when television commercials show steel balls rolling precisely along body panel seams.

PRODUCT ARCHITECTURE

Since the architecture phase of product development determines 60 percent of the cost and has significant effects on quality, reliability, serviceability, flexibility, customizability, and time to market, it is imperative to view early concept decisions as pivotal aspects of product development. Early concept decisions are the strategic decisions that determine the architecture for hardware, software, and their interactions.

Hardware architecture for Mass Customization is heavily dependent on common parts and modules, plus clever ways to customize products beyond modularity. Software architecture for Mass Customization can be based on modular strategies such as object-oriented software or, as recommended by Hewlett-Packard's Software Re-use Group, domain-specific "modules and kits" where each kit (for each product line) would contain several modules with well-defined interfaces.

Product architecture would be determined by strategic decisions such as the following (which include some common extremes in parentheses):

- Product customization/variety/configuration strategy.
- Team composition and timing (complete team active early, or not).
- Product definition methodology (systematic or ad-hoc).
- Part combination/integration strategy (many discrete parts, or very few integrated parts).
- Parts strategy (design/build in-house or buy from catalogs).
- Product cost strategy (part/labor cost focus or total cost focus).
- Manufacturing strategy (flexible or lots; make or buy; tooling strategy).
- Quality strategy (quality from testing or quality from design and process controls).
- Reliability strategy (inherent quality or burn-in and redundancy).
- Service/repair strategy (design responsibility or user's responsibility).
- Vendor strategy (low bidder or vendor/partner relationships).
- Measurement of product development (time to market measured to first customer ship or to stable production; intermediate progress measured by design quality or predetermined deadlines; product cost measured by part/labor cost or total cost).

For example, early concept decisions that would determine product architecture for an electronic system are as follows:

- Customization strategy (modular, mother/daughter-board options, various printed circuit board assembly scenarios on common bare boards, program PROMS on the fly, etc.).
- Product configuration strategy (switches, jumpers, software settings, automatic, or universal).
- Level of integration (many discrete integrated circuits on many circuit boards or very few. VLSIs or ASICs on one circuit board).
- Interconnection strategy (card cages, cables with connectors, or hand-soldered wires).
- Cabinetry strategy (design and build cabinets, doors, card cages, fans, etc., or buy modular components from catalogs).
- Heat flow/dissipation strategy (fans, conductive, convection, refrigeration, etc.).
- Printed circuit board size and bus standardization (arbitrary size with unique bus or standard size and standard bus; design and build unique boards or purchased off-the-shelf boards for processing, I/O, memory, etc.).
- Printed circuit board assembly strategy (all components automatically placed, soldered and cleaned, or not).
- Power supply (custom or standard shape, voltage, and wattage; separate power supplies for different countries or universal power supply).
- Test strategy (ATE "bed-of-nails" diagnostic tests or quality assured by process controls with final go/no-go system test only).
- Reliability strategy (inherent reliability or redundancy; "hot" replaceable boards and power supplies or not).
- Regulatory compliance strategy including all current *and anticipated* regulations.

DESIGN FOR MANUFACTURABILITY

Design for manufacturability (DFM) is the practice of designing products for ease of manufacture.[9] Narrowly interpreted, DFM focuses on designing for assembly (DFA), which concentrates on designing products to be easily assembled. For instance, combining many separate parts into a single integrated part eliminates the labor necessary to assemble all the separate parts.

Broadly interpreted, as will be done here, DFM focuses on designing for all aspects of manufacturing: fabrication, assembly, quality, regulatory compliance, material and supply chain logistics, shipping, distribution, service, repair, and so forth. Much of the focus of DFM is to design cost out of products from the beginning.

Some of the key principles of DFM are summarized below. Note that each of these techniques can have a significant effect on minimizing a product's total cost.

Part Commonality

A key principle of DFM is parts commonality as discussed in Chapter 5. Fewer types of parts simplifies assembly, minimizes the chances of using the wrong part, and simplifies part procurement and distribution logistics. This results in lower costs for assembly, quality, and material overhead.

Eliminating Right-Hand and Left-Hand Parts

Results similar to part commonality can be achieved by designing right-hand and left-hand parts to be identical. Often it is easy to incorporate the features required by right and left parts into a single part. A related principle is to design "pairs" of identical parts, such as the top and bottom parts of briefcases and suitcases. This technique results in three benefits compared to the practice of using different parts for right and left, or top and bottom:

1. *The number of part types is cut in half,* thus simplifying part procurement, delivery to points of use in the factory, service, and spare parts logistics.

2. *The quantities of these parts is doubled,* thus resulting in higher economies of scale and purchasing leverage. Further, doubling quantities can result in better delivery, which may be crucial to just-in-time operations.

3. *Tooling costs are cut in half,* since only one die or mold is needed instead of separate tooling for right/left or top/bottom parts.

Symmetrical Parts

Design parts to be symmetrical so that they do not need to be oriented. This simplifies automation and eliminates errors for manual assembly. Often it is easy to add the same features to each end of a part to make it symmetrical. An extra hole or groove would not cost much because the production process is already set up to make that hole or groove on the required end. Even if there was a noticeable cost to making parts symmetrical, it would probably be more than offset by the benefits if costs were calculated on a total cost basis. A little known example of symmetrical parts is the felt-tipped pen, in which the felt tip is pointed on both ends so that automatic assembly machines do not have to orient the felt.

Make Part Differences Very Obvious

If parts cannot be common or symmetrical, make sure that part (or end) differences are very obvious. The worst part shape is almost square, which invites incorrect assembly. Similar *looking* parts, with different threads, ratings, or strengths should be distinguished from each other by clear markings, lettering, or coloring.

Combining Parts

The number of parts can be minimized if many functions or "parts" can be combined into a single one. Threaded fasteners can be purchased with "captivated" washers and/or lock-washers that are permanently affixed but still able to spin when the fastener is tightened. This eliminates the assembly of screw to washer and eliminates the chance that a screw would be assembled without a lock-washer.

Creative design of casting and molding can integrate many functions into a single piece, often with minimum cost for each additional function. The main chassis part for the Hewlett-Packard DeskJet printer accomplishes 30 functions by combining what might have been separate parts to mount gears, motors, shafts, rollers, control mechanisms, paper guides, wiring, and covers.

Provide Access for Parts *and* Tools

Some parts, such as fasteners, may be small, while efficient tools to install them may be quite bulky. Not providing adequate access for tools forces less efficient manual assembly.

Use Catalog Parts

A general rule, known as Anderson's Law, is "never design a part that is available from a catalog."[10] Experienced suppliers of catalog parts are usually more efficient at the design and manufacture of their parts. Not only would *total* cost be lower, but there are also improvements in quality and delivery. Development time and cost for the parts would be zero if the part has already been designed by the supplier. Customers like to be able to buy standard replacement parts from multiple suppliers. Finally, unnecessary parts manufacture can distract a plant from its real mission: building products.

But many engineers are misled by inadequate cost systems. They look up "cost," which is really only labor and materials, and then conclude their company can design and manufacture parts less expensively than experienced suppliers.

Adhere to Process Design Guidelines

Fabrication processes have specific design guidelines to ensure that parts are designed for manufacturability.[11] Processes such as molding, casting, forging, forming, machining, and surface mount assembly[12] have many specific design guidelines that must be followed to minimize cost. In many cases, these guidelines must be followed exactly to be able to use the process.

Optimize Tolerances

Tolerances are key determinants of cost and quality. And, yet, most tolerances are specified arbitrarily and unscientifically. When many design engineers do not know how to methodically specify tolerances, they will "overspec" the tolerances, "just to be on the safe side." However, *this is a very expensive way to achieve quality!* Other engineers may not even be aware of quality effects of specifying average tolerances or the default tolerances printed on drawing paper. This can cause quality problems, which raise costs, sometimes catastrophically.

There is a way to methodically specify tolerances *to achieve high quality at low cost*. The methodology, called *robust* design or Taguchi Methods®, was developed by Japanese quality expert Genichi Taguchi. Basically, it systematically analyzes the effect of all tolerances on the total system to methodically determine the tolerances that are really necessary to achieve high quality. Since the tolerances are optimized, they are neither too tight, which is expensive to make, nor too loose, which is expensive to repair. It uses an efficient statistical technique called *design of experiments* to perform the computations. A good introduction to the subject, written by a journalist, is Lance Ealey's *Quality by Design*.[13]

Minimize Costs Related to Drawings and Documentation

Good documentation control can save cost by making documentation creation and management as cost-effective as possible. Good documentation encourages reuse of engineering detail, parts, modules, and software, which saves the costs of "reinventing the wheel."

It also maximizes make/buy flexibility if all designs are documented well enough to be fabricated by outside vendors. Poor documentation limits production to the in-house people who "just know how to make it," even if this is not the most cost-effective solution.

Documenting changes promptly will save the cost of repeating mistakes or finding out the hard way about undocumented changes. Proactive procedures to minimize risk from data loss will avoid costly delays.

If drawings are *unambiguously* conveyed to production, with Geometric Dimensioning and Tolerancing (ANSI Y14.5), there will be less chance of costly errors and misinterpretations. Properly dimensioned drawings with optimal datum references will save fabrication costs by allowing the shop to design tooling quickly, fabricate the parts, and conduct first article inspections with coordinate measurement machines.

Mistake-Proof Design

"Poka-Yoke" is a Japanese concept that originally evolved to prevent mistakes in manufacturing.[14] *Poka-Yoke* can be used as a design methodology to "mistake-proof" the design so parts cannot be assembled wrong or products manufactured incorrectly. These design features need only be designed once, but these features go on to prevent mistakes in manufacturing and service for the life of the product. Part symmetry is a design technique that can eliminate the possibility of assembling a part backwards. Part standardization, with fewer types of parts, will minimize the chance of

picking the wrong part. Clever design features can actually prevent incorrect assembly.

Design to Support Efficient Manufacture

Designing products for production on existing equipment *within process capabilities* will save the cost of purchasing new equipment, the expediting costs to get it shipped and installed in time for the ramp-up, and the debugging costs usually associated with new equipment. As mentioned earlier, the development team for the 1994 Ford Mustang had a senior manufacturing manager whose job was to ensure that the new product did not exceed the capabilities of existing equipment.[15]

Processing costs can be minimized if designers design for the *minimum process steps:* For example, mixed-technology printed circuit boards (with both leaded and surface-mount parts) must be built by all the required machines for *both* processes. This is why, a few years ago, personal computers jumped, in one generation, from all leaded parts to virtually all surface-mount parts.

Ease of Service and Repair

Products can be designed to lower service and repair costs. Products, manufacturing processes, and their service and repair procedures can be *concurrently* designed. Parts should be able to be replaced independently, at least the parts most prone to failure. Tool commonality can minimize the number of tools necessary for field repairs. Designing for tool access is as important for assembly as for service and repair. The product can be designed with self-test or remote diagnostic capabilities. Common parts will simplify repair part logistics and increase the probability that the replacement parts will be readily available.

Design for Reliability

The following techniques can be used to design reliability into products:

- Concept simplicity is the key to *inherent* reliability, which will be maximized with the fewest parts, interfaces, interconnections, and lines of code.

- Approach system reliability as a primary design consideration.

- Use proven standard parts and design features that have been used before.

- Select parts on the basis of substantiated reliability data; existing parts and previous engineering have more reliability data available than new parts and designs.

- Use proven, precertified modules that can be combined to result in a certified assembly; reuse object-oriented software modules that have already been debugged.

- Simulate/predict reliability performance early in the design process.

- Use manufacturing processes that are in control and have a history of producing reliable parts.

- Use total quality management to maximize quality/reliability.

- Design to minimize errors in fabrication, assembly, and installation.

- Design to minimize quality degradation during shipping and installation.

- Minimize mechanical contacts in electrical connections, especially for low voltage: Combine circuit boards to eliminate cables and connectors; use connectors with the minimum mechanical connections (e.g., flex cable); minimize use of sockets.

- Eliminate all hand soldering for cable connections or interconnecting circuit boards.

- Use *burn-in* or *run-in* to induce early failures with the goal of using this as a diagnostic tool, not a production step, to isolate problems and then solve them.

AGILE PRODUCT DEVELOPMENT MANAGEMENT FOR MASS CUSTOMIZATION

Implementing the above principles should establish a strong product development methodology. Mass Customization places additional demands on the product development process.

A key element of any mass customization strategy is modularity. Some products are *inherently* more modular than others, for instance, personal computers, which could be assembled from various motherboards, memory chips, hard drives, power supplies, monitors, keyboards, option boards, and software. But, in most cases, modularity is not inherent and will have to be designed into the product line.

The other key element of a mass customization strategy is the customizable aspects, those portions of the product that can be customized by programming, configuring, mixing, or cutting to fit. Again, this will have to be designed into the product line. The design of the modularity and customizability is a prime example of an *investment* in product development.

Organizationally, the simplest approach would be to structure a single product development project that, starting with the product definition for the product family, would decide the amount of customization that could be achieved with modularity and the amount that could be achieved with easily customizable features, as discussed in Chapter 10. The project would then simultaneously design the modules, the customizable features, and the processes to assemble the modules and "customize" the remainder.

If this approach proves impractical because of timing or project scope, then multiple product development teams would have to be coordinated with central task forces working on modular design and standardization. Each of these scenarios will be discussed next in more detail.

SIMULTANEOUS DESIGN OF THE PRODUCT FAMILY

This approach would embark on the simultaneous design of the whole mass customization product family. The major steps are presented below (these will be discussed in more detail in the next chapter).

1. Methodically define the product for the product family citing customer preferences for the range of customization to be offered.

2. Determine how to achieve the customization through an optimal balance of modularity and rapid customizability (programming, configuring, mixing, cutting to fit, etc.).

3. Establish an optimal product family architecture.
4. Simultaneously design
  a. Modules with standard interfaces.
  b. Processing for module fabrication and assembly.
  c. Customizable features.
  d. Processing for customizable features.
5. Simultaneously design products based on above architecture.

The process may require some looping back to refine the architecture before embarking on product design. After standard modules are designed, it is important for all product development teams to precisely adhere to the standards. Individual product designers may be tempted to alter modularity standards to make their particular product "better." But deviating from modular standardization for slight improvements in one product or product version might devastate the overall mass customization plan and thus result in a net loss for the company. If such "improvements" are truly better for all products, they should have been considered in the architecture phase or, if discovered later, should be incorporated in a loop back to earlier steps. Once the modular architecture has been determined, modular standards should be strictly followed in all product development activity.

Of course, all the above steps should be practiced within the advanced product development methodologies described earlier.

COORDINATED TEAMWORK

This approach assumes that products in the mass customization family will be developed by *separate but coordinated* product development teams, possibly over time. Ideally, the process should follow the above model as closely as possible, especially the first four steps, with extra attention paid to coordination in step 5 (above).

Regardless of how the products are developed, the process must begin with a methodical product definition for the product family citing customer preferences for the range of customization to be offered. The customization strategy (step 2) still needs to determine the optimal balance of modularity and rapid customizability. Further, all product/process designs should be pursued up to the point that the architecture can be optimized (step 3). The simultaneous design of modules, customizable features, and their processing (step 4) needs to be completed. The architecture and interfaces of modules need to be well defined to ensure the greatest probability of success in designing future modules. The design of the products could then be leveraged to parallel development projects with some of them possibly being deferred to future developments.

An inherent danger for developments that span time is insufficient effort up front on the architecture and module development. This may result in difficulty later when designing products around poorly defined modules or architecture.

Parallel developments must be well coordinated to ensure that projects utilize standard modules properly, design around standard processes, and generally design products compatible with all aspects of the overall mass customization plan.

DEVELOPING MASS CUSTOMIZED PRODUCTS AROUND EXISTING MUDULES

In some companies, it may be advantageous to develop a mass customized product line around existing modules. The modules have already been designed and may be in production, perhaps at high enough volume to benefit from some economies of scale. However, the scope of the customization may be limited somewhat by existing products, modules, and processes. A limited effort could be successful if its aim was to expand the product line into niche markets, even though falling short of customizing products for individual customers. This may be a stepping-stone on the way to full Mass Customization.

Industries with well-designed modules and well-defined interfaces may benefit from the utilization of existing modules. For instance, the development of a mass customized line of automobiles would probably utilize existing engines and transmissions, possibly with various existing performance options. Electronic systems (such as computers, instruments, and communications equipment) might utilize existing processing and memory boards while adding a choice of configurations and other options (add-on boards, software, firmware, etc.).

Again, the first steps would be to methodically define the product family and decide if a family of customized products could be built around existing modules. The decision process would converge on the best scenarios for the utilization of existing modules. The decision to proceed with mass customization based on previous engineering should be constantly reevaluated to make sure it still makes sense. If not, the plan should be revised to include newer modules. In extreme cases, the plan may have to be abandoned or postponed to a more opportune time.

Then, the optimal product family architecture should be established based on the optimal utilization of existing products. Part of this effort will be to standardize the specifications of the chosen modules and their interfaces and not let them "evolve" unless such improvements are compatible with the mass customization plan. The needs of the mass customization family may have to be reconciled with products using the existing modules. When evaluating such trade-offs, the overall good of *all products* should be the decision-making criterion. If the existing modules are manufactured in a flexible manufacturing environment, it may be possible to efficiently produce different versions of the modules, one for existing products and one for the new mass customization family.

New modules and their manufacturing processes may need to be designed as per step 4 above. The design of the product family can then proceed by simultaneous or parallel design teams as discussed above.

There may be a temptation to think that any existing modular products could be transformed into a mass customized product line merely by offering various combinations of existing modules. However, the manufacturing process must be scrutinized for feasibility to ensure that it is flexible enough to build products to order. Issues that might be impediments would be excessive internal variety of parts, modules and processes. If there are more different parts than can be distributed at all points of use, then the factory is not flexible and will not be able to build mass customized products to order.

NOTES

1. James Womack, Daniel Jones, and Daniel Roos, *The Machine that Changed the World* (New York: Rawson Associates, 1990; paperback edition, Harper Perennial, 1991).

2. Michael L. Dertouzos, Richard K. Lester, and Robert M. Solow, *Made in America, Regaining the Productive Edge* from the MIT commission on Industrial Productivity (New York: Harper Perennial, 1989).

3. *Industry Week*, "The Complete Guide to America's Best Plants," Cleveland, OH: Penton Publishing, 1995), p. 12.

4. From a speech by Boeing President Philip M. Condit, presented May 7, 1993, at the Haas Graduate School of Business at the University of California at Berkeley.

5. *Industry Week*, "The Complete Guide to America's Best Plants."

6. Artemis March, "Usability: The New Dimension of Product Design," *Harvard Business Review*, September–October 1994, p. 144.

7. This was the case with the 1994 Ford Mustang development. The entire product development team of 400 actually reported to the team leader for the duration of the project. (From a speech by and discussion with project team leader William W. Boddie, October 18, 1993, at the Haas Graduate School of Business at the University of California at Berkeley).

8. Presentation by and discussion with William W. Boddie, October 18, 1993, at the Haas Graduate School of Business at the University of California at Berkeley.

9. David M. Anderson, *Design for Manufacturability, Optimizing Cost, Quality and Time-to-Market* (Lafayette, CA: CIM Press, 1990).

10. Ibid., p. 82.

11. Ramon Bakerjain, ed. *Tool and Manufacturing Engineers Handbook*, Volume 6, *Design for Manufacturability* (Dearborn, MI: Society of Manufacturing Engineers, 1992); and James G. Bralla ed., *Handbook of Product Design for Manufacturing, A Practical Guide for Low-Cost Production* (New York: McGraw-Hill, 1986).

12. Ray P. Prasad, *Surface Mount Technology, Principles and Practice* (New York: Van Nostrand Reinhold, 1989); and Phil P. Marcoux, *Surface Mount Technology, Design for Manufacturability* (Sunnyvale, CA: PPM Associates, 1989).

13. Lance A. Ealey, *Quality by Design, Taguchi Methods® and U.S. Industry* (Dearborn, MI: ASI Press, a division of American Supplier Institute, 1988).

14. Nikkan Kogyo Shimbun, Ltd./Factory Magazine, *Poka-Yoke, Improving Product Quality by Preventing Defects* (Portland, OR: Productivity Press, 1987).

15. Presentation by and discussion with William W. Boddie, October 18, 1993, at the Haas Graduate School of Business at the University of California at Berkeley.

CHAPTER

Designing Mass Customized Products

Before starting the design of mass customized products, it is important to make sure that all the prerequisites are in place or will be in place by the time the products go into production, specifically: Related products have been rationalized (Chapter 4); standardization programs are well under way (Chapter 5) as well as improvements in manufacturing flexibility (Chapter 7) to lower the cost of variety (Chapter 3); all decisions are being made on the basis of total cost (Chapter 6); and product development itself has become an important core competency (Chapter 9).

THE IMPORTANCE OF GOOD PRODUCT DEFINITION

The first step in any product development is to translate the voice of the customer into product design specifications and resource prioritizations. For Mass Customization, this step is even more important and more complex since the voice of the customer must be translated into families of products that define the range of customizability needed to satisfy customers.

Contrary to the common temptation, the first step is not concept work. But unfortunately, product development is often launched because of intoxicating concepts that may or may not satisfy customers.

In a survey of 12 large technology-based companies, managers were asked, "What are the causes of product development delays?" The number one response, with 71 percent of managers responding, was poor product definition.[1] If the product is not defined well, then the product definition may have to change later to really satisfy customers. Late changes in product definition usually result in costly and time-consuming engineering change orders (ECOs) because of the amount of engineering and possibly tooling that have been based on the original product definition. An equally unpleasant alternative to late changes in the product definition is to proceed based on the poor product definition and introduce the product that does not really satisfy customers.

A good product definition will become a consistent focus for the *whole company synergy* that is the source of competitive advantage in product development. One company waited until the prototype stage for Marketing to say, "That's not what we wanted." The result was much rework to redesign the product to reflect what was "wanted."

The proper procedure for an intriguing concept or technological strength would be first to thoroughly investigate the market potential. For Mass Customization, the scope and range of customization–the universe of possibilities—will need to be optimized for the greatest potential of success in the marketplace without wasted effort for unnecessary customization.

EXECUTIVE OVERVIEW OF QFD

Quality function deployment (QFD) is a tool for systematically translating the voice of the customer into product design specifications and resource prioritizations.[2] Its strength is to translate subjective customer wants and needs into objective specifications that engineers can use to design products.

In the most general sense, the input to QFD is a set of subjective customer preferences; the outputs are product specifications and resource prioritization (see Figure 10–1). The values in the

FIGURE   10–1

QFD Executive Overview

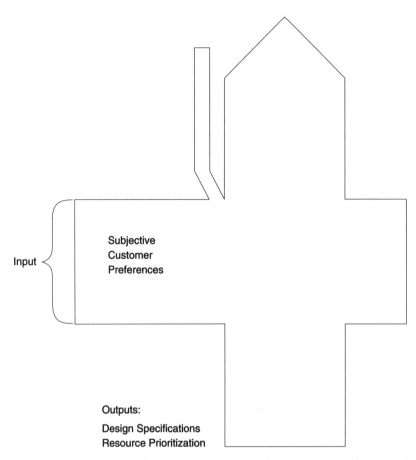

"design specifications" row are the actual values engineers will use to design products. The "resource prioritization" row is the percent of the design team's effort that should be spent on each aspect of the design. Using this prioritization will ensure that the design team devotes its efforts toward features that customers want the most. And, thus, they will not waste effort "polishing the ruby" more than the customer wants it polished. This can be a temptation when engineers are personally excited about certain new technologies that are being used in the product.

QFD FOR DISCRETE PRODUCTS

It would be better to use some methodical tool to define products than none at all. Even if the full QFD methodology appears too overwhelming, the first few steps can generate tremendous insight.

Figure 10–2 shows the completed QFD chart with each area labeled according to its function in the methodology. The "subjective customer preferences" are listed, one per row, in words that are meaningful to the customer, not in "specsmanship jargon."

One of the most valuable aspects of QFD is also the easiest to obtain: simply asking customers for the "relative importance" of

FIGURE 10–2

QFD for Discrete Products

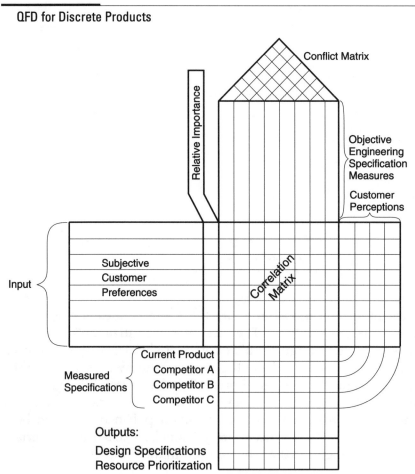

their preferences, from a low of 1 to a high of 10. The result is a customer ranking of what is most important and what is least important. This ranking is very important to help neutralize any internal biases in Engineering toward exciting technology or in Marketing toward "pet" features.

Customers are then asked how they would rank the current product against the competitors' products. The result is entered in the chart under "customer perceptions." Comparing this competitive ranking with the customers' "relative importance" ranking can give valuable insight into resource allocations. The full QFD uses these inputs to calculate an optimal percentage of the engineering budget to devote to various tasks, but even a subjective comparison of customer importance to competitive ranking would be very insightful.

If a competitor was ranked best about something important to the customer, the company would be wise to measure that product and try to learn how it achieved customer satisfaction. The things to measure would be the specifications that appear in the columns in Figure 10–2 labeled "objective engineering specification measures." These contain the objective measurements that will eventually have target numbers for discrete products or ranges for mass customized products. The objective measures would be in engineering units that quantify dimensions, force, torque, energy, decibels, and so on. All of those objective measurements are then actually measured for the current product and several competitors and entered in the chart under "measured specifications."

The "correlation matrix" correlates which customer preferences are affected by which engineering specifications. Symbols are placed in the square to indicate the type of correlation. Usually two to four rankings are listed: "positive" or "negative" correlation; "strong," "some" or "possible" correlation; or "strong positive," "medium positive," "medium negative," "strong negative" correlation. Roughly half the boxes should be checked. Results become less valuable as one approaches either extreme of all boxes checked or no boxes checked.

The "conflict matrix" tabulates any specifications that might be inherently in conflict with others, to aid in making trade-offs of one feature versus another. An example would be a more powerful car engine that may hamper handling because of its extra weight.

Various cells in a QFD chart are used to make calculations and normalize them to useful percentages. One of the "bottom lines" is the design target row (labeled "design specifications"), in this case, a single value for discrete (noncustomized) products. The other is the resource prioritization, which can be given in a percentage of the engineering budget or hours spent achieving the various design targets.

PRODUCT DEFINITION FOR MASS CUSTOMIZATION

For Mass Customization, all products in the mass customization family must be defined so that customers can actually receive custom products. Thus, the product definition is not a single definition but is a range of product definitions that represent various combinations of modules, standard parts, custom parts, custom configurations, and customized dimensions.

To design products and processes for Mass Customization, the scope of product-family breadth must be understood. It is important to establish the *optimal* scope of product-family customization. It may not be necessary or even feasible to offer every possible variation of products in a product family. Since customers may need only certain variations (as indicated by their inputs on "importance"), it would be a waste of effort to offer more variation than is really appreciated. Thus, mass customized product families must be defined with the *optimal scope* of customization.

QFD FOR MASS CUSTOMIZATION

Mass Customization needs a methodology that will translate the voice of the customer for families of customized products. Figure 10–3 shows the QFD chart for Mass Customization, with the "design specs" expanded into five rows. The first new row, "to be customized by," indicates if the product is customized in the factory (F), at the dealer or distributor (D), at the point of sale by the user (P), by the user's technical staff (T), by the actual user (U), or self-adjusting (S). Other symbols representing other customization scenarios can be used as appropriate. A blank or a question mark could mean "to be determined."

The purpose of these entries is to identify where and by whom the customization will be done. The design team will have

FIGURE   10–3

QFD for Mass Customization

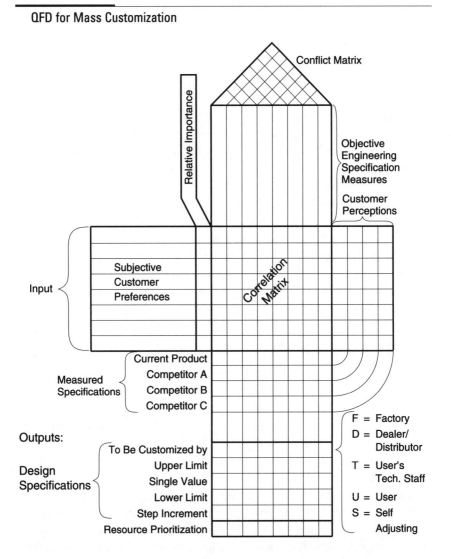

to design the product for compatibility with this customization strategy. Factory customization would rely on flexible manufacturing to be able to quickly build any configuration that is called for. Dealer/distributor customization would have to consider the tools, parts, patience, and skill level present at *all* dealers and distributors. User customization would have to be designed for the anticipated range of users' skill level, patience, and tools needed, if any. A variation of user customization would be a situation common in large companies where technical staffs or departments would perform the customization, for instance, configuring computers for all office workers or customizing production tools for factories. Self-customizing products literally adjust automatically to "fit" the user.

The next three rows in Figure 10–3 contain the "single value" row, which would be used for those engineering specifications that can be expressed by a single value and not a range of values. The upper and lower limits specify the range of dimensions for applicable specifications. The "step increment" would specify the steps or increments that could be appropriate for values within the range. A "zero" entry would indicate infinitely variable dimensions between the upper and lower limits.

As with discrete QFD, the design team would base the design on the design specification target values or ranges and steps. Understanding how each range would be customized will help develop the resource prioritization.

ISSUES RESOLUTION

Following the Japanese model cited in the last chapter, it is important to raise and resolve issues throughout product development *as soon as they are identified*. This is especially important in the early steps such as product definition. In addition to technical feasibility, several other issues should be considered early (when they are easier to resolve) rather than later (when they are harder to resolve). One of the values of starting product development with a *complete* multifunctional team is the variety of opinions that are available from people with diverse backgrounds, education, and experience.

Typical examples of issues for product development, in general, are questions like: How valid are our assumptions? How could we become more confident about these assumptions? How good is our product definition? What were the real reasons for previous successes? What were the problems with previous product developments and their introductions into production? What are the most likely things that could go wrong? What would we do if they did? From a consequence standpoint, what is the worst thing that could go wrong? What would be our plan B if that happened? What are the most likely changes that might occur with respect to the market, customers, competitors, and regulations? Can we objectively justify proceeding?

Some of the key issues for Mass Customization would be how to efficiently accomplish the customization specified by the product definition. What would be potential modularity? What machines, tooling, or people would perform the actual "cutting to fit" customization? What will be our documentation and information flow strategy?

EARLY CONCEPT WORK

After the product is well defined, then begins the highest-leverage activity in product development: concept simplification and architecture optimization. As shown in Figure 6–1, this is the stage that will determine 60 percent of the cumulative lifetime cost of the product plus significant impacts on quality, reliability, serviceability, flexibility, and customizability. For Mass Customization, this is the stage that determines how easily and effectively products can be customized. Specifically, this stage will determine how products will be customized and who will perform the customization.

An important part of architecture optimization is determining how and when the product will be customized. Hewlett-Packard uses the concept of *postponement* to defer customization as late as possible. Dr. Corey Billington, manager of HP's strategic planning and modeling group, defines postponement as follows: "In its simplest form, postponement means to stock a product in a generic, uncompleted form until a customer order is received and then to convert the generic product into a final product while the customer waits."[3] The following sections will discuss various ways to customize products.

Ways to Customize Products

To be effective at Mass Customization, optimize the proportion of the following customization categories: *modular, adjustable,* and *dimensional.* Each will be described briefly, followed by expanded definitions.

1. *Modular.* Modules are building blocks. Usually modules are building blocks that can customize a product by assembling various combinations of modules. Examples of modules would include many components in automobiles: engines, transmissions, audio equipment, tire/wheel options, and so on. In electronics, modules would include processor boards, power supplies, plug-in integrated circuits, daughter-boards, disk drives. In software, code could be written in modules (objects) that can be integrated into various combinations.

2. *Adjustable.* Adjustments are a *reversible* way to customize a product, as in mechanical or electrical adjustments. Adjustments could be infinitely variable. Discrete adjustments, or configurations, would represent few choices, such as those provided by electronic switches, jumpers, cables, or discrete software-controlled configurations. Adjustments and configurations are reversible. These adjustments and configurations make the product customizable, as pointed out in Chapter 1.

3. *Dimensional.* Dimensional customization involves a *permanent* cutting to fit, mixing, or tailoring. Dimensional customization could be infinite or have a selection of discrete choices. Examples of infinite dimensional customization would include the tailoring of clothing, drilling holes in bowling balls, grinding eyeglasses, mixing of paints or chemicals, the cutting of wire or tubing, and machining metal parts. Examples of discrete dimensional customization would be hole punching, soldering selected electronic components onto a printed circuit board, and downloading selected software code onto "read only" firmware (PROMs).

For Matsushita's National custom bicycle, the modular contributions to the customization were the wheels, pedals, drive chain, derailleur, seat, handlebars, and controls. The adjustable contributions were adjustments for the height and angle of the seat and handlebars. The dimensional contributions were the lengths of the frame tubing, which were cut to fit.

Firmware could be any of these three categories depending on the application. Programmable integrated circuits could be (1) programmed and then stocked as modules; (2) used as a configuration device, for electrically erasable programmable read only memory (E^2PROM); or (3) permanently programmed, as in "programmable read only memory" (PROM).

Virtual Modularity

A variation of modularity would be *virtual modularity,* which does not limit modules to physical building blocks. Drawings of virtual modules (known in CAD as components, symbols, or blocks) could be combined and "assembled" in CAD systems; in fact, some CAD systems, like Pro/ENGINEER, use the *assemble* command to assemble *components.* Layers in application specific integrated circuits (ASICs) can be combined as modules in CAD to form custom products.

For printed circuit boards, certain groups of traces and their components (integrated circuits, resistors, capacitors, etc.) could be a *virtual* module in a CAD system, perhaps segregated by CAD layers. Combining various virtual modules could customize PC boards with a minimum of special design work.

Hidden Modularity

In some markets, obvious modularity may be desirable, such as with stereo modules called components. Customers can choose their favorite amplifier, tuner, CD player, and speakers and simply connect them together.

In other markets, customers would prefer an integrated product, or at least *the appearance* of an integrated product. Internal or *hidden modularity* really could be transparent to the customer, but still be of value throughout the value chain. Products could be assembled from various choices of modules, but then be assembled into what appears to be integrated products. Electronic systems could be sold as an integrated "system," but with a high degree of modularity inside the cabinetry. OEM (original equipment manufacturer) products could assemble standard modules inside off-the-shelf enclosures or cabinets (as emphasized in Chapter 5) to produce custom products. For instance, custom test equipment modules can be assembled in standard cabinetry ("racks") to produce custom "rack systems."

Personal computers have some obvious modularity: monitor, keyboard, and central processing unit, which contains hidden modularity inside: various combinations of motherboard, memory, disk drives, video controller, and option boards.

Module Commonality

Just as with parts commonality, discussed in Chapter 5, commonality of modules should be an important consideration, especially when modules are stocked in inventory. If modules are cleverly designed, they could be used in many products. Further, multiples of the same module could be used in the same products, such as memory modules in computers.

Minimizing module types will reduce many forms of manufacturing overhead costs and supply chain costs. Similarly, maximizing the order quantity of modules takes advantage of economies of scale.

Adjustable Customization

Adjustments can be automatic, as discussed in Joe Pine's *Mass Customization*: the Gillette Sensor razor; the Schick Tracer brand; and the Braun Flex Control electric razor that always keeps the razor head at a 90-degree angle to the user's face.[4] As pointed out in Chapter 1, Matsushita has developed a washing machine that can automatically choose one of 600 washing cycles.

Alternatively, adjustments can be set by the plant, dealer, or user. Examples of user-controlled adjustments include seat positions in cars or office chairs; bicycle seat and handlebar height and angle; the Reebok Pump tennis shoe; table saw cut adjustments; and all the adjustments on machine tools.

There may be an optimal balance of automatic adjustments and manual adjustments: Basic users may want automatic adjustments, but advanced users may want to be able to configure the product to meet their advanced needs. Many PC software applications are installed with the most popular *default* settings, which can be reset by more advanced users.

One caution about adjustability: Make sure adjustments are not *coupled* in such a way that one adjustment will affect another. Too many interconnected adjustments may frustrate dealers or users and, in extreme cases, might result in an adjustability "Catch 22," where several adjustment attempts have rendered the product unusable. Another problem with multiple adjustments might be worst case incompatibility: Designers must be sure that no adjustment will be incompatible with any other adjustment to the point of degrading product performance.

Dimensional Customization

Some examples of dimensional customization were cited in Pine's *Mass Customization:* Englert, Inc., of Wallingford, Connecticut, markets a machine that makes custom house gutters by feeding aluminum sheet metal, from a coil, through rollers that form it into the desired shape and then cut the length to fit the house; Custom Cut Technologies mass customizes suits by cutting each component to fit; the Peerless Saw Company developed a computer-controlled laser system to cut custom teeth profiles on cutting saws; the National bicycle plant custom cuts the tubing for the frame to fit the body of the customer.[5]

Dimensional customizability can be performed manually, but care must be taken to plan operations to avoid setup changes. For instance, tubing could be cut to the required length by a worker who reads the dimension on a computer monitor and then manually positions the tubing in a saw.

Many dimensional customizations can be performed by computer numerical controlled (CNC) equipment, such as machining, hole punching, laser cutting, wire cutting, and circuit board assembly. This "programmable customization" is a valuable set of tools for quickly customizing parts or modules. The programs that control these machines can be changed instantly, without a setup change, thus permitting flexible manufacturing of these parts or modules, such as printed circuit boards. However, to be flexible, all parts used must reside in the machine. This underscores the importance of part commonality for anything that will be assembled by programmable automation. For materials that are cut to fit, there should be raw materials commonality, such as the same size bar stock or tubing. With materials commonality, one machine could be set up to programmably cut bar stock or tubing to length without having to change the setup for different sized stock.

The other caveat is that fixturing (for positioning and clamping) be common for parts that are machined and products that are automatically assembled. Common fixturing results from common part geometries for metal parts and common "form factors" (shape and size) for printed circuit boards.

Using this programmability of PC board assembly equipment, a cleverly designed "bare" printed circuit board could be assembled in a variety of ways, as shown in the example product in Chapter 2, with different parts to produce a variety of assembled printed circuit boards. The main advantage of this approach is that the number of bare board variations can be minimized; this is important because of procurement lead time and the large setup cost incurred when ordering a batch of bare boards. If the lead time and board fabrication setup are too much, bare boards would have to be stocked, even in a just-in-time "pull" system. Therefore, minimizing the number of types of versatile bare boards would minimize raw parts inventories and yet still allow many customization scenarios.

Who Performs the Customization

An important part of a mass customization strategy is to determine, in the early design stage, who actually will perform the customization. Thinking this through thoroughly, considering the trade-offs (next section), and exploring various scenarios will help optimize the customization strategy.

Modular Customization
- Factory assembles product from building block modules.
- Dealer/distributor adds modular "options" to base product (such as audio equipment in automobiles or add-in boards in PCs).
- User adds modular options to owned products (such as wool seat covers or "mag" wheels on a car or expanded memory and option boards for PCs).

Virtual Modular Customization
- Factory builds products based on virtual modules in CAD systems (for instance, "assembling" CAD drawings or combining circuitry/component "groups" on printed circuit boards).
- User/dealer could input factory CAD systems to customize factory products in the design stage.

Adjustable/Configurable Customization
- Factory configures or adjusts products for niche markets or individual customization; operation is either programmable or manual.

- Dealer/distributor configures or adjusts products to reflect local market demand or to customize for individual customers (e.g., drilling holes in bowling balls, grinding eyeglasses, etc.).
- User directly adjusts products (such as automobile seat positioning); product is self-adjusting (such as various shavers); or user configures product (such as personal computer configurations).

Dimensional (Cutting-to-Fit/Mixing/Tailoring) Customization

- Factory can use programmable tools to cut materials, mix chemicals, or program read-only firmware.
- Dealer/Distributor could customize product by tailoring clothing or by mixing various "flavors" with the "vanilla" product (like the old soda fountain making milk shakes or a paint store mixing pigments into white paint).
- User permanently "cuts" or "configures" parts to fit by breaking out plugs (like the break-out hole plugs in house electrical wiring boxes) or by breaking off extra length (like breaking off the extra length in hanging file folder support rails that can accommodate various file cabinet drawer lengths).

Trade-Offs

Some trade-offs regarding modular, adjustable, or dimensional customization are presented below with positive and negative issues related to each. The following list can serve as a baseline list, which can be modified to more closely correspond to specific products.

Modular Customization:

+ Economy of scale benefits for widely used modules lower cost and improve deliveries, with just-in-time deliveries more likely.
+ Overhead cost savings: procurement, inventory, floor space, production planning.

+ Widely used modules have less vulnerability to lead time delays.

+ Plug-together modularity can simplify some assembly.

+ Easier test, diagnosis, repair, and maintenance.

+ Encourages JIT and flexible manufacturing.

+ Easy to farm out module fabrication and even design.

+ Using existing modules lowers the cost and time of product development.

+ Easy to customize products for many customers needs.

+ Potentially broader product line.

+ Modular customized products are reconfigurable.

+ Opportunities to upgrade products.

− Product architecture limitations.

− Interface design and fabrication may add cost.

− Interfaces may compromise functionality by adding weight or weakening structures.

− May not be able to cover all customers' needs.

− May require more assembly than an integrated design.

− The extra interfaces may result in undesirable visual aesthetics (such as seams, joints, etc.) or undesirable acoustics (such as squeaks and rattles).

− Requires thorough design of modules and interfaces and consistent application.

− More connectors on critical electrical circuits may lower reliability; the most reliable circuitry may need to be on a single circuit board.

− Modular circuitry may be slower if connection between modules is too long a path.

Adjustable Customization.

+ Easy to configure/adjust to customers' needs.

+ Customization can be postponed further down the value chain (e.g., to the dealer).

+ Product is more readily returnable and can be resold to another user who can readjust product.

- Configurations may be in steps or choices that can satisfy some customers but not all.
- Adjustments may add cost compared to a nonadjustment variation.
- Adjustments may compromise functionality by adding weight or weakening structures.
- Distributor adjustment or configuration may require too great a skill level or too much equipment.
- User adjustment or configuration may require too great a skill level or patience from users.

Dimensional Customization

+ May be the most effective way to satisfy customers' exact needs.
+ Avoids functional compromises of module interfaces and adjustments.
- May be difficult and costly fabrication to cut or tailor to fit; but some CNC equipment could automate the process.
- May be difficult to postpone customization, except for certain products such as mixing paint color.
- Permanent: not reversible, not returnable.

PRODUCT LINE ARCHITECTURE

By this point in the development process, the product will have been methodically defined to reflect the voice of the customer, everyone is constantly raising and resolving issues, and the team understands various ways of customizing products. The next stage is to establish an optimal architecture *for the product line* or product *family.* Since this stage determines 60 percent of the cost, product line architecture should be optimized *thoroughly.* To do this, it is extremely important to have a *complete* product development team with *all specialties active early.*

Product Definition

Start with the product specifications and resource prioritizations generated by the production definition process. It may be necessary to rationalize that, using the techniques of Chapter 4, to make sure minor market opportunities are not compromising the overall project.

Determine Scope

Determine the optimal scope of the product line customization: how broad it is; how ambitious it is; whether this is a pilot or integrated into the mainline operations; the stages of evolution.

Explore Scenarios

Explore *many* scenarios with respect to how to customize the product, as discussed above. Use creativity and brainstorming techniques to do this. Sometimes outside facilitators can act as catalysts and get people thinking in new ways. The team must avoid the temptation to jump at the first or most obvious idea. The goal is to optimize the balance of modular, adjustable, and dimensional customization. Some people automatically equate Mass Customization with modular design. Others may lean too heavily on adjustments. And yet most may not fully explore dimensional customization, especially using programmable equipment.

Concurrency

Keep thinking about the "big picture" including the manufacture and distribution. This is the ultimate application of *concurrent engineering* where the design team has to design an *entire family of products* and *flexible processes* to make them. Various scenarios must include consideration to the flow of parts, products, and information through manufacture, procurement, and distribution. For leading scenarios, make sketches or drawings, such as Figures 2–1 and 2–2, which were drawn as "solid models" in AutoCAD. The first step in this process is to draw the necessary blocks (or components or symbols) such as a generic parts bin, certain large parts, a computer symbol, and various machine tools and hand tools. Then these blocks can be copied or "arrayed" to illustrate many scenarios. The value of such drawings is that they can be common focal points to which everyone on the team can relate.

Design Philosophy Goals

Establish *design philosophy goals*. These are not design goals per se, but rather goals about the overall design approach, for instance:

Maximize the utilization of common parts; specify key common parts early and use them whenever possible. Standardize on one size screw for entire subassemblies or even products to encourage autofeed screwdrivers, as shown in Figure 2–1. Maximize use of off-the-shelf hardware instead of "reinventing the wheel." These decisions need to be made early, since many design aspects may have to accommodate the off-the-shelf hardware. Optimize flexibility with "extra" holes, signal ports, power ports, utility capacity, and convenient mounting spaces. For electronics, allow no hand soldering, minimize or eliminate cables, and minimize the number of circuit boards, preferably to only one.

Modular Design Strategy

It is very important for mass customized products to be *partitioned* optimally. Custom assembly of physical modules is not the only mass customization strategy available. There are many ways to partition a product, which will be discussed below.

Some partitioning criteria may even be counterproductive to mass customization. Many product development books recommend partitioning the products for ease of management by dividing the team into several subteams, so they can design all the subsystems in parallel. But this approach usually fails to optimize system architecture. For example, when the author conducted a manufacturability review for the design of an electronic system, he found that the largest cost subassembly was the wiring harness that linked all the subsystems. It was very complex, *and costly,* because the individual subteams designed their subassemblies independently and simply specified their demands on the wiring harness, instead of optimizing the wiring of the product as a system.

Partitioning for project management will probably not produce the optimal modular product architecture for mass customization. Partitions have a way of turning into modular boundaries. Thus, a product partitioned for project management might be poorly partitioned for mass customization. Mass customized products need to be designed by a multifunctional team, not loosely coordinated affiliations of subteams.

The traditional criteria for partitioning products is along functional lines, such as (for an electronic system) input/output, processing, memory, power supply, chassis, peripherals, and so forth. As with management partitions, this will probably not be optimal for mass customization. Different groups used to design automobile bodies and frames. Until the 1950s, General Motors advertized "bodies by Fisher." But with such an organizational partitioning, how could anyone be able to combine bodies and frames into today's "unit-body" construction?

Teams designing mass customized products need to consider other partitioning criteria, such as the following:

Assembly

The product could be partitioned so that various physical modules could be combined to form custom products. However, other considerations may affect this module design strategy.

Off-the-Shelf Parts

Off-the-shelf parts may be modules themselves and force surrounding design features to conform to keep these parts truly standard.

Integrated Subsystems

Optimizing the integration of subsystems can minimize costs of assembly of electrical connections. For instance, for the above-mentioned example of the electronic system with the expensive wiring harness, this approach would specify multiple standard off-the-shelf cables to perform all the subsystem interconnections. Several $20 cables would certainly be a better solution than this single $1,800 wiring harness. In Mass Customization, the standard cables could be assembled as modules, whereas the wiring harness approach would require multiple versions or a single version containing all the wires for all customizations. This approach would have to be implemented at the system level, with appropriate connectors incorporated into all subsystems.

Service

Service considerations could determine partitioning, with failure-prone subsystems designated as modules that are easy to replace and repair. Failure-prone components could even be congregated together into one easy-to-replace module. The most frequently serviced modules could be designed to be the easiest to access and replace.

Risk and Debugging

Modular design could minimize risk by locating new and untried technologies in an easy-to-replace module. If problems surfaced before the product was offered for sale, engineering fixes would be confined to the design and manufacture of one module. If problems occurred in the field, the same considerations would apply in addition to the considerable benefit resulting from the ability to swap out the problem module. This is one of the significant advantages of object-oriented software: Bugs tend to be confined to single modules rather than rippling through the entire code.

Upgradability and Obsolescence

A modular design strategy could be oriented around making upgrades easier and minimizing the impact of the obsolescence of certain parts and technologies. Modular upgradability could be implemented by the user, by the dealer, or by the manufacturer as field upgrades. Upgradability may be transparent to users and dealers; it may simply allow the manufacturer to introduce more "new" (really upgraded) products more easily by limiting new engineering to certain modules.

Part Availability and Cost

Parts and subassemblies that may have availability problems could be added when they become available if the product was designed for such a contingency. This could allow manufacturing to keep operating despite critical part shortages. Similarly, if product architecture allowed high-cost parts to be added last, this would minimize the amount of time that the factory would have to "carry" the cost of these parts.

The Design of Modules

A modular architecture can now be developed based on considerations of these partitioning criteria, plus any others deemed relevant. The modular architecture should be optimized for customer satisfaction, manufacturability, cost, serviceability, risk, distribution, sales, and future opportunities.

Chapter 8 of Joe Pine's *Mass Customization*,[6] citing the work of Karl Ulrich of MIT,[7] discussed various types of modularity.[8] In *component sharing* modularity, a common module is used on (or shared by) many different products; common parts and subassemblies discussed in Chapter 5 encourage component sharing modularity. In *component swapping* modularity, a product can be customized with various choices of components that can be "swapped" in and out, such as various radio options in an automobile. In *sectional modularity*, entire products or systems can be formed by appropriate combinations of modules, for instance, with software objects, plumbing fittings, or any type of "building block" modularity (Lego™ toys are the simplest example). In *bus modularity*, components with standard interfaces can be attached or plugged into a standard structure, like a computer bus (standardized back-plane connectors) that can accept any bus-compatible circuit board.

If modular architecture is a critical element of a mass customization strategy, then the design of the modules should be staffed and funded accordingly. Modules may have general usefulness beyond current product development efforts. A single product development, with its budget and time constraints, may not be able to design versatile modules "for the good of the company." Therefore, module design teams may have to be funded and formed with designers with broad product development experience. The module designs would have to be coordinated with all products that currently and potentially could use them.

In addition to optimal partitioning, modules must be designed to be as versatile as possible to encourage use on as many products as possible, even products that may not be part of the mass customization family. This expanded use raises order quantities and generates economy of scale benefits for all users. Versatility for future opportunities can be enhanced, at not much extra cost, by providing extra holes, signal ports, power ports, and utility capacity. If a machine tool is already set up to drill .25-inch holes, the cost of drilling additional .25-inch holes is relatively small.

In addition to versatility, hardware and software modules must be designed to be robust so that manufacturing tolerances and operating parameters are carefully determined to minimize the chance of problems from worst case tolerance combinations or any form of intermodule incompatibility.

Module interfaces, both for hardware and software, must be well designed and robust. Hardware modules should be easy to assemble and disassemble. Software modules should easily combine without the need for additional intermodule code, debugging, or "patches." Examples of well-defined interfaces include the following: the National Electrical Manufacturers Association established standard interfaces for mounting motors and bolting them to gearboxes; audio equipment has standard electrical signals and standard connectors between preamplifiers, amplifiers, and speakers; computer "busses" have signal and connector standardization that allow a wide variety of printed circuit boards to be plugged together; telephones have standard interfaces between the phone and the wall plug and also between the phone and the receiver.

The modules and their interfaces *must remain standard.* Individual design teams must avoid the temptation to "improve" modules for one project, unless the improvement is so good that it warrants a universal module upgrade and change of the standard, considering the impact on all projects using or planning to use the module.

If intermodule variability is a problem that threatens to compromise a modular strategy, inter-module adapters can be allocated space between the modules. For example, in shipbuilding, modules are very large and expensive; to compensate for "tolerance stack" and other interface problems, inexpensive intermodule adapter sections are built to "take up the slack." For automobiles, both engines and transmissions are very expensive to design and tool up for; the interface between these inflexible modules is an inexpensive "bell housing" (for manual transmissions) or adapter plate. In fact, aftermarket part vendors sell a broad range of bell housings and adapter plates to accommodate their customers' needs for help with engine "swapping."

DEVELOPING MASS CUSTOMIZED PRODUCT LINES

The first two steps are to be accomplished by a multifunctional task force that includes, at the minimum, Engineering, Manufacturing, Finance, Purchasing, and Materials. The remaining steps are to be accomplished by a *complete* multifunctional product development team that has product line responsibility.

1. *Rationalize product lines;* eliminate products that don't fit into a flexible environment, have low sales, have excessive overhead demands, are not really appreciated by customers, have limited future potential, or may really be losing money, using method-ologies presented in Chapter 4.

2. *Standardize* parts, processes, features, fixtures, tooling, and raw materials for new designs, using methodologies presented in Chapter 5, and for existing products, eliminating duplicate parts and implementing "better than" substitutions of standard parts and materials, as discussed in Chapter 7.

3. *Thoroughly understand how customers use products* **in their** *environments.* Research potential opportunities for customization from the customers' point of view. Because customers may limit their stated wants and needs to what they believe to be possible, mass customizers may have to ask "what if" questions and specu-late on how customers would appreciate customizations that they cannot now comprehend.

4. *Identify potential families of products to mass customize* based on a *balance* of *capabilities and opportunities* in marketing/distribu-tion, engineering, and manufacture. Ask the following questions:

- What are our core competencies and strengths? Look for opportunities that utilize these strengths and minimize the new strengths that need to be added.

- What customization is needed now or may be appreciated if offered? Brainstorm on *all* possible customization possi-bilities; ask, What if we could offer . . . .? Be sure to couple this brainstorming with the possibilities in design, manu-facture, and distribution.

- What customization could be feasible in design and manu-facture? Again ask, What if we could design, build, and distribute . . . .? Consider how technology and improve-ment programs could affect the feasibility of:
  - Standardization of parts, processes, features, fixtures, tooling, and raw materials.
  - Development of hardware and software modules useful for many products.
  - Agile manufacturing capabilities: JIT, lot-size-of-one, build-to-order.
  - Configurators.
  - Parametric CAD.
  - CAD/CAM.
  - Computer numerically controlled (CNC) equipment: available or specially developed.

■ What if we could build-to-order, ship directly to stores or customers, and eliminate much of the current distribution chain? Would customers benefit? How would these distribution cost savings affect price and profits?

5. *Determine* what *needs to be customized from the customers' point of view.* Focus on *what* is needed without excluding any ideas yet on feasibility grounds. Feasibility judgments may be based on current perceptions of the way things are; new technologies and programs may change several aspects of feasibility.

6. *Brainstorm* how *to accomplish the customizations.* Propose several scenarios, identifying modular, adjustable, and dimensional aspects of the customization. Translate the identified needs into their implications in engineering, manufacturing, marketing, and distribution for all scenarios. Compare estimates of *differences* in *total cost* for all scenarios.

7. *Pursue leading candidates and narrow the choices.*

■ Sketch or generate basic drawings or solid models of products to help with analysis and offer common focal point.

■ Sketch or generate symbolic drawings or solid models of operations showing the flow of parts and information, like those shown in Figures 2–1, 2–2, and 7–1, which are AutoCAD 3D solid models drawn in perspective. Note that solid model components (blocks, symbols) can be easily moved, copied, and modified to illustrate many scenarios.

■ Arrange to have the *complete* team raise and resolve the issues, as discussed in Chapter 9.

■ Evaluate throughput times and delivery possibilities. Can operations build to order a product and get it to the customer as fast, or faster, than currently from finished goods inventory?

■ Explore marketing, advertising, and ordering possibilities. Make sure that *customers* will be able to comprehend that this is really possible.

■ Estimate *total* costs for the leading scenarios, using the total cost philosophy and tools presented in Chapter 6. Remember to consider all distribution costs, whether or not they are within the manufacturing company itself.

- Obtain early customer feedback, being sure to address credibility issues: If we really could . . . . , would you buy it?
- Select the most promising candidates. Multiple scenarios could be pursued until the "winner" becomes apparent.

8. *Methodically define product families* to generate resource allocations and engineering specifications that reflect the voice of the customer. Chapter 9 presents the QFD methodology.

9. *Optimize product line architecture.* As shown in Figure 6–1, the concept/architecture phase determines at least 60 percent of a product's lifetime cost and a large proportion of functional desirability, quality, reliability, and time to market. Commit to significant effort for this phase *proportional to its effect*.

- For modular aspects of the customization, invest in the development of versatile modules that are consistent with modular product architecture.
- For adjustable aspects of the customization, determine the optimal amount of adjustability, target ranges/steps, how the adjustability is performed, and conceptual design and manufacturing implications.
- For dimensional aspects of the customization, investigate ways to cut to fit, mix, or tailor with programmable CNC equipment manual operations directed by on-line instructions, mixing by distributors, or easy "snap-off" tasks performed by users.

10. *Design fabricated parts and specify procured parts* so they can be made flexibly enough or be procured quickly enough to be "pulled" into assembly operations on demand.

For batch mode fabrication, internally fabricated parts do not necessarily need to be made in a lot size of one to support built-to-order product assembly. If the parts are small, inexpensive, and not likely to deteriorate or become obsolete, they can be made in batches as part of a *kanban* resupply (see Chapter 7, step 9). Kanban bins for small, cheap, and stable parts can be sized with enough parts to never cause a work stoppage, even at peak demand. Only rough estimates of this peak demand are necessary, so part resupply does not require forecasts and MRP-based procurement cycles.

Parts that are large, expensive, or prone to deterioration or obsolescence may have to be made flexibly as needed to minimize space, cost, or risk.

Programmable machine tools can provide a versatile source of dimensional customization by "cutting to fit" bar stock, tubing, sheet metal, cloth, leather, and so on.

To eliminate setup and make these machines flexible, fixturing geometries and raw materials must be standardized. Further, all operations for all parts built must be within the capabilities of the machine, including automatic tool changers, for instance, for machining centers and punch presses.

Versatile programmable machine tools can reduce processing steps by performing several functions in one machine, such as sheet metal laser cutting and using machining centers for drilling, taping, and milling.

Flexible operations must have the ability to quickly and easily generate CNC programs, sometimes for each part, from CAD/CAM systems.

If plastic molded parts and cast metal parts can not be supplied by kanban or are providing some dimensional customization, then the molding or casting process needs to be flexible.

The first step would be to consolidate molded and cast shapes to the minimum number of different parts that are used in the maximum number of products. To maximize versatility, each of these parts may have extra metal, functions, "hooks," or circuitry.

Decisions about these part consolidations may be difficult if the cost system does not quantify total cost. The extra features will show up immediately and clearly as an *"extra"* cost. However, the substantial benefits may not show up anywhere in the current cost system. Until total cost accounting arrives, Figure 10–4 may help itemize the benefits of these consolidations and serve as a basis for quantification or, at least, for educated "leap of faith" decisions.

One technique to achieve flexible molding/casting would be to minimize setup with quick die changes, using techniques pioneered by Shigeo Shingo, know as Single Minute Exchange of Dies (SMED).[9]

There are many ways to minimize die-change times, such as clever, universal mounting/locating geometries to facilitate quick changeovers and mechanized means for moving dies quickly in and out of presses and molding machines.

Too great a variety in mold/die shapes also might cost too much to build and slow down die-changing operations. It may be possible to make single-use molds and dies, possibly modeled after the old Linotype machines, which cast lead blocks of type for

FIGURE 10-4

Cost Trade-Offs for Part Consolidations

Cost Added:

- Extra cost/part on some of the parts for extra material, circuitry, etc.
- Onetime cost of making the change

Cost Saved:

- Economy of scale savings (purchasing leverage) for ordering n times the volume at $1/n$th of the number of part types
- Tooling cost cut by a factor of n if n parts can be consolidated
- Material overhead savings on n fewer parts
  - BOM/MRP expenses
  - Ordering expenses
  - Warehousing/stocking cost for raw materials inventory
- Setup cost saved by not having to set up the eliminated part(s)
  - Setup labor reduction
  - Machinery utilization improvements
- WIP inventory savings from processing fewer part types
- Design cost of eliminated parts for new designs
- Prototyping cost savings from fewer new designs
- Documentation cost of eliminated parts for new and existing designs
- Value of less chance of running out of fewer part types
- Value of the consolidation's contribution to flexible operations

---

each line of newspaper type and then melted them down for the next usage. Patterns for such molds, or the molds themselves, could be machined by CNC equipment and then recycled for the next mold.

If only one portion of the mold or die is unique to each customer, then custom "inserts" could be substituted into standard cavities in the molds or dies. This technique could also enable molds and dies to be changed more quickly, since the bulk of the tooling could remain fixed.

Procured parts and materials, preferably, should be resupplied by kanban if they meet the above conditions. For parts and materials with lead times too long for kanban:

- Identify parts with long lead times.
  - Explore ways to minimize the lead time (listed in order of the easiest first):

  – Expedite deliveries; apply pressure; offer incentives;
    make delivery a key condition of doing business.
    Commonality efforts result in fewer part types with
    higher order quantities, which makes expediting efforts
    more focused and, ultimately, successful.
  – Look for faster suppliers.
  – Work with suppliers to improve their lead times. Most
    delivery delays are caused by paperwork delays and
    processing inefficiencies.
  – Establish vendor/partner relationships with fast lead
    times as a key criteria.
  – Bring production in-house. Doing so may be the only
    way to shorten lead times and may complete the "miss-
    ing link" in a flexible operation. But it may not be a core
    competency and, thus, a distraction of focus.

- As a last resort, carry a stock of the long lead time parts,
  the size of which would be based on sales forecasts. As
  with any forecasting paradigm, this approach is dependent on forecast accuracy, which varies. Therefore, this
  approach is more appropriate for inexpensive parts, which
  can be stocked in excess without much penalty. Although
  stocking expensive parts may incur a high inventory carrying cost and may incur risks of deterioration and obsolescence, production planners must resist the temptation
  to minimize stocks, especially if this increases the chance
  of running out and halting production. Work stoppages
  may cost much more than the extra inventory carrying
  costs to ensure raw material availability.

11. *Design product assembly* to be able to assemble/configure
all product variations in the family without any setup to retrieve
parts, position parts, download programs, calibrate anything, or
find and understand instructions. Assembly, adjustments, and
configurations will probably all occur at some assembly operations
for subassembly or final assembly. For flexible assembly:

- *All parts must be available at all points of use.* This underscores
the importance of part standardization. If there are too many different parts, it may not be possible to make them available at all
points of use, or doing so would make the assembly area crowded
and confusing.

- *Parts are resupplied automatically* without any setup to retrieve or order them, as with the kanban systems. A cost-effective alternative for inexpensive parts, such as fasteners, is "breadtruck" resupply, where a supplier is contracted to keep the bins full, much like bread is resupplied to food stores (see Chapter 7, step 8). The supplier comes to the plant periodically to fill the bins and then bills the company at the end of the month for the amount consumed.

- *Fixtures and fixturing geometry are standardized* to eliminate setup related to fixturing. Universal mounting/locating geometries apply to both parts and fixtures. Examples on parts include locating bosses on castings and tooling holes on printed circuit boards. Examples on fixtures include locating surfaces on machine tool fixtures and tooling pins on circuit board tooling plates or pallets. Note that clever fixtures can be designed to accommodate a wide range of shapes and sizes.

- *Tools are standardized* so all tools needed at each assembly operation are readily available. If each assembly station uses only one type of screw, then "auto-feed" screwdrivers can be used to automatically advance the next screw into the powered screwdriver (see Figure 5–3).

- *Process steps are standardized* to avoid confusion and setup, for example, torque settings, dispenser quantities, timed steps, calibration procedures, and so on. The Japanese call this *poka-yoke*.

- *Assembly/configuration instructions are displayed on-line* to eliminate the setup of finding and understanding instructions. This is especially applicable to service operations.

Displays for manual assembly instructions can be generated from two-dimensional CAD drawings, 3-D CAD solid models, drawn illustrations, or digital photographs that can be touched up to emphasize certain points. At the very minimum, the monitor can display text instructions that could be exported from appropriate documents in word processing or database applications. Instructions can be made available in multiple languages for multilingual work forces and to ease the transition when pilot production is transferred to the plant in another country.

If graphical representations are important, the monitors can show selected "views" from CAD drawings. They can be displayed on CAD "viewer" programs, like *Autodesk View*, which sell for a tenth of the cost of AutoCAD itself. Current multimedia tools could even animate important processing sequences, if needed.

The view would be advanced to the next instruction when the worker presses a "next" or "page down" button on an input device. The input device could be a foot pedal to keep hands free for assembly work. Keeping track of the timing of these steps can subtly provide good statistical data for subsequent task analysis.

Assembly instructions must be quickly changed. In a "pull" (demand flow) system, the change can be triggered by wanding the bar code of a key part (like a circuit board), pallet, or some kind of "traveler" card or documentation. This is preferable to entering work order numbers on a keyboard because it is faster and not prone to entry errors. In a "push" system (where work is scheduled and sequenced), the next set of instructions could be displayed after the previous job is finished.

12. *Establish flexible CAD and CAD/CAM capabilities* (as discussed in Chapter 8) to allow CAD "templates" to be updated instantly with customer or niche market input. Updated part drawings would then update assembly drawings and relevant manufacturing programs.

13. *Establish order entry procedures* (as discussed in Chapter 8) summarizing rules for allowable combinations of modules and limits/steps for adjustable and dimensional customization. Create an order entry database or *configurator* to accommodate all the rules and constraints and instantly generate valid orders for transmission to the factory.

14. *Establish the capability to print customized documentation* for various industries, market segments, countries, languages, or individual customers.

15. *Implement flexible routing and shipping capabilities*, for example, based on bar codes that trigger file servers to route parts or products within the plant or print shipping labels.

16. *Plan the optimal flow of parts and products* into a truly flexible factory, like the vision presented in Figure 2–2.

IMPLEMENTATION

The above steps were presented in a logical order. This should not imply that product development teams need only go through these steps once. As in all product developments, design is an iterative process. *All* these steps should be explored for *many scenarios* and then, as the team converges to an optimal scenario, keep improving the design activity in all these steps.

This should all be part of the architecture phase. Before any parts are designed, the architecture must be finalized with everyone's buy-in. Thoroughly optimizing the above procedure should minimize any possibility of needing to change the architecture.

NOTES

1. Ashok K. Gupta and David L. Wileman, "Accelerating the Development of Technology-Based New Products," *California Management Review,* Winter 1990.

2. John Hauser and Don Clausing, "House of Quality," *Harvard Business Review,* May–June 1988; reprint number 88307.

3. Dr. Corey Billington, "Strategic Supply Chain Management," *OR/MS Today,* April 1994, (published jointly by the Operations Research Society of America and the Institute of Management Sciences), pp. 20–27.

4. B. Joseph Pine, II, *Mass Customization, The New Frontier in Business Competition* (Boston: Harvard Business School, 1993), p. 180.

5. Ibid., p. 203–4.

6. Ibid., chap. 8.

7. Karl T. Ulrich and Karen Tung, "Fundamentals of Product Modularity," working paper 3335-91- MSA, Sloan School of Management, MIT, September 1991.

8. This book categorizes "cut-to-fit modularity" and "mix modularity" as *dimensional* customization rather than modularity.

9. Shigeo Shingo, *A Revolution in Manufacturing,* The SMED System (Portland, OR: Productivity Press, 1985).

The Future of Mass Customized Products

B. Joseph Pine II
Founder, Strategic Horizons LLP

Effective product development is not only an imperative today for a company to truly embrace Mass Customization but, it also will be crucial to where business competition will go in the future. Reconsider the framework given in the first chapter (Figure 1–1). Note that it takes us from Craft to Mass Production with the Industrial Revolution, from Mass Production to Continuous Improvement with the quality revolution of the past few decades, and then on to Mass Customization in recent years of increasing market fragmentation and customer demands. But it doesn't stop there: Business competition will not cease its progression once this new business model is mastered. Rather, as one can surmise from the figure, it will go back to Invention! The next logical step in business competition is a markedly higher degree of inventive capability, one that builds on mass customization techniques to enable the rapid, constant, efficient creation of new, innovative products—not just customized versions of existing products. We might label this "Continuous Invention."

For mass customized variations within a given product architecture, virtually instantaneous development cycles with efficient production are already a reality.[1] However, it may be science fiction to think of instantaneously creating the architectures themselves, inventing new product categories, or even developing major innovations for well-established products. But there are a number of promising lines of research and practice that will, now and in the future, yield marked improvements in this direction. A few are discussed below.

MODULAR DESIGN

Component modularity, based on physical elements, is already being widely used to develop architectures for mass customizing products. Taking it up a level, Susan Walsh Sanderson of Rensselaer Polytechnic Institute, describes how design modularity—what she calls "virtual" design—can modularize *functional elements* to reuse them across product families.[2] Higher and higher levels of modularity will yield greater and greater degrees of innovativeness. One can envision certain classes of "functionalities" being reused across very different products, with tools in place to make their reuse quick, efficient, and effective.

In fact, this is rapidly becoming a reality in software development thanks to object-oriented programming systems (OOPS). Software objects are essentially distinct functionalities with certain properties that allow them to be quickly integrated with other objects to create increasingly complex and diverse programs. And other industries are using similar concepts. Computer Products, Inc., of Boca Raton, Florida, provides a growing library of modules to its customers, so they can quickly design their own power supplies, reducing the development time of whatever product is being designed. Similarly, LSI Logic Corporation of Milpitas, California, has developed CoreWare building blocks that allow its customers to quickly develop whatever custom integrated circuit modules they need for whatever product they are developing. Thanks to modular design, the mass customization of these kinds of component products—software, power supplies, and application specific integrated circuits (ASICs) are only the beginning—will in turn yield tremendous advances in the development cycle times of those products for which they are components, such as personal computers, set-top boxes, wireless communicators, and new classes of products yet to be invented.

Essential to design modularity is incorporating more and more of the product essence inside of information technology, as Motorola has made great strides in doing with its Fusion Factory. A key tenet of mass customization is *anything that can be digitized can be customized.* Once something resides in the realm of bits—ones and zeroes—it can be instantly changed on demand to a different, but still meaningful, set of ones and zeroes. In some cases the product itself can be digitized, such as with greeting cards, sheet music, and other information-based goods (not to mention telecommunications, insurance, and financial services that are all fundamentally information-based). In other cases, as with Motorola pagers, the specifications for the product design and its manufacture can be digitized for almost instant instantiation in a physical, customized product. In the future, as information technology continues to advance, greater and greater functionality will be digitizable, yielding virtual design and something that could easily deserve the label of "Continuous Invention."

INVENTION DATABASES AND EXPERT SYSTEMS

Many functions, however, cannot be digitized or even modularized and may never be. Many stubborn development problems, for example, require resolving fundamental engineering contradictions for which there are no easy solutions. But what if you could attack it from every possible angle, quickly apply various inventive principles and physical effects to the problem at hand, have an expert system suggest alternatives, and learn by analogy from thousands of innovative creations?

That is exactly what one software product, called *Invention Machine Lab* from Invention Machine Corp. of Cambridge, Massachusetts, is already on the market to do.[3] It has three modules. The first, IM:Principles, helps developers find solutions to engineering contradictions by presenting inventive principles gleaned from analyzing more than 2.5 million patents. The second module, IM:Effects, contains a knowledge base of more than 1,350 physical, geometric, and science-engineering effects to assist users in understanding the ramifications of alternative approaches. And the third, IM:Prediction, helps developers predict the possible technological evolution of their invention to lead them down the path of creating entirely new products. Motorola, for example, has licensed more than 1,000 copies of Invention Machine Lab to speed the creation of new, innovative products from its various R&D labs.

But surely such software is only the beginning. Fast-moving technologies—including intelligent agents to find the right information wherever it may reside on the Internet, fiber optics to instantly transmit it, CD-ROM drives to store it, and multimedia systems to learn and apply it—hold the promise of widely applying the lessons of not only past innovations but also real-time new creations almost instantaneously to current development projects. As MIT Media Lab head Nicholas Negroponte is fond of saying, if you can envision some possibility for applying information and communications technologies that can't be done right now, "just wait a few months!"

COLLABORATIVE TECHNOLOGIES

Of course, not everything can be solved by looking at past solutions or techniques. The key for most truly inventive creations lies not in accessing the past but in collaborating with those with the right skills, experiences, and expertise to pull it off. Here again, new technologies are rapidly coming on-line that can drastically reduce the development time while increasing the effectiveness of collaborations. In his book *No More Teams!* Michael Schrage, research associate at the MIT Media Lab, has extensively discussed how such technologies as groupware, liveboards, argumentation spreadsheets, and rapid prototyping, are but a shadow of what will come as these technologies merge into collaborative environments:

> Picture a holographic projection of a new product—an automobile, a cereal package, a point-of-purchase display—in the center of a conference table that the participants can rotate, shrink, expand, detail, manipulate, modify, alter, stretch, and multiply according to whatever design criteria they desire. A tap on the keyboard, a spoken command, a conversation lead to side-by-side displays of various alternatives. Tap another key, and the group is literally inside the laser-generated product, viewing it from angles and perspectives that were previously inaccessible. This conference room turns an idea into a virtual reality . . .
>
> Use high-bandwidth satellite and fiber-optic telecommunications capacity to put those three-dimensional images in New York, London, and Tokyo simultaneously, and it's clear that this technology is designed to foster collaborative communities—not just networks. Distance becomes irrelevant. People can choose to collaborate in real time or to make their collaborative contributions off-line by annotating the texts or editing the screen and asking the others to comment on these changes at their convenience.

This is where the real value of collaborative interaction can reside. The shared creation of possibilities and perspectives empowers this global group to look at an opportunity in ways that were once impossible.[4]

Collaborative technologies will have two effects on product development processes: They will enable many activities to be done that could never have been done before, and they will allow activities that could be done to be completed much faster, more efficiently, and more effectively.[5] Included in this latter group will be the ability, through virtual reality and other simulation technologies, to rapidly examine and test new product concepts without having to build the physical components. Combined with design modularity, the potential time savings in the testing phase of new product development are enormous. As just one example of what possibilities are fast becoming achievable, professors at the University of Illinois at Chicago have created a virtual reality system they call CAVE (for CAVE Automatic Virtual Environment) that enables researches to walk around—without bulky headsets—three-dimensional representations of products.[6] General Motors, Caterpillar, and other companies are already using CAVE in their new product development activities.

But perhaps the greatest benefit yet to be realized from virtual reality and other collaborative technologies is the ability to work together directly with customers in the marketing, design, and production of their own customized products. When customers can enter a collaborative environment to touch and feel, manipulate and create their very own product, the issues of information overload and lack of competitive space may simply disappear.

BREAKDOWNS AND BREAKTHROUGHS

Given all of the above, the greatest potential for significant and sustained cycle time reduction of major innovations is still human commitment and ingenuity. Necessity is still the mother of invention; if people *believe* they *must* innovate something particular by a specific date commitment—whether from competitive pressures, internal beliefs, or a focus on meeting some market window—then they will usually figure out a way to do so no matter how difficult that task truly is.

This is not just wishful thinking, but reality. Allan Scherr, former IBM fellow and now with EMC Corporation of Hopkinton,

Massachusetts, has developed a framework for creating break-through achievements—major innovations created within specific time and cost windows.[7] One key insight is that breakthroughs happen because of *breakdowns:*

> Breakdowns are defined as situations where the circumstances are inconsistent with and fall short of one's committed goals. A break-down occurs whenever there is a gap between a committed result and the predictable outcome of the current circumstances . . .
>
> A breakdown is a demand for extraordinary action. It causes people to shift attention and see things differently. This perceptual change is often the opening that lets people see opportunities for previously unconsidered actions.[8]

A breakdown can only be resolved either by decommitting or by achieving a breakthrough. If people maintain their commitments, then breakthroughs can indeed happen with some regularity. In more than 20 engineering and programming projects undertaken with this model, productivity increased almost three times on aver-age, with equivalent quality and markedly higher morale.[9] Greater acceptance of this model, which many managers and professionals understand intuitively, will yield greater breakthroughs, both in terms of innovativeness and in the time it takes to be innovative.

As one macro-example of this, consider Moore's Law, which Dr. Gordon Moore of Intel formulated in 1965 to describe the appar-ently relentless advance of semiconductors. In a famous article for *Electronics* magazine, Moore showed that the complexity of memo-ry chips had been doubling every 18 to 24 months and speculated that this would continue into the foreseeable future.[10] The same law held for microprocessors and other kinds of semiconductors as well and quickly became universally known in the industry. So much so that, I believe, Moore's Law became a self-fulfilling prophecy! Once convinced of its essential truthfulness, executives at semiconductor companies—most notably Intel itself—began plotting it out and set-ting targets for their design teams that would in fact fulfill the law. Commitments to these targets made by those design teams yielded countless breakdowns, from which emerged the vast number of breakthroughs that have been generated in this most innovative of industries. If Gordon Moore had never articulated his Law over 30 years ago, it is not at all clear that the extent of advancement we see today would have occurred!

THE FUTURE LANDSCAPE

Of course, breakdowns will not always yield breakthroughs, technology will not solve all invention or collaboration issues, and not all innovations are amenable to digitization or modular design. No matter what technologies or techniques are developed in the future, many development projects—and certainly the most important and the most inventive among them—will still take significant amounts of time to complete. And while development times for most anything can be greatly lowered from where they are today, they often cannot be rushed without detrimental consequences.[11] There is more than wine that cannot be sold before its time.

But nonetheless, there is still a tremendous amount of progress that can be made in the direction of Continuous Invention. With new systems, technologies, and techniques one can indeed envision the day not too far in the future—sometime in the 21st century—when the development and life cycle times of major new platforms such as automobiles and computers are measured in months, consumer electronics products in weeks, and many products in days. Like many mass customized products today, custom variations created in minutes will be common. And if there is any problem with achieving these numbers, it will come—as it should—from customer acceptance issues, not from the inability of producers to do it.

While true Continuous Invention is still far into the future with many design issues left unresolved, the only path to it leads directly from Mass Customization. And that is doable today indeed. By putting into practice the concepts and techniques that Dave Anderson has laid out in this book, you are beginning a long and profitable journey into the art of efficiently serving customers uniquely. Where it will end no one truly knows today.

N O T E S

1. See Christoph-Friedrich von Braun, "The Acceleration Trap," *Sloan Management Review*, Fall 1990, pp. 49–58, and "The Acceleration Trap in the Real World," *Sloan Management Review*, Summer 1991, pp. 43–52 for an interesting and thought-provoking argument that decreasing the life cycles of new products can be very detrimental for a company's health. While his argument is inherently sound, it

assumes that there is always a natural limit to how quickly new products can be developed, and therefore to how low life cycles can go. I believe that this assumption is false, thanks to such techniques as are discussed here. However, it is clear through von Braun's work that such an environment will become increasingly turbulent with potentially large ups and downs in revenue and profits (as new products attract customers to buy before they might otherwise purchase, reducing revenue in the future).

2. Susan Walsh Sanderson, "Cost Models for Evaluating Virtual Design Strategies in Multicycle Product Families," *Journal of Engineering and Technology Management* 8 (1991), pp. 339–58.

3. Bryan Mattimore, "The Amazing Invention Machine: Software for Creative Geniuses," Success, October 1993, p. 34, and Audrey Choi, "Invention Machine's Software Wins Orders for Picking Brains of Inventors," *The Wall Street Journal,* February 12, 1996, p. B10a. According to the latter, the Invention Machine Lab "codifies the invention principles behind some 2 million international patents and the inventive techniques of some of the world's greatest inventors."

4. Michael Schrage, *No More Teams! Mastering the Dynamics of Creative Collaboration* (New York: Currency Doubleday, 1995), pp. 185, 186–87.

5. Of course, the time it takes to do new activities will detract from the time savings of doing old activities faster. Whether it is leisure time at home or working time at the office or on the road, we continually find new things to do as technology frees up time on the more mundane tasks.

6. See Carolina Cruz-Neira, Daniel J. Sandin, Thomas A. DeFanti, Robert V. Kenyon, et al, "The Cave: Audio Visual Experience Automatic Virtual Environment," *Communications of the ACM* 35, no. 6, (June 1992), pp. 64–72; and Gene Bylinsky, "The Digital Factory," *Fortune,* November 14, 1994, pp. 92-110.

7. Allan L. Scherr, "Managing for Breakthroughs in Productivity," *Human Resource Management* 28, no. 3, (Fall 1989), pp. 403–24.

8. Ibid., pp. 407–8.

9. Ibid. p. 403.

10. For a fascinating recount of the history of the microchip and its impact today (including its capabilities for mass customization), see Michael S. Malone, "Chips Triumphant," *Forbes ASAP,* February 26, 1996, pp. 52–82.

11. See J. Utterback, M. Meyer, T. Tuff, and L. Richardson, "When Speeding Concepts to Market Can Be a Mistake," *TIMS Interfaces* 22, no. 4, (July–August 1992), pp. 7–13.

ABOUT THE AUTHORS

Dr. David M. Anderson, P.E., is a management consultant who specializes in seminars, workshops, and consulting on implementing Agility and Mass Customization. He shows companies how to rationalize product lines, standardize parts, and concurrently develop products and flexible processes for all the agile paradigms: Build-to Order, Niche Markets, Just-in-Time, Continuous/Demand-Flow Manufacturing, Agile Manufacturing, and Mass Customization.

David Anderson co-teaches the one-week course (with Joe Pine), "Achieving Competitive Advantage Through Mass Customization," for the Executive Education Program at the University of Michigan. At the Haas Graduate School of Business at the University of California at Berkeley, he created and taught the course "New Product Development, the Management and Design of Manufacturable Products" as part of the Management of Technology Program.

Dr. Anderson has over 23 years of industrial experience and counts as clients many leading companies including several divisions of Hewlett-Packard, Emerson Electric, Bausch & Lomb, United Technologies, Loral, Kaiser Electronics, Guidant, Freightliner, and many others. When he was Manager of Flexible Manufacturing at Intel's Systems Group, he initiated successful programs for Design for Manufacturability (DFM) and standardization of parts and tooling.

He wrote the book, *Design For Manufacturability, Optimizing Cost, Quality, and Time-to-Market* (CIM Press, 1990), the opening chapter in the SME handbook on DFM (TMEH, Vol 6), and the chapter of DFM and Mass Customization in the *Quality Function Deployment Handbook* (Wiley, 1996). His next book will be on low-cost product development.

From 1977 to 1983, his company, Anderson Automation, Inc., generated design studies and built special production equipment for companies such as IBM, FMC, Clorox, and Optical Coating Labs. He holds professional registrations in Mechanical, Industrial, and Manufacturing Engineering and a Doctorate in Mechanical Engineering from UC, Berkeley.

B. Joseph Pine II, the founder of Cleveland-based Strategic Horizons LLP, is an author, speaker, and consultant. Through seminars, workshops, and ongoing consulting, Mr. Pine helps clients see the world differently—from the perspective of what individual customers increasingly value. He helps them develop the right strategic initiatives, build the appropriate organizational structures and operational capabilities, and overcome the inevitable obstacles to business transformation.

Mr. Pine wrote the book *Mass Customization: The New Frontier in Business Competition* (Boston: Harvard Business School Press, 1993) and has authored numerous articles for *The Wall Street Journal, Planning Review,* the *IBM Systems Journal, Chief Executive,* and *CIO,* among others. One recent article, "Do You Want To Keep Your Customers Forever?" was his second as lead author for the *Harvard Business Review,* appearing in the March–April 1995 issue, with a third *HBR,* co-written with his partner Jim Gilmore, due the fall of 1996. His clients have included Hewlett-Packard, USAA, Eaton, IBM, Roadway Logistics, Lincoln Life, Northern Telecom, Tennant, and Winnebago Industries.

Mr. Pine's book details the shift companies are making from mass producing standardized offerings to *mass customizing* goods and services that efficiently fulfill the wants and needs of individual customers. *Financial Times* named *Mass Customization* one of the seven best business books of 1993 and the American Association of Publishers, Professional and Scholarly Division, named it Best New Book in Business and Management of 1993. The book, which also received the 1995 Shingo Prize for Excellence in Manufacturing and Research, has been translated into Japanese, German, Portuguese, Korean, and Spanish, with other translations underway.

INDEX